CORNISH LIGHT

The Nottingham 1894 Exhibition Revisited

Nottingham Castle

Penlee House
Gallery & Museum
Penzance

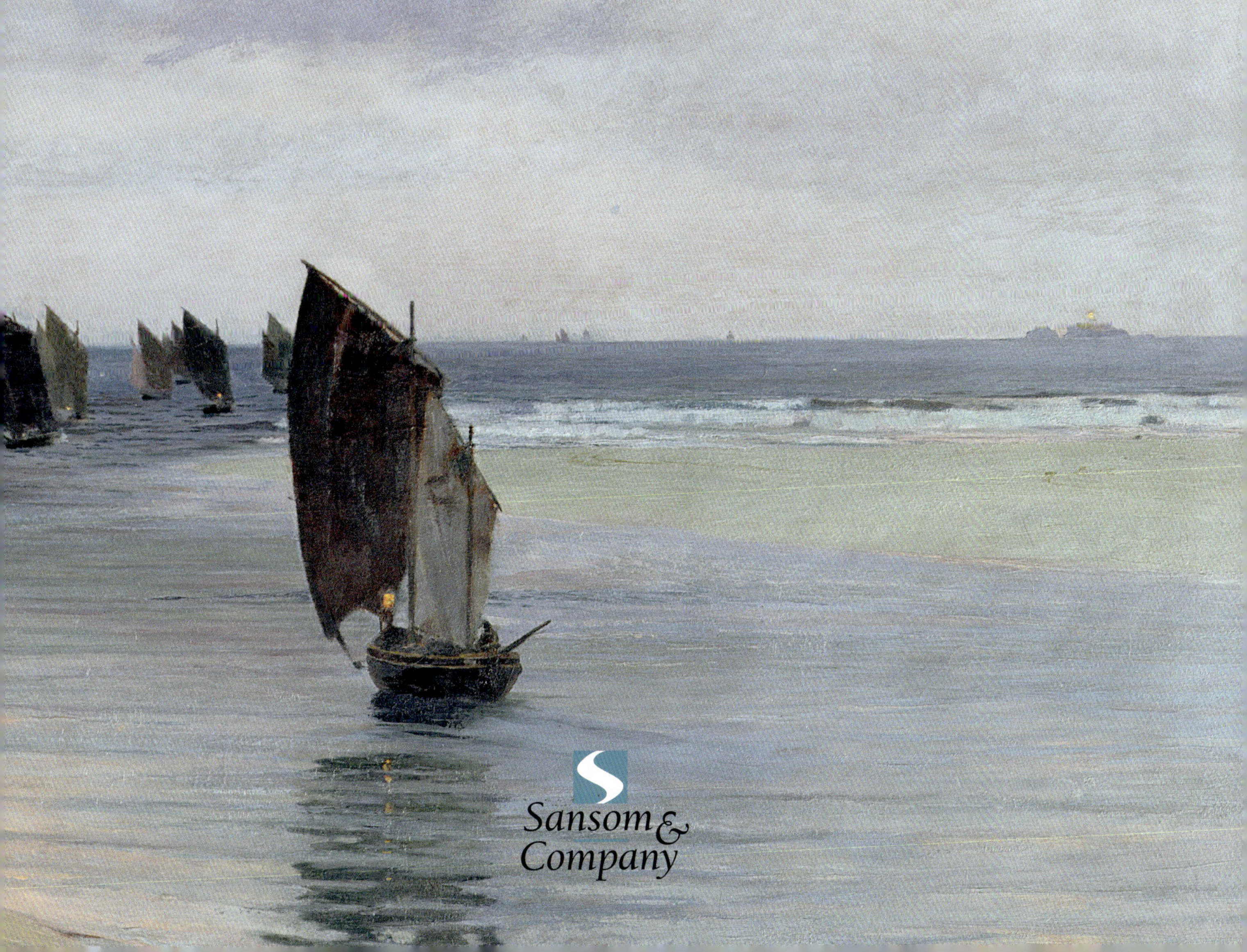

Sansom & Company

First published in 2015 by Sansom & Co,
a publishing imprint of Redcliffe Press Ltd.,
81G Pembroke Road, Bristol BS8 3EA

info@sansomandcompany.co.uk
www.sansomandcompany.co.uk

ISBN 978-1-908326-70-6

Published in conjunction with the exhibition 'Cornish Light'
at Nottingham Castle Museum and Art Gallery (3 April–7 June 2015)*
and Penlee House Gallery and Museum, Penzance (20 June–5 September 2015)

Exhibition sponsored by

MESSUM'S

*Supported by

Nottingham City Council

British Library Cataloguing-in-Publication Data
A catalogue record for this book is available from the British Library

Printed by Zenith Media

Frontispiece: Adrian Stokes, *The Harbour Bar*
Leeds Museum and Galleries (Leeds Art Gallery)

CONTENTS

FOREWORD

In 1894, a visionary Curator named Harry Wallis brought together an unprecedented number of paintings by artists from Cornwall in a single exhibition at Nottingham Castle Museum & Art Gallery. Many of these artists, such as Stanhope Forbes, Fred Hall, Frank Bramley and Edwin Harris had been at the forefront of the avant-garde in the 1880s, with their revolutionary techniques of painting the figure out of doors with square-tipped brushes, methods acquired from their admiration of the French artist Jules Bastien-Lepage and their education at the ateliers and studios in France and Belgium.

Less inclined to Impressionist colour and techniques, this loose association of artists who colonised the Cornish fishing port of Newlyn were social realists, painting the local people and places in a characteristic grey, even light. By the 1890s, however, this community of artists and the common ethos that held them together was beginning to wane. The 'French manner' that defined the group in the 1880s was becoming more relaxed, painters such as Henry Scott Tuke in Falmouth and William Osborn in St Ives, and even Stanhope Forbes in Newlyn, were working with fragments of colour and light with much greater fluidity than before, creating a truly 'Cornish Impressionist' style that is still practised by artists in Cornwall today. The 1894 Nottingham show, therefore, represented a watershed in Cornish art.

The idea of re-visiting the 1894 exhibition was proposed by Cornish painting specialist David Tovey and is based on an extensive period of research, during which he traced many of the pictures shown in the original exhibition. *Cornish Light* therefore brings together some of the best pictures from this period alongside other representative works in a new exhibition whose title captures the spirit and aspirations of this generation of artists, drawn to the Cornish coast because of its particular quality of light.

Cornish Light is also the result of an exciting collaboration between Nottingham Castle Museum & Art Gallery and Penlee House Gallery & Museum in Penzance. Penlee House is the only gallery in the UK dedicated to collecting and exhibiting the work of the Newlyn School of artists and has published extensively on the subject. In Nottingham, the exhibition arrives just as the Castle is embarking on major plans to develop the site and re-present its rich, thousand-year history. A focal point in this history was the transition of the Castle from a private Ducal Palace into a public art gallery and museum in 1878. Its mission was to showcase the best of current and historic art and design from Nottingham and around the world and Harry Wallis' 1894 Cornish painting exhibition epitomised this pioneering spirit. It not only brought work by contemporary artists from Cornwall to Nottingham, but also prompted the acquisition of paintings directly from the exhibition for the Museum's fledgling Fine Art collection.

Cornish Light provides the opportunity to see ground-breaking Cornish painting from the 1890s in two very different contexts: on the Cornish coast where it was made, and in the land-locked urban city where it was first presented on an ambitious scale. It shows that you don't have to visit London to see great art; Harry Wallis would have approved.

Louise Connell
Penlee House Gallery & Museum

Deborah Dean
Nottingham Castle Museum & Art Gallery

Exhibition sponsored by Messums

Acknowledgements

Nottingham City Museums and Galleries and Penlee House Gallery and Museum are grateful to all the lenders to the exhibition and would like to thank everyone who has assisted with the exhibition and catalogue: Joanne Chamberlain, Stephen Whittle, Atkinson Art Gallery, Bonhams, Bowerman Charitable Trust, Christies, Katie Boyce, East Gallery, Kettering, Henrietta Boex, Natalie Rigby, Falmouth Art Gallery, Rachel Boyd of Richard Green, Graham Bazley of W.H. Lane and Son, Rebecca Herman, Leeds Art Gallery, Siân Millar, Manchester City Galleries, David Messum, Johnny Messum, Carol Tee, Messums, Newlyn School Gallery, Deborah Dean, Andrew King, Maria Murphy, Tom Price, Sarah Skinner, Pamela Wood, Nottingham City Museums and Galleries, Andrea Kusel, Paisley Art Gallery, Ian Parfitt of E&P Design, Louise Connell, Katie Herbert, Penlee House Gallery and Museum, Duncan Walker, Russell-Cotes Art Gallery, Bournemouth, Peter Ogilvie, Salford Art Gallery, Clara Hudson and John Sansom of Sansom & Co, Tim Craven, Southampton Art Gallery, Stephen Litherland, St Ives Art Club, Louise Dowe, St Ives Town Council, Alice Calloway, Caroline Collier, Christopher Higgins, Tate, Sandra Penketh, Godfrey Burke, Walker Art Gallery, Liverpool, all the private collectors who have lent to the exhibition and with special thanks to David Tovey.

David Tovey would like to thank: The ever-efficient Katie Herbert of Penlee House Gallery and Museum, Penzance, who is always a tower of strength in such ventures, and, of course, my co-authors and to all at Nottingham Castle Museum and Art Gallery, who embraced my vision for this project. I am most grateful, once again, to Exeter historian, April Marjoram, for genealogical research on the artists Ernest Ireland Blackburne, Jessie Davidson, William Dickson and Ernest Fox. I am also very grateful to Mark Jones for photographing for me letters from the Nottingham City Museums and Galleries Archives.

Nottingham Castle Museum and Art Gallery stands on the site of a Castle built by the Normans to establish the rule of law over a famously rebellious city, where the Robin Hood legends began. The present building is an elegant seventeenth-century Ducal Palace, built for the Duke of Newcastle but gutted by fire in 1831 by protesters demanding electoral reform. For forty years it was left untouched by the Duke as 'a monument to the folly of the people' but was remodelled in the 1870s as the first municipal art gallery and museum outside London. It opened its doors in 1878 to great acclaim and has since continued to be the base for the City's important collections of Fine and Decorative Arts. Today, as in 1878, historical and contemporary art are shown side by side and the first floor gallery spaces present temporary exhibitions of regional, national and international artists. See website for site information and opening hours, which vary from summer to winter.
www.nottinghamcity.gov.uk/Castle
nottingham.castle@nottinghamcity.gov.uk

The award-winning **Penlee House Gallery and Museum**, Penzance, is the only Cornish public gallery specialising in the world famous Newlyn School artists (c.1880–1940) including Frank Bramley, Stanhope and Elizabeth Forbes, Walter Langley, Harold Harvey and Laura Knight. In recent years, the Gallery has built an international reputation for its year-round programme of temporary exhibitions, which offer the unique opportunity of viewing major Cornish works, borrowed from public and private collections across the UK, a stone's throw from where they were created. Changing displays always include a selection from Penlee House's permanent collection, ensuring that the Newlyn School are represented in at least one gallery. Set in an elegant Victorian house and park, Penlee House also covers West Cornwall's archaeology and social history, and offers an excellent café and shop, with full wheelchair access throughout. Open Monday to Saturday throughout the year.
www.penleehouse.org.uk | **info@penleehouse.org.uk**

THE CORNISH GROUP OF ANGLO-FRENCH PAINTERS

David Tovey

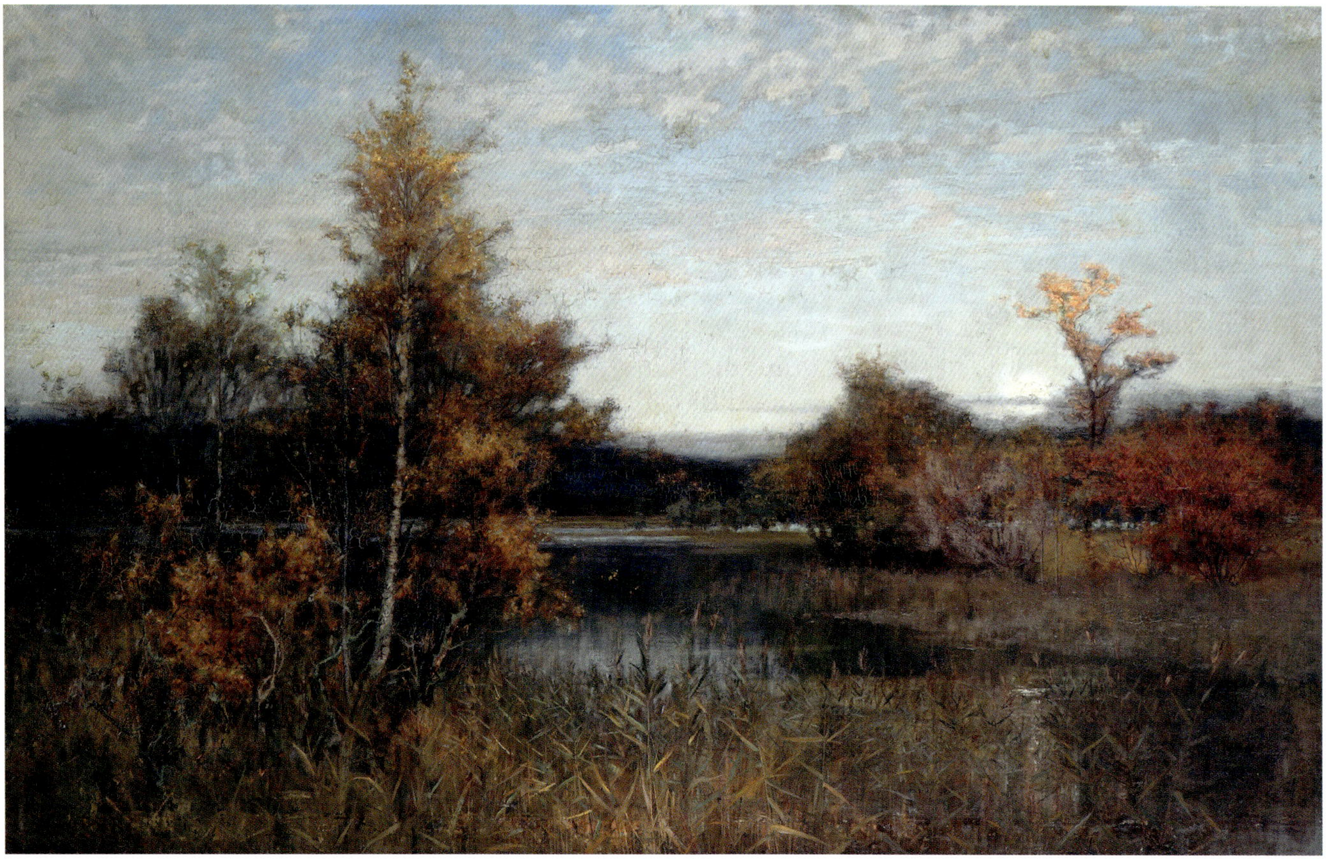

Alfred East
An Autumn After-glow
1886 • oil on canvas • 100 x 151 cm
Dudley Museum and Art Gallery, Dudley MBC

The status of Cornish art in 1894

One of the most fascinating features of the archival material relating to the 1894 exhibition retained by Nottingham Castle is the light that it throws on how the Cornish artists were viewed by themselves and others at the time. Of particular interest is how the Cornish artists did *not* want to be viewed, by virtue of their stipulation that, in the pre-publicity for the show and in the catalogue, Harry Wallis should not use the term 'Newlyn School' – the description still most often used when referring to Cornish artists.

Whilst late-nineteenth century Cornish art, particularly that produced in Newlyn, has seen a resurgence of interest in the last few decades, with many visitors from around the country making regular pilgrimages to Penlee House Gallery & Museum, Penzance, to see the exceptional shows that its dedicated staff put on time and time again, it still receives very little exposure outside Cornwall. Accordingly, the exceptionally high regard in which late Victorian Cornish art was held at the time of the 1894 Nottingham exhibition, will come as a surprise to many. For instance, the show was promoted as containing 'many of the principal pictures of the last few years and several that rank with the chief works of the century', whilst the artists themselves were labelled 'revolutionaries'. In conclusion, it was stated, 'It is certain that there never was a more significant body of painters in England than the 'Newlyners' of today. Individually, there is perhaps greater prominence, but collectively, there unquestionably is not.'[1] Accordingly, the exhibition was said to showcase many of the finest works of the whole nineteenth century by the most significant body of painters in England ever!

Albeit the pre-publicity notices, printed in a vast range of papers, vary in length, the similarity of wording used indicates that it was Harry Wallis who drafted and sent out a standard notice. Naturally, he wanted to arouse interest in the exhibition, but some of the sentiments expressed would appear to result from conversations with the artists about the trials and tribulations that they had faced before they ultimately gained recognition. The *Daily Guardian* was one of the papers to feature a significant section of Wallis' draft:

> *The Cornish School of Painters ... have a common ideal, and that ideal is poetry with reality in art, whether it is of the figure or the landscape. Earnestness, insight, unremitting labour, and the most complete abandonment of personal ease, to accomplish the art they adore, have been their watchwords and, so to speak, the esoteric signals of their craft ... There is no conventionality amongst them, but in an almost invisible manner, figure painters are drawn to Newlyn, while the votaries of the aerial landscape, the conflict between the sea and earth and sky, have found in St Ives their ground of gathering. There is much to be said of the individual work of many, especially of the women whose work is of the highest distinction; and the canvases of Mrs Adrian Stokes, Mrs Stanhope Forbes and others directly challenge the male members of the brotherhood. The Cornish school of painters have had a most difficult and wearisome task. They have had to contend against trickery and falsity, and above all against the dreaded commercial spirit which had entered into English art, and which for many years had 'boomed' certain clever but shallow artists as the be-all and end of all British pictorial art. It is to the lasting merit of this school that they have by some dint of genius broken down this 'corner' in the world of art. The market can no longer be rigged in favour of a few whose ideas of art lack the vital elements of truth and self-sacrifice. The whole horizon of English art is being changed in the recognition of the work of the Cornish school.*[2]

The Cornish artists are here being presented as revolutionary geniuses, who have changed the face of British art. Clearly, there is some journalistic licence in these pronouncements, but it is a reminder that there was a time when Cornish art was considered *avant-garde*.

1. *Nottingham Express*, 29 September 1894.
2. *Daily Guardian*, 17 July 1894.

Further evidence that the Cornish artists had ruffled a few feathers was provided at the Opening Luncheon by the 'celebrity' guest speaker, the art critic, Henry Blackburn, whose book on *Breton Folk* will have been essential reading for many of the Cornish artists, during their earlier trips around Brittany, and who published annual notes on the Academy, New Gallery and Grosvenor Gallery exhibitions. In an unimpressive performance, during which he appears to have committed the cardinal sin of getting some of the Cornish artists' names wrong, he demonstrated that he was not necessarily a great admirer of the new techniques that the Cornish artists had introduced into British painting. Quoting the viewpoints of other art critics, seemingly with approval, he commented, 'They were told by some of the great critics that the Newlyn School if not impressionist, at least took their impressions from nature, and when they felt that they had arrived at a certain point, they stopped, and some people said they did not finish their pictures. At any rate many men were wise enough to say that they very often left off painting where the difficulties began.'[3] This criticism that the work of the early Cornish artists lacked the requisite high degree of finish required for academic painting was one typically levelled at them in the 1880s, but most art critics had now come to accept that such apparent sketchiness, which left broad brushstrokes visible and outlines fuzzy, was actually the result of the artists' in-depth observation of the effects of light and atmosphere in nature. The eye did not see the hard outlines considered correct in academic painting. It was for this reason that one of the newspapers also referred to the Cornish artists as 'the wet cat school'.[4]

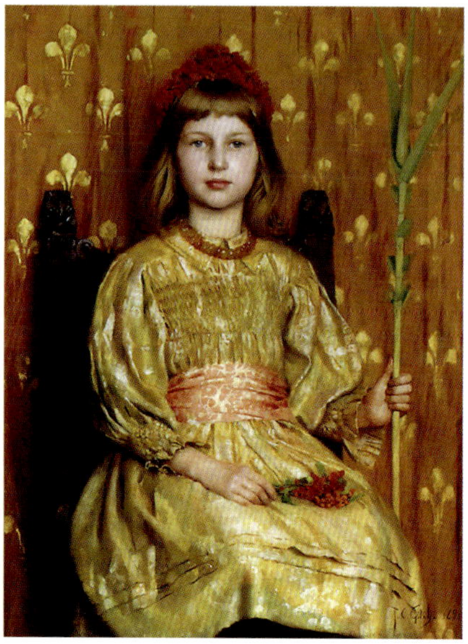

Thomas Cooper Gotch
My Crown and Sceptre
1891 • oil on canvas • 95 x 68 cm
Art Gallery of New South Wales, Sydney; image courtesy the Artist's Estate

Why Cornwall?

One question that fascinated reviewers was what was so special about Cornwall that it should attract such gatherings of artists and inspire them to produce such ground-breaking work? This was an issue that was referred to on a number of occasions during the speeches at the Opening Luncheon. Blackburn expressed himself slightly bemused, given that there was nothing very Cornish about certain paintings in the show, such as one of a London dinner party (Chevallier Tayler's *A Summer Dinner Party*), or a portrait of an artist's daughter as a medieval saint done in Italy (Thomas Gotch's *My Crown and Sceptre*) or some comic work by Fred Hall. However, Thomas Gotch and William Titcomb, in their speeches, tried to define the common characteristics that bound the Cornish colonies together.

The report of Thomas Gotch's speech included the section:

> *Perhaps it might not be thought that he had got far in explaining who the Cornish painters were and why they were. He wished to say they were not a sect; they were a section, a branch of a large body of young painters located in the wilds of Cornwall for various reasons. But they were not distinct from their brethren all over the kingdom. Their pedigree was somewhat curious; there was something of French ancestry about them... The movement received its first impulse in this island about the time of Gainsborough, Constable and Sir Joshua Reynolds. By some means, a picture by Constable found its way into Paris and it revolutionised art in France. The movement was carried on by Corot, by Millet of Barbizon and had found its most marked expression with Bastien-Lepage. Paris again became the centre of the art world and he was rather inclined to think that it remained so. Amongst others, a great number of English painters made their way to the studios in Paris, which were a great contrast to the studios in England. In Paris, a distinguished painter esteemed it to be an honour to be the professor of a great number of pupils. Many of those who were now at Newlyn had studied in these French studios. The result was that about ten years ago a band of British and Franco-British 'savages' came over to this country prepared to snap their fingers in the face of all the established painters of Great Britain and Ireland. Some of these, owing to curious incidents, found their way to the West of Cornwall and settled at St Ives, Falmouth and Newlyn.*

3. *Nottingham Evening Post*, 28 September 1894.
4. *Nottingham Express*, 29 September 1894.

> *When they got there, they found the conditions for working were so favourable – the natural character of the scenery, the extremely interesting type of character, the old-world industry that was maintained there, the conditions of light so much in contrast to the shocking fogs where Mr Blackburn elected to reside (Laughter) – all these things combined with the warm and temperate climate in winter caused them to remain there to form friendships and to take root deeper and deeper every year.*
>
> *He thought he had now offered some explanation of why they were there and why they remained. It was due not to their having a desire to preach a special creed in art, but because they found it uncommonly convenient, and that they were surrounded by very good friends (Hear, hear). But he would like to say that they felt very much in touch with the men of their generation who for very various causes had made their homes in different parts of the kingdom, in London and the provinces, in Scotland and in Ireland. Speaking of Scotland, reminded him of another school of painters – the Glasgow School. They were strongly in sympathy with the Glasgow School and were very glad to find that the English art of the day could display such vitality in so remote a country as Scotland (Hear, hear).'*[5]

William Titcomb went further than Gotch, stating that the Cornish artists 'had derived *all* their inspirations from France'. He felt that the feature that could be said to characterize their work best was their commitment to painting out of doors; 'One of our first aims is to attain absolute truth of tone by posing our models and painting them in the exact background and surroundings which it was intended the picture should represent.'[6] Whilst, in truth, by this juncture, the difficulties experienced in painting large canvases out of doors had led to a number of artists watering down, or even abandoning, their strict adherence to *plein air* painting, there were still vehement supporters of this method, which had been so championed during their sojourns in France.

Shared experiences in France

Both Gotch and Titcomb indicate that one of the defining characteristics of the Cornish artists was their debt to their French training and their experiences in that country. In the late 1870s and 1880s, aspiring artists in England became dissatisfied with the quality of teaching in art schools in this country, with its emphasis on drawing from the antique, and so joined the throng of artists from around the world that were flocking to Paris, which, as Gotch indicated, was considered to be the art capital of the world. There, they sought to study in one or more of the *ateliers* that sprang up to meet the extraordinary demand, and to experience for themselves the latest trends in a fast changing art market. Given that the Ēcole des Beaux Arts was largely closed to foreigners, students from outside France tended to enrol at the large *ateliers* for both men and women run by Rodolphe Julian, whose tutors included Robert Fleury, Jules Lefebvre and Gustave Boulanger, or to select particular masters whose classes were recommmended, such as J.P. Laurens, Carolus Duran, or Léon Bonnat, whilst female artists often preferred Colarossi's, as they were allowed there to draw from the nude model. Whilst it is clear that spells spent by a number of the Cornish artists in these various *ateliers* overlapped, there was not a single master who was a major influence. In any event, the master's presence in these *ateliers* was very limited, often just once a week, and, when there, he could only pass comment on a few works. Accordingly, in the main, the students helped each other, reacting positively to the general enthusiasm that a new dawn was breaking in the art world and to the sense of competition, which masters such as Julian sought to engender. As a result, strong friendships and a keen work ethic developed.

Whereas students in the *ateliers* concentrated almost exclusively on drawing and painting the figure, clothed and nude, the vogue at the time was for out-of-doors

5. *Nottingham Evening Post*, 28 September 1894.
6. *ibid.*

painting. As Gotch indicated, this movement had begun in the art colony of Barbizon, Seine-et-Marne, France, with painters, such as Corot and Millet, wishing to dispense with academic conventions and studio trickery, and, instead, seek direct inspiration from nature. To obtain absolute truth in nature, the view developed that one must not only do one's preliminary sketches out of doors, but also execute one's exhibition pieces on the spot as well. However, it is interesting that whilst acknowledging the debt due initially to the Barbizon School, Gotch placed emphasis on the fact that the Barbizon painters had themselves been influenced by Constable, so as to argue, for the sake of a British audience, that the original impulse had come from British art, and that the Cornish artists were not merely importing wholesale a French approach to painting.[7]

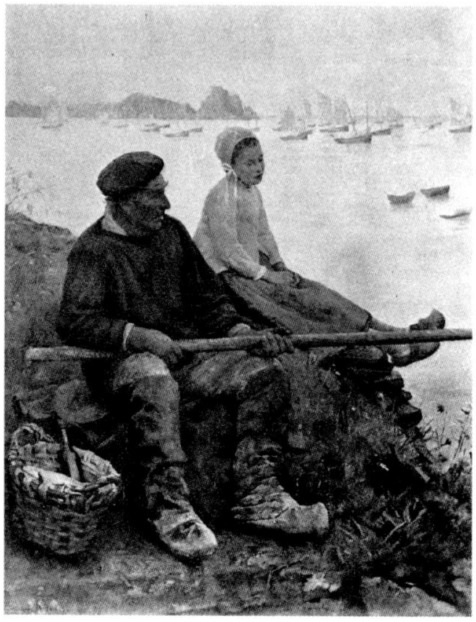

Stanhope Forbes
Grey Rocks and Grey Mullet
from *Royal Academy Pictures*, 1892

Gotch also mentioned in his speech Jules Bastien-Lepage who was, without doubt, the single biggest influence on the Cornish artists (and many of the other 'Franco-British savages'), as, during the period when most of the Cornish artists had been working in France in the early 1880s, he was regarded as something of a cult figure. Bastien-Lepage argued that figure painters, who, for practical reasons, had tended to paint their figures in their studios, even if placing them in a landscape setting, should also adopt a *plein air* approach for their major exhibition pieces. The very different and significant problems that resulted from such an approach, with the passage of the sun perpetually altering the areas that were either lit up or in shade, not to mention coping with changing weather conditions, could not be resolved in an *atelier*; students had to experience these difficulties for themselves by painting 'under the open sky', and to find their own solutions with the aid of their companions. Accordingly, many artists found the time spent away from the *ateliers* was often more instructive than long days spent in their crowded, smoky, atmospheres.

Inspired by the writings of Emile Zola and others, there was also a feeling of nostalgia for the past, as industrial progress and greater commercialisation threatened to destroy traditional ways of life. Cities, to which ever greater numbers of workers thronged, were dirty, noisy, polluted places, leaving residents dreaming of rural idylls. Accordingly, artists were attracted to remote places, where they could still capture ancient customs and quaint modes of dress in rustic settings. Given that such places tended to lack the cultural refinements of the metropolis, the company of like-minded artists made the experience much more pleasurable. Colonies, therefore, started to proliferate, and established artists continually searched out fresh destinations, which could provide appropriate new motifs. For the vast majority of the artists who later settled in West Cornwall, the art colonies of Brittany, particularly those at Pont-Aven and Concarneau, had been the initial attraction. Accordingly, the Newlyn artists Frank Bramley, Edwin Harris, Walter Langley and Elizabeth Forbes and the St Ives artists Adrian and Marianne Stokes had worked in Pont-Aven, whilst Stokes and many of the early St Ives settlers, who included Harry and Dorothy Robinson, had worked in Concarneau. Stanhope Forbes had opted first for Cancale and then Quimperlé, where he had socialised, on different occasions, with Ralph Todd and Trythall Rowe, whilst Norman Garstin had also worked in Quimperlé. Alfred East and Adrian Stokes, both to become leading landscape painters, had not unnaturally opted to work in Barbizon itself for a while, and several artists had also worked in Normandy and in other Continental art colonies.

Having enjoyed the colony lifestyle abroad, young English artists on their return to Britain decided to explore their own remote outposts to see if there were places which contained the right old-world, quaint subject matter, which would appeal to middle-class picture buyers, as well as offering pleasant, cheap living. For the reasons that Gotch listed, Cornwall proved eminently suitable, but it was not the only destination of choice and the Cornish artists shared affinities with a number of different groups of artists around the country, such as the Glasgow School. Many of these young artists became exasperated by the constant rejection of their French-inspired works by aged reactionaries on the Royal Academy Hanging Committee, and so a group of them, which included Thomas Gotch, Henry Tuke and other Newlyn residents, launched a campaign to set up a rival exhibition

7. Constable's three paintings at the Paris Salon of 1824 were so popular that they were moved to the principal exhibition room shortly after opening and he was awarded a gold medal. Thereafter, his work had a direct influence on a number of the Barbizon painters.

society. This resulted in the formation in 1886 of the New English Art Club, but one of the names seriously considered for the new venture was 'The Society of Anglo-French Painters'. As Gotch indicated, therefore, the Cornish artists were part of a wider movement, which is why I consider the term 'The Cornish Group of Anglo-French Painters' far more apposite than the ubiquitous 'Newlyn School', which has been bandied about so readily, by auctioneers, dealers and some public galleries, to describe almost any form of Cornish representational art, that it has become meaningless.[8]

The attractions of Cornwall

Newlyn, St Ives and Falmouth, as busy fishing ports, all satisfied the artists' requirement for 'old-world industry' and the fisherfolk proved 'exceedingly interesting types of character'. What is more, the major fishing seasons – mackerel in the spring, and pilchards, and then herring, in the autumn – required different boats and different fishing gear and involved different techniques, and so there was a never-ending wealth of different subjects for the artists to tackle. The fishermen, with their bushy beards and weather-worn countenances, had a certain nobility in their bearing – they were often compared to Old Testament prophets. Whether in smocks or sou'westers, they made very paintable subjects, particularly as picture buyers were aware that they constantly risked life and limb in their battle with the elements, as they sought to earn themselves a crust and bring fish to the country's markets. Accordingly, an artist did not need to use much invention to confer upon them a heroic status.

The fisherwomen also made fine subjects. Just a month after his arrival in Newlyn, Stanhope Forbes told his mother 'that the average of good looks is very high. I never saw so many really nice looking girls in a small place.'[9] They also wore a distinctive set of clothing that was picturesque. An ankle-length dress or skirt was always covered by a white or pale-coloured apron, whilst older women tended to wear a colourful heavyweight plaid shawl. Headgear varied enormously from sun bonnets. headscarfs (often plaid) and shawls to the distinctive, wide-brimmed Cornish gook.

As the son of an an Anglican Bishop, Titcomb had a life-long fascination for displays of faith, whatever the denomination, and he also felt that the Cornish temperament gave rise to scenes that appealed to the figure painter.

> *One reason why Cornwall was such a particularly good place for us to have chosen to paint was on account of the natural life of the Cornish people. They were an emotional people, too unsophisticated to hide their feelings. Then there was the tragic life of the sea, such as it was impossible to find elsewhere. In Cornwall too, they had an extraordinary state of feeling arising out of the intensity of the religious life of the people. It was one of the few parts where the people had not lost their belief in religion.*[10]

Due to the fact that until 1877, Cornwall was part of the diocese of Exeter, Anglicanism had little following in Cornwall, and the principal religion of the county was Methodism, albeit there were a variety of different denominations. All, however, had strict rules relating to the observance of the Sabbath, and the artists soon learnt that sketching on a Sunday would not be tolerated. A dowsing with a bucket of water was a frequent disincentive, whilst some miscreants are even recorded as having been thrown into the harbour. Religion was considered 'the brightest and best part' of life and the artists needed to respect the locals' faith, however boring they found Sundays in Cornwall to be. Given the uncommerciality of faith as a subject, only Titcomb made it a field of study. He was particularly taken with the fervency of the Primitive Methodists, and one of his exhibits in the 1894 exhibition, *Piloting Her Home*, was one of a trio of works that made this sect famous around the world.

8. Key questions as to the scope of the term, upon which one is likely to receive differing answers, are: i. Does it just include Newlyn-based painters? ii. Does it just relate to figure painters? iii. Does it just relate to painters in oils? and iv. What period does it cover?

9. Letter postmarked 1 February 1884, TGA 9015.2.1.222.

10. *Nottingham Evening Post*, 28 September 1894.

Among the other principal attractions of south-west Cornwall that Gotch listed was the quality of its light. This had both a warmth and an intensity, even on grey days, that was noted by all artist visitors, from Turner onwards. With both Newlyn and St Ives being situated on the narrow West Penwith peninsula, light reflected over the land from the sea on both coasts, which, as it had come across the Atlantic, was unadulterated by sediment and so was pure and clean. Its colour had a richness that was often equated with that of the Mediterranean. In addition, in St Ives, there were four sandy beaches, all facing in different directions, and so, from any view point at any time, light was also reflecting from the crystals in the sand. Filson Young, later a pioneering producer for the British Broadcasting Corporation, commented, 'Perhaps the crowning charm of St Ives and that which, with its entirely unique and characteristic composition, makes it the most interesting town in England to the artist, is its atmosphere ... There is something in the air of the place itself, alternating between extreme transparency and a mysterious haze, that gives unending wonder and value to its simple features'.[11] The impressive cloud formations, which crossed the narrow foot of Cornwall 'like a march of emperors', with 'their stately processions, their almost intolerable majesty,' also provided inspiration.[12] Cornish light, with its special atmospheric envelope, therefore, has been an enduring attraction to artists and played a key role in the ongoing success of the colonies.

Gotch also mentions the mild winter climate, which made for a pleasant lifestyle and resulted in unique exotic flora. However, this was principally an attraction for keen *plein airists*, who wanted to sketch out of doors for as long as possible. Accordingly, local businesses found that the artists generated a year round industry, for no sooner had the summer sketchers returned home, than the long-stay winter visitors settled down to work on their major exhibition pieces for the coming year's shows.

As word spread, significant colonies grew up both in Newlyn and St Ives. Newlyn was south-facing and had the advantage of being close to Penzance, not only a town of some substance, but also the terminus of the railway, so that travel north was more convenient. St Ives, on the other hand, was reached only by rail via a branch line and had no large town nearby. It also had in the early 1880s a rather poor reputation as a dirty, stinking fishing village, with an inadequate water supply and poor drainage, but once these issues were addressed, it became a haven for marine painters, because its north-facing location meant that the sun lit up the waters of St Ives Bay from dawn until dusk. The coastline in both directions was also very attractive, rugged headlands to the north, dune-backed sands to the south, whilst the wild, bleak, gorse-clad moors in what was called the Hinterland, with their Celtic remains, had their own solitary, brooding majesty, particularly in winter, when the bracken had taken on a cinnamon tint. The romantics dubbed this 'faerie country'.

The artists' lifestyle

Whilst agreeing with Gotch that colony life led to valued friendships, Titcomb, in his speech, felt it important to stress some of the disadvantages of being in a remote cultural outpost.

> *Living in Cornwall, we miss the cultivated life of London. We have no music, no drama, no pleasant wickednesses; we are fearfully moral and fearfully uncomfortable; we live in miserable lodgings and are at the mercy of Wesleyan landladies, whose forte is certainly not cooking – but we have the compensation of painting side by side with many congenial spirits.*[13]

In order to raise a laugh, Titcomb was probably recalling his early days lodging with Mrs Pearson at 6 The Terrace, St Ives, rather than his current state of affairs, which saw him living with his wife in an attractive newly-built property

11. Filson Young, 'An Aquatint', article in *The Outlook*, reproduced in *St Ives Times*, 5 June 1914.
12. C. Ranger-Gull, *Portalone*, London, 1904, p. 145.
13. *Nottingham Evening Post*, 28 September 1894.

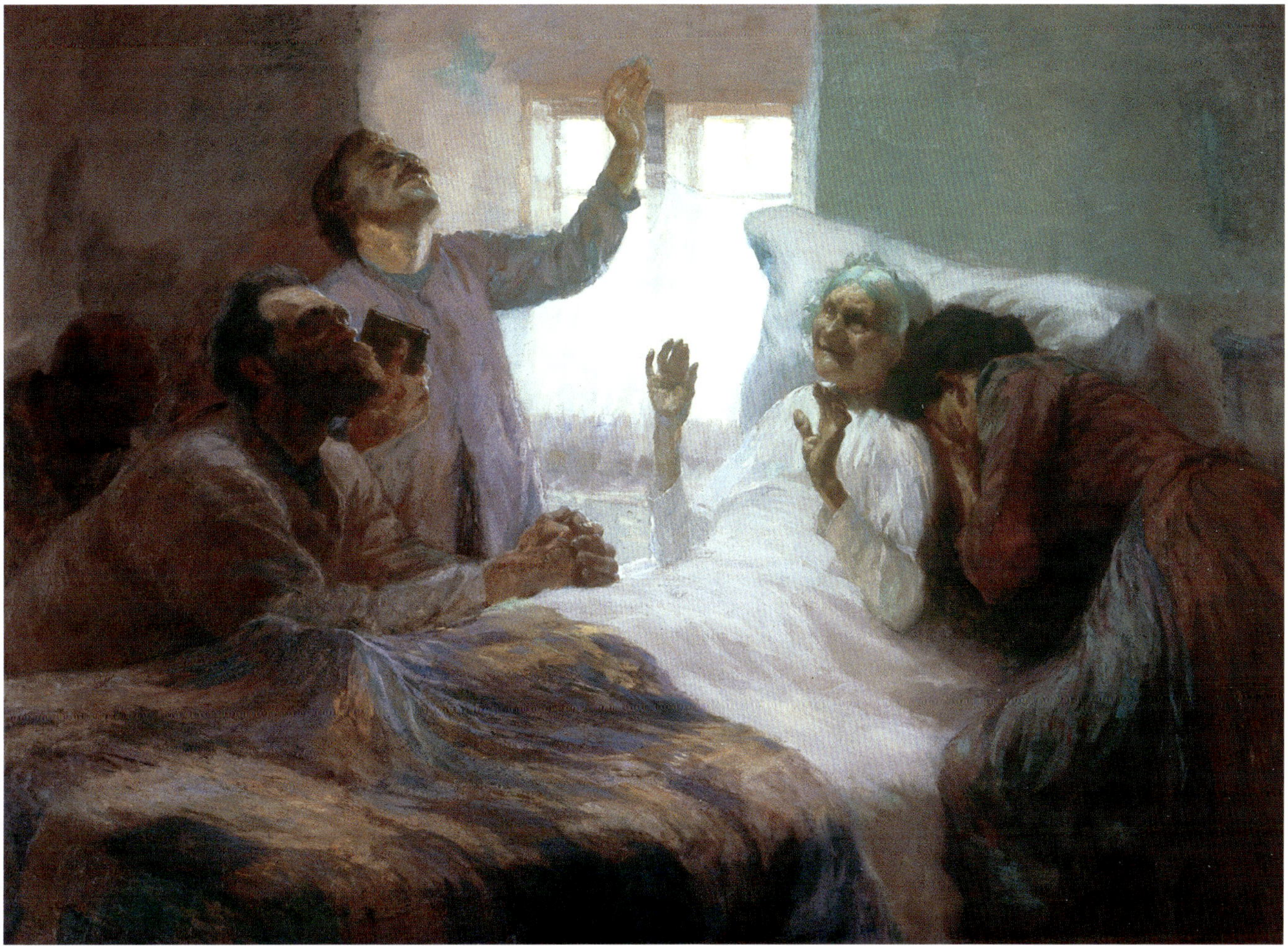

William Titcomb
Piloting Her Home
Art Gallery of Ontario, Toronto; image courtesy the Artist's Estate

This scene, which features the old lady, Janet Rouncefield, who had modelled for Titcomb a number of times, was actually witnessed by him as he came to pay his last respects before leaving the country for a year's visit to Italy. He told an enquirer, 'I found the old woman apparently dying, her daughter crying by her bedside. Presently the door was flung open and four fishermen entered to pray with her. We all knelt, and between my fingers I could not but watch the scene, being delighted with its beauty and interest, at the contrast between the bronzed, hard men and the frail old woman almost in ecstasy at death's door, waving her arms and talking familiarly to Jesus, as only Methodists can.'' On his return, he found that the woman had survived and he got the participants to re-enact the scene in his studio, having over 40 sittings from them.

* The letter has been framed and hangs in the Fore Street Methodist Chapel.

in Richmond Terrace in the town, flanked by other artists. In the early years of the colonies, artists tended to come and go, returning to their family homes or exploring other colonies in Britain and abroad. This meant that they did not wish to commit themselves to long leases of either homes or studios, and so ended up taking rooms with landladies, because this gave them maximum flexibility. The arrangements made with such landladies, as to the number and type of rooms offered, and the culinary arrangements, varied considerably, but, as it was not unusual for artists to end up based in such rooms for as much as nine months, it is not surprising that the particular eccentricities or deficiencies of their landlady began to pall after a while. However, after a few years, artists began to feel more committed to their Cornish life and so decided to become more independent by taking leases of both homes and studios; this was particularly the case, naturally, after artists had got married.

Whilst it is clear that artists soon made friends amongst local members of their class in their villages, they relied to a considerable degree on their fellow artists for their social life. Dinners, musical and card-playing evenings, billiards and amateur dramatics were among the interior pastimes that made the winter evenings pass, whilst cricket, golf, tennis and walking were outdoor activities for long summer days. Accordingly, they soon had settled down to a way of life that seemed very attractive to a city dweller, as a correspondent to the *Westminster Gazette* reported, after a visit to St Ives, in 1896, 'I can say without hesitation that more genial, kindly, hospitable society does not exist in England than in the artist colony, who dwell in the villas and terraces on the heights above St Ives. Simplicity of life, refinement and cultivated taste, love of outdoor nature, and freedom from convention, combine to form a moral atmosphere which is like a tonic, an antiseptic, after the sickly "decadence" of much of the artistic society of London'.[14] The lifestyle in Newlyn was just as attractive, the principal difference between the two colonies being that the artists in St Ives had formed, in August 1890, the St Ives Arts Club, and tended to meet for their entertainment, particularly on a Saturday night, in the Club's premises on Westcott's Quay, whilst the arrangements at Newlyn were less formal.

The colonies were particularly vibrant during the winter months, when the artists settled down to work upon their major exhibition pieces, and the highlight of the artistic calendar was Show Day, a date selected in March. This was when the artists opened their studios to the public to display the paintings that they intended to send to the leading exhibitions of the year, principally the Royal Academy and the Paris Salon. The fact that the fisherfolk were not only welcomed to partake in the spectacle by the artists, but were sufficiently intrigued by the crowds to do the rounds of studios themselves, says much for the mutual respect that developed between them. The result was, in the words of Charles Vulliamy, a student at Newlyn, 'a most curious, a unique crowd of picture-gazers. Pallid high-brows, with their black stocks and floppy hats, stand by the side of chubby old fishwives; and ladies who would cut a seemly figure in the tea room at the Trocadero are elbowed by tough sailor men from the quay. Thus, in a strong smell made up of fish, tar, creosote, oil-paint, and things which are better imagined than described, a truly democratic set of sight-seers moves from studio to studio.'[15]

Painting in Newlyn prior to 1894

The date of the formation of the art colony at Newlyn is normally given as 1882, but locals will have seen very little change in the habits of artists this year from previous years. Ever since the completion of the rail link to Penzance in 1859, artists had been a regular sight around the town and Henry Martin (1835–1908), a painter of coastal landscapes and fishing subjects, had been a resident of the village for all of the 1870s. However, the first of the artists with a more modern approach to base himself in the village for a significant period was Walter Langley, from Birmingham. After visits in both 1880 and 1881, he settled in Newlyn in 1882

14. Reproduced in *St Ives Weekly Summary*, 19 September 1896.
15. Charles Vulliamy, *Unknown Cornwall*, London, 1925, p. 75.

and was always recognised by his fellow artists as the first 'Newlyner'. He also achieved conspicuous success in 1883 with some of his first Cornish watercolours. When Stanhope Forbes, who was to become the leader of the colony, 'stumbled upon' Newlyn in January 1884, he found Langley, his Birmingham friend, Edwin Harris and Ralph Todd, whom Forbes had met previously in Quimperlé, already in residence, but, as the year passed, more and more artists, arrived, for reasons which Forbes could not precisely determine.[16] These included Frank Bramley, Henry Tuke, Chevallier Tayler and a further Birmingham friend, William Wainwright, who was included in the 1894 exhibition, despite having worked in Newlyn for only some six months or so during 1884.

The colony at Newlyn first attracted significant attention in the London art world, when Stanhope Forbes' *A Fish Sale on a Cornish Beach* was hung at the Royal Academy in 1885. This received considerable praise from the critics, who thought that it warranted being bought by the Chantrey Bequest for the nation, but the Trustees were put off by the clear French influence upon the artist's technique. The painting, which is still regarded as the seminal 'Newlyn School' work, showed fish laid out and groups of fisherfolk conversing on the beach at Newlyn, which, still wet from the receding tide, was like 'a shining mirror', as it reflected light from the grey sky. Painted on the spot by Forbes, who had to cope with fainting models, rain storms, howling wind and blowing sand, it set the benchmark for what became the Newlyn style, as his colleagues sought to replicate his success. Because of the difficulties of painting large pictures out of doors in bright sunlight, grey days were seen as the optimum time for working and so low-toned paintings became the trade-mark of the colonists, whose ranks were swelled in 1885 by Fred Hall, Henry Detmold, and William Fortescue, amongst others.

Whilst the mild climate in Cornwall made *plein air* painting practicable for the majority of the year, there were, naturally, still periods of poor weather, when the artists were forced to work indoors. In their interior scenes, the Newlyn artists tended to make a feature of the contest between light coming through a small cottage window, usually placed in the background to the picture, and the artificial light in the room from candles or oil lamps, which might be aided by the warm glow of a fire in the hearth. A recent analysis of these interiors suggests that, although many aspects correctly reflect what would have been typical cottage interiors of the time, the artists, in their selection of features to be incorporated, did have in mind the expectations of the general public. In view of the poor light in many cottages, the scenes may also have been rigged up in artist studios. In the main, such interiors are populated by women, seen by Victorians as 'the angel of the household', and the subjects selected cover courtship, motherhood, bereavement and lonely old age, with themes of stability, work, dignity, mutual support and thrift.[17]

In 1886, Stanhope Forbes, Thomas Gotch and Henry Tuke were actively involved in the formation of the New English Art Club, which was intended to challenge the Royal Academy by showcasing the works of the young 'Franco-British savages', and Newlyn artists made significant contributions to its initial show, but a dispute with Henry La Thangue as to its ambitions led to most resigning in 1887, and adopting the conventional route of accepting the Royal Academy Summer Exhibition as the ultimate goal for one's major works. This decision was made easier by the fact that more Cornish works were now deemed acceptable, and Forbes soon found his work was in demand, selling one of his 1886 Academy exhibits, *Off to the Fishing Ground*, to the Walker Art Gallery, Liverpool.

In 1888, the Newlyn artists finally were recognised by the art establishment in Britain, when Frank Bramley's *A Hopeless Dawn* was bought by the Chantrey Trustees for the nation. Whilst this displayed the 'square brush' technique criticised by lovers of academic painting, its subject matter, full of sentiment and pathos, and its reference to a John Ruskin poem, which enabled a full narrative story to be read into the painting, meant that it was just the sort of work that the Victorians appreciated. For a while, as a result, bereavement scenes became rather too commonplace in the Newlyners' output.

16. *The Cornishman* records on 4 September 1884 that there are at least 27 artists in the village.
17. See Mary O'Neill, *Cornwall's 'Fisherfolk'*, Sansom & Co, Bristol, 2014, pp. 13–42.

Thereafter, honours came the way of the Newlyners thick and fast. In 1889, Stanhope Forbes won a gold medal at the Paris World Exposition, which, as it celebrated the centenary of the French Revolution, was the greatest exhibition of the decade, and sold *The Health of the Bride* to Henry Tate and *The Village Philharmonic* to Birmingham Art Gallery. He now had little trouble selling his work and started to produce vast canvases. His new wife, the Canadian, Elizabeth Armstrong, also won a medal at the 1889 Paris World Exposition. Frank Bramley too achieved some notable successes, selling works to both Durban and Auckland art galleries and winning a medal in Paris in 1892. A number of other Newlyners, such as Henry Detmold and William Fortescue, also sold work to public galleries. Their journey from rebels to part of the establishment was completed when Forbes was made an Associate of the Royal Academy in 1892 and Bramley in 1894.

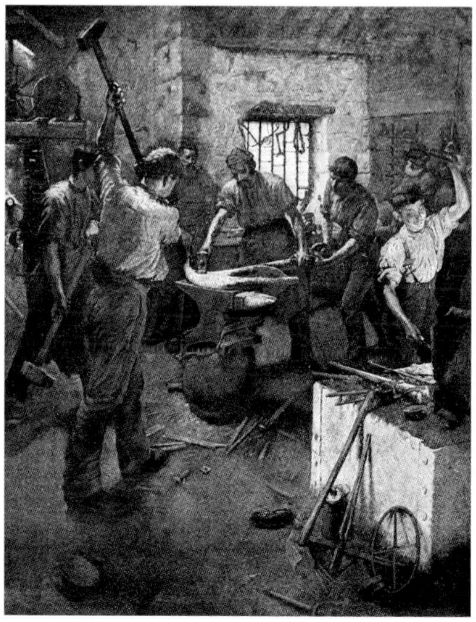

Stanhope Forbes
Forging the Anchor
from the 1894 exhibition catalogue

Just prior to the Nottingham show, the French Government had tried to acquire Stanhope Forbes' *Forging the Anchor*, which had been shown at the Paris Salon that year, but Forbes had already sold it to leading collector, George McCulloch, who lent it to the Nottingham exhibition, whilst the Chantrey Trustees had been keen on Walter Langley's *Ne'er morning wore to evening but some heart did break* at that year's Royal Academy, but had been beaten to it by a private buyer. However, R. Jope-Slade, in his review of the 1894 Academy exhibition, had no doubt that Thomas Gotch's *The Child Enthroned*, a work done in a very different style, was 'the most sensational Newlyn picture of the year'. It had 'something of the conventionality of the early Florentines and something of the naturalism of West Cornwall, and in intense lapis-lazuli blue, rose pink, sap green and gold presents a composition of amazing brilliancy'.[18] Newlyn pictures were very much in demand.

Painting in St Ives prior to 1894

Although artists had been sufficiently prolific in St Ives in the early 1880s for a guide book to the village, specifically directed at them, to have been produced in 1884, the date normally selected for the formation of the colony is 1885, being the first year that artists over-wintered there. Those artists were the Scot, William Eadie, the Yorkshireman, Harry Robinson, and his Irish fiancée, Dorothy Webb, by far the best artist of the three. In 1886, the Robinsons, now married, were joined by a group of friends of varying nationalities from their days in Concarneau and, as this visit proved enjoyable and successful, that group returned in 1887, along with further friends from Brittany, who included the English landscape painter, Adrian Stokes and his Austrian wife, Marianne, whom he had met and married in Pont-Aven. This meant that, from the outset, the St Ives colony had been an international community, and some of the early settlers, such as the Americans Edward Simmons and Howard Russell Butler, the Swedes Anders Zorn and Emma Lowstadt Chadwick, and the Finns Helene Schjerfbeck and Maria Wiik, had achieved considerable success for the colony at the exhibitions of the Paris Salon, including the Paris World Exposition of 1889. There had also been medals in Paris for English members of the colony – Adrian Stokes, Alfred East, William Titcomb and Louis Grier, the latter's success, *The Night Watch*, featuring in the 1894 exhibition.

Marianne Stokes, whose early figure paintings tended to feature children in rustic naturalist settings, had also achieved significant successes since settling in St Ives. Her Pont-Aven work, *The Parting*, was bought by the Walker Art Gallery, Liverpool in 1885, and she also won medals in Munich in 1890 and at the 1893 Chicago World Columbian Exhibition, where her husband, Adrian, and William Titcomb were also medalled.

International members of the colony who took part in the 1894 exhibition, in addition to Marianne Stokes, were the Americans Lowell Dyer and Sydney Laurence, one of whose works had just gained an Honourable Mention at the

18. R. Jope-Slade, *The Royal Academy and its Recruits, Black and White Handbook to the Royal Academy and New Gallery Pictures*, 1894.

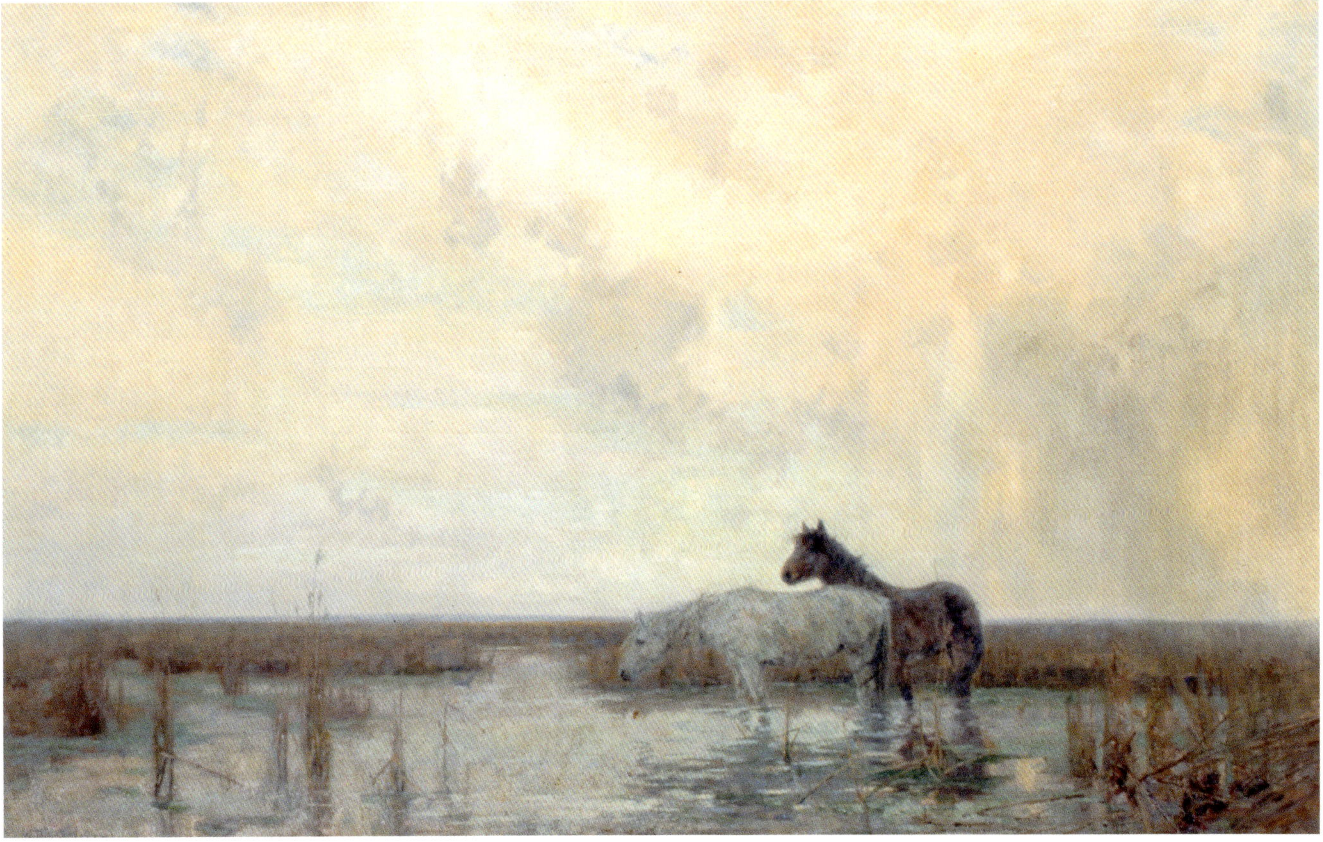

William Dickson
Wide, Wild and Open to the Sea
1893–4 • oil on canvas • 121 x 184.5 cm
The Royal Pavilion & Museums, Brighton & Hove

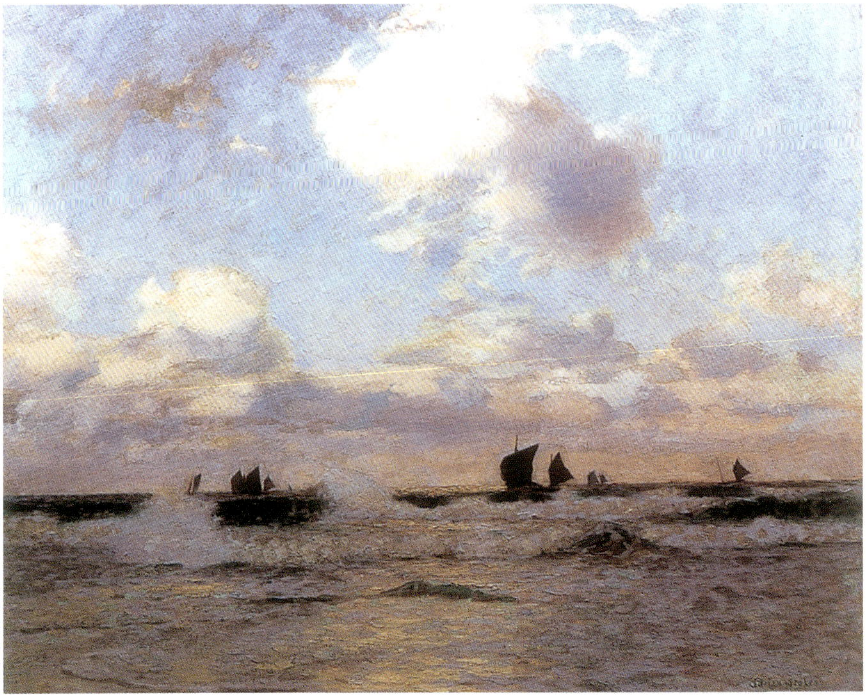

Adrian Stokes
Off St Ives
private collection; image courtesy Messums

Salon that year, and the Canadian, Mary Bell, who had recently married fellow St Ives artist, Charles Herbert Eastlake.

St Ives' development as a centre for landscape and marine painting owed much to Adrian Stokes, whose painting *Upland and Sky* was bought by the Chantrey Trustees for the nation in 1888 – the same year as Bramley's success. He had followed this success up with a series of fine landscape and marine exhibits at the Royal Academy and the New Gallery, such as *The Harbour Bar* (1889), which had been bought by Leeds Art Gallery, and *Off St Ives* (1890), and these established him as one of the leading artists in these genre in the country. As the Barbizon School influenced style and technique of his paintings and their emphasis on atmospheric effect, rather than subject, were considered quite revolutionary, students of landscape painting, particularly from the Herkomer Art School in Bushey, started to make trips down to St Ives to work alongside Stokes. These included Greville Morris, Arthur Meade, Algernon Talmage and, most importantly, John Arnesby Brown, from Nottingham. As these visits proved rewarding, students, like Brown and Talmage, who both went on to become Royal Academicians, decided that they no longer felt the need to study in France, as they could learn all they needed to about *plein air* landscape painting from an acknowledged master in St Ives, who was joined, from time to time, by Alfred East, another rising landscape painter with similar ideals. This young group of landscape and marine painters, which included also John Noble Barlow, Edmund Fuller, Will Osborn, Julius Olsson and Louis Grier, had earned, by the time of the 1894 exhibition, the sobriquet 'The School of Moonrises', because their interest in evoking mood and poetic associations had led to a series of depictions of sunsets, afterglows, twilight and moonlit scenes. However, it was at the 1894 exhibition that they made a significant impact as a group for the first time.

Whilst, by 1894, the number of landscape and marine artists based in St Ives meant that this style of work was most closely associated with the colony, there were still a number of figure painters from St Ives who were represented in the 1894 exhibition, including the first settlers Harry and Dorothy Robinson, and William Eadie, another early settler, William Titcomb, who was consistently referred to in the press as 'a Newlyner', because his work shared the same influences as his Newlyn colleagues, Marianne Stokes, Mary Bell, who inclined towards decorative fancies, and her husband, Charles Eastlake, albeit he later became better known as a landscape painter.

Painting in Falmouth prior to 1894

Falmouth is famous for its harbour, which, together with the Carrick Roads, is reputed to be the third largest natural harbour in the world, and is the deepest in Western Europe. Although the Falmouth Packet Service, which had operated out of the port for over 160 years between 1689 and 1851, had now ceased, it still attracted a lot of shipping as it was the most south-westerly good harbour in Great Britain. Accordingly, it was often the first port for returning Royal Navy ships. It had also enjoyed a good rail service from 1863.

Whilst Falmouth had been the home of a number of prolific pre-colony marine and coastal watercolourists, such as Thomas Hart and James George Philp, it did not seem to attract that many of the 'Franco-British savages', and the art colony there at the time of the 1894 exhibition was restricted to Charles Napier Hemy, who had settled there in 1880, William Ayerst Ingram (1855-1913), who was based there from 1882, albeit having brief flirtations with both Newlyn and St Ives subsequently, Henry Tuke, who had moved across from Newlyn in 1885, William H. Humphris (1851–1917) and John Herbert Eva Downing (1859-1932). When asked in 1895 whether he identified with the Newlyn School, Tuke responded, 'No, we consider ourselves quite a distinct branch of the brotherhood, and we are a congenial set too.'[19] Of these five, only Hemy and Tuke were represented in

19. Flora Klickman, 'The Life Story of a Famous Painter', *Windsor Magazine*, 1895, pp. 608–9.

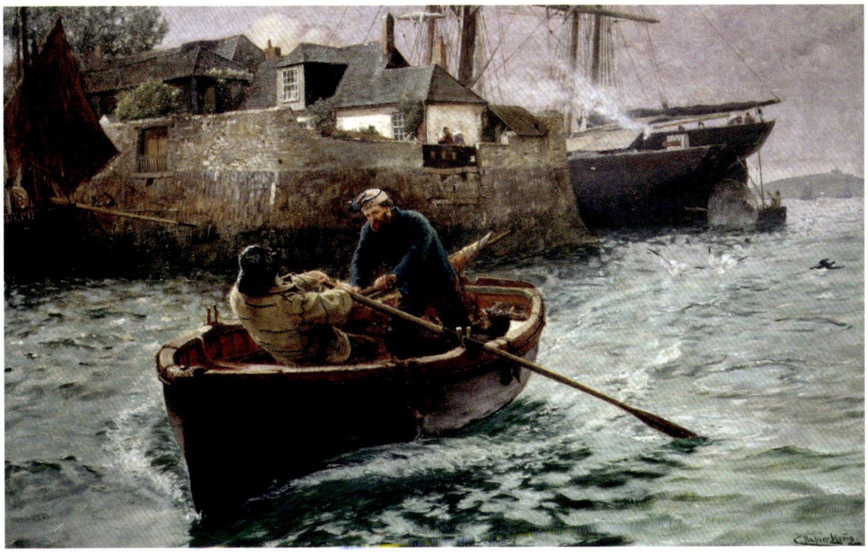

Charles Napier Hemy
Homeward
1885 • oil on canvas • 91 x 137.5 cm

the 1894 exhibition. Although Jack Downing was a good friend of Tuke and had been involved with Tuke and Ingram in setting up Falmouth Art Gallery in 1894, his omission is not a surprise, as he was little more than an amateur. However, both Humphris and Ingram had been included in the Cornish Artists' exhibition at Dowdeswells in 1890 and Ingram's omission is particularly strange, as he was well represented in the contemporaneous marine exhibition at Birmingham.

Hemy's decision to base himself in Cornwall had nothing to do with art, but resulted from his desire to acquire a good Catholic wife to provide the home life that he craved after the death of his first wife. As Amy Freeman, the girl recommended to him by his priest, lived in Falmouth, he chose to live there. In fact, as he had always had a hankering after the sea, the fishing industry operating from the port there proved ideal as subject matter for him. Initially, he was forced to make his sketches in an open boat, which tested his endurance to the limits, but, having hit on the idea of a floating studio, he was able not only to work far more comfortably, but also to explore other sections of the Cornish coast. Accordingly, he came to specialize in depictions of the fisherfolk going about their business off shore, and had made a number of sales to public galleries by the time of the 1894 exhibition.

Tuke, who knew Falmouth well from visits with his family as a young man, was a keen sailor also and he too decided to acquire in 1886 a boat – a French brigantine – for use as a studio. For the first few years of his time in Falmouth, his style resembled closely that of the Newlyn painters and, in 1889, his large painting, *All Hands to the Pumps*, was bought by the Chantrey Trustees. However, *The Bathers*, which was bought by Leeds Art Gallery in 1890, and was included in the 1894 exhibition, marked a change of style. This featured naked boys getting ready to swim off his boat in bright sunlight. Henceforth, this was to be his speciality, and his boat enabled him to sketch his models in hidden away sandy coves on the Fal estuary, only reachable from the sea, so that he could work undisturbed. At the Royal Academy in 1894, another fine work in this vein, *August Blue*, was bought by the Chantrey Trustees, providing respectability for such subjects. Accordingly, whilst the Falmouth contingent was small, both Hemy and Tuke were highly acclaimed artists.

The 1894 exhibition had the clumsy title 'Special Exhibition of Pictures by Cornish Painters of Newlyn, St Ives, Falmouth, etc'. The 'etc' seems to have been for the benefit of Ernest Fox of Marazion, albeit he had decided to leave Cornwall by the time the exhibition actually opened, and for Walter Jevons, who had moved from St Ives to St Martins on The Lizard.

With this exceptional array of talented artists, who had been much in the news recently, no wonder Nottingham was so proud and delighted to have persuaded the Cornish Brotherhoods to exhibit in their beautiful new Gallery.

Memories of the Dowdeswells 'frost'

The 1894 exhibition was not the first time that the Cornish artists had shown together outside Cornwall. In December 1890, Dowdeswells, the New Bond Street dealers, had devoted an exhibition exclusively to their works. However, this had met with a poor critical reception and very few sales. Gotch, in a letter to Wallis, called it 'a failure', whilst Titcomb, in his speech at Nottingham, was damning in his assessment. He called it 'a frost literally and metaphorically, for it was held in the last week of December. It was badly arranged, nobody sent a representative picture, and I am afraid our enemies called it a pot boiling exhibition.'[20] The *Pall Mall Budget* was also minded to look back at the Dowdeswell show, when reviewing the Nottingham one, and concluded that it had shown the Newlyners at their worst. 'They were like a flock of sheep, blunderingly following one, or at the most, two shepherds, repeating their errors without the excuse of novelty, and revealing a monotonous taste for mournful subject and dismal colour that was depressing.'[21] Whilst the plethora of mournful subjects tended to emanate from Newlyn, Arnesby Brown recorded that grey, low toned works had become rather a fashion for the St Ives landscapists as well, it being thought the height of vulgarity to paint sunlight!

Such reactions to the Dowdeswells show had hurt, but the criticisms had been taken on board and, in the intervening four years, a number of the artists had taken a conscious decision to move away from rustic naturalism and emphasize their own individual vision. For some, this meant introducing more symbolism into their works; others chose subjects from the realms of fancy or from history, literature, myth or legend, whilst landscape and marine painters looked to produce what they termed lyrical, idealist or neo-romantic mood pieces. Accordingly, having widened considerably the range of their work, the artists from Newlyn were uneasy with the term 'Newlyn School', for the word 'School' suggested a common mode of painting. In his speech at the luncheon, Thomas Gotch commented, 'That term, given to them by a generous press, had been a continual source of worry to those of the Newlyn School and they had had some hesitation in adopting it.'[22] Furthermore, not unnaturally, the artists of St Ives and Falmouth did not take kindly to being bracketed with the Newlyn artists, with all the associations that now brought, and desired that the very different make-up of the various colonies should be recognised. Accordingly, it is clear from the pre-publicity for the exhibition that the artists had banned the use of the term 'Newlyn School'; instead, Wallis was forced to use the phrase 'Cornish Brotherhoods' – for the artists had previously referred to 'the Brotherhood of the Palette'.

However, whereas Wallis could influence the advance notices about the exhibition, which in general did refer to the Cornish Brotherhoods, he had no control over the reviews of the exhibition, which invariably labelled the exhibition a 'Newlyn School' show, despite in many instances praising the landscape work of the St Ives artists as being the most interesting aspect of the exhibition. For instance, the critic at the *Nottingham Express* commented, 'What struck me most, perhaps, was the strength of the landscape section'. These works, he felt, were 'a revelation of the meaning of Newlyn principles applied to landscape'.[23] This is a fascinating comment, given that the term 'Newlyn School' these days is nearly always used to refer to figure painters only. What the critic presumably meant was that the

20. *Nottingham Evening Post*, 28 September 1894.
21. *Pall Mall Budget*, 4 October 1894. This was clearly written by R. Jope-Slade, who had said much the same thing in *The Royal Academy and its Recruits, Black and White Handbook to the Royal Academy and New Gallery Pictures*, 1894.
22. *Nottingham Evening Post*, 28 September 1894.
23. *Nottingham Express*, 5 October 1894.

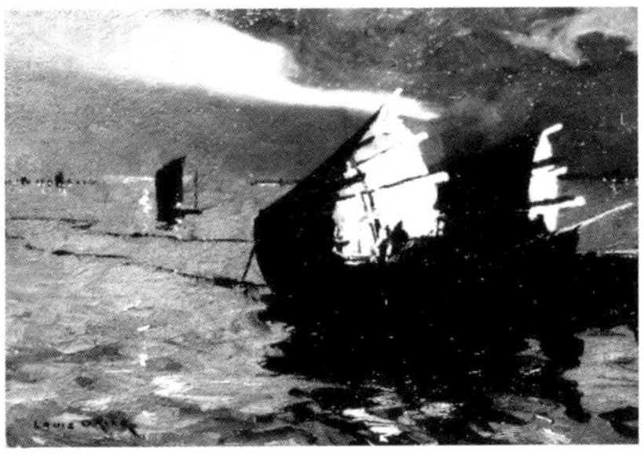

Louis Grier
The Night Watch
location unknown: image from private collection

St Ives landscapists, like their figure painting colleagues, were not interested in highly finished works with solid outlines, but used broad brushes, produced fuzzy edges and had an over-riding interest in capturing light and atmosphere – all consequences of their French-influenced training. They too, therefore, fit neatly into the term 'The Cornish Group of Anglo-French Painters'.

Impending changes

In retrospect, the Nottingham exhibition can be seen to have captured the Cornish artists at the very point at which change was occurring. There can be little argument that, whatever successes the St Ives artists had enjoyed on the international stage prior to 1894, the artists of the Newlyn colony were better known and more successful in the British art world. At the time of the exhibition, Newlyn was vibrant and, on Show Day the next year, an artist, probably Thomas Gotch, in conversation with Herbert Thomas, who went on to become editor of *The Cornishman*, said, 'Newlyn, you know, is really progressive. Every year, there is a greater assertion of individuality amongst the younger men; and we are changing our methods and subjects as we discover wherein lie our individual strengths.'[24] That year, the philanthropist, Passmore Edwards, also arranged for the Newlyn artists to have their own gallery in the village, so that their works could be seen to better effect. However, 1895 also saw the beginning of an exodus from the colony, for reasons that are unclear, and, within a couple of years, Bramley, Harris, Hall, Chevallier Tayler, Frank Richards, Craft, Da Costa and Ireland Blackburne had joined Detmold and Bourdillon in moving away, and Gotch followed in 1900. At the turn of the century, therefore, the only significant artists in the Newlyn colony were Stanhope and Elizabeth Forbes, Walter Langley, Henry Rheam and a disconsolate Norman Garstin, who was unable to sell his work.

This was in stark contrast to St Ives, where, from 1895, Schools of Painting devoted almost exclusively to landscape and marine painting, run by Julius Olsson, Louis Grier, Algernon Talmage and John Noble Barlow, had led to in an influx of young, talented newcomers. This resulted in the following comparison between the colonies to be made in April 1900. 'At Newlyn, the artists – at any rate those who are left – are mostly veterans, men who have won their spurs or have begun to think wistfully of the grey in their beards and the many milestones they have passed. At St Ives, some of the strongest wielders of the brush are broad-shouldered, alert, sanguine, bright-eyed young men who are strenuously working their way to the front. But while at Newlyn, the gaps in the ranks are not being filled by talented newcomers, at St Ives one meets many new names and the younger men are forging ahead and bidding their seniors look to their laurels.'[25] This influx of new talent into St Ives continued until 1914, by which time it had developed an international reputation as the 'Mecca' of the seascapist.

Falmouth continued much as before. The colony did not really grow in size, but Hemy and Tuke continued to enhance their reputations, and so it was not forgotten. Newlyn's decline was reversed by the establishment of the Forbes School of Painting in 1899, which began to attract some talented young artists to the colony. St Ives' dominance, though, was not challenged until the Lamorna colony became established in 1912.

24. *The Cornishman*, 4 April 1895.
25. *St Ives Weekly Summary*, 7 April 1900.

WHEN CORNWALL CAME TO NOTTINGHAM: THE 1894 EXHIBITION

Sarah Skinner

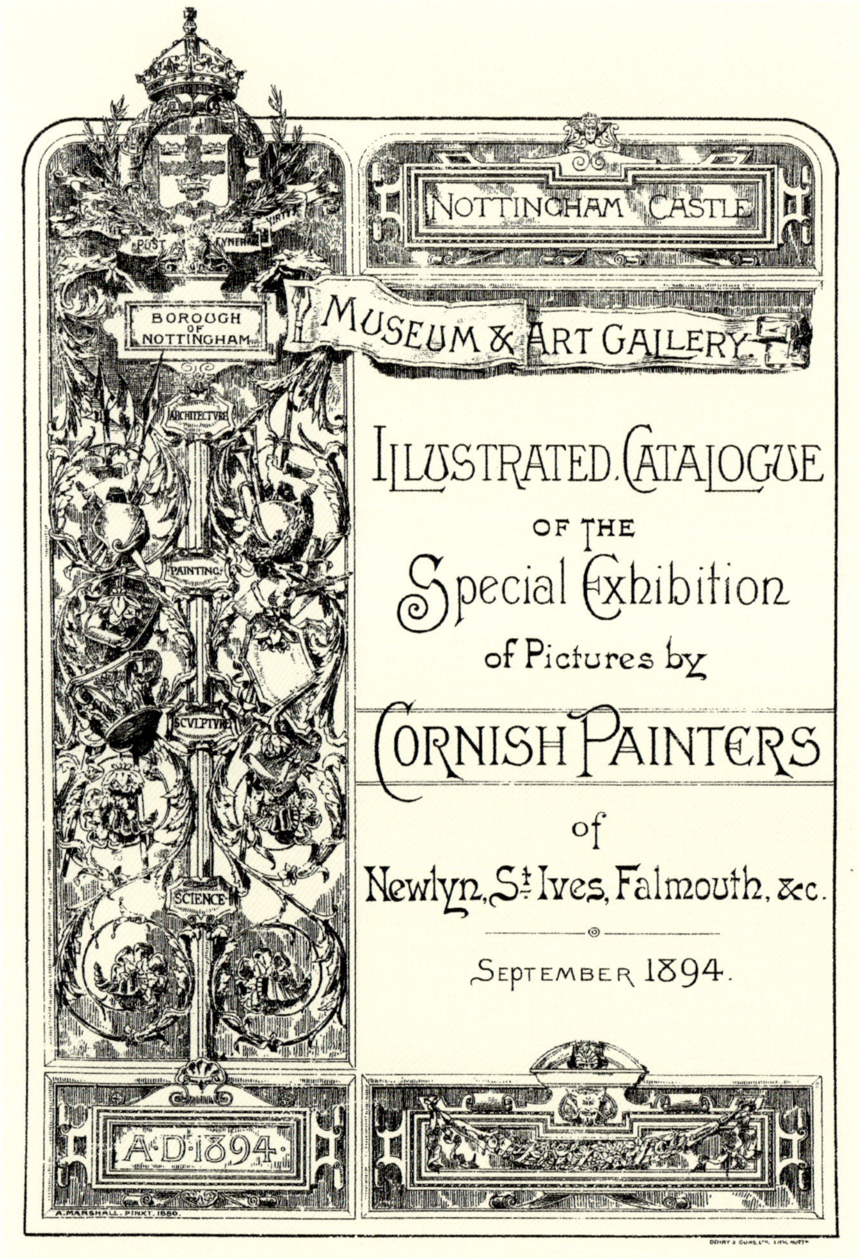

1894 exhibition catalogue cover
private collection

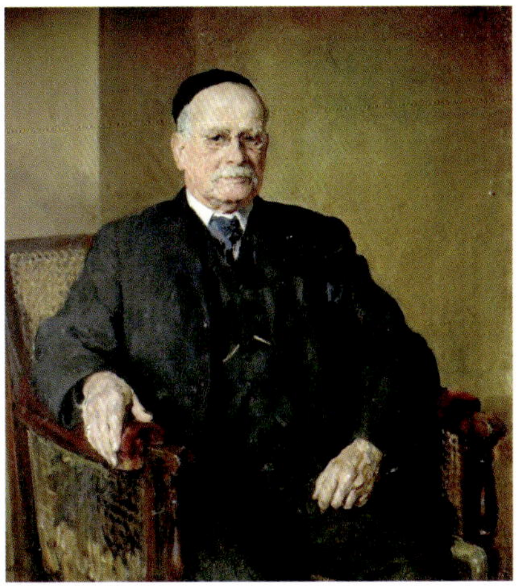

T.C. Dugdale
Portrait of George Harry Wallis
Nottingham City Museums and Galleries

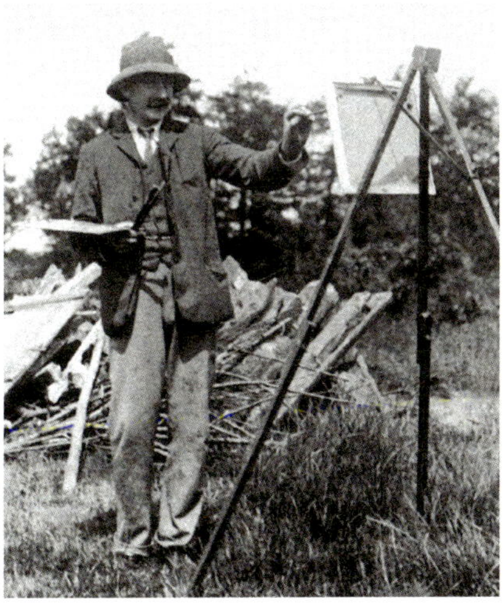

John Arnesby Brown painting
en plein air
private collection

Perhaps it is best that such an exhibition should be held in such a central town as Nottingham ...

On Saturday 29 September 1894 Nottingham Castle Museum and Art Gallery opened a 'Special Exhibition of Pictures by Cornish Painters of Newlyn, St Ives, Falmouth etc.'

The exhibition consisted of 234 paintings[1] by 50 different artists who were based permanently in Cornwall or were working regularly there. Cornwall then was a remote and little-known area of the country. The exhibition was a major undertaking for the Art Director and Curator of the Museum and Art Gallery, George Henry (Harry) Wallis, and there must have been an element of risk: why bring Cornish art to the Midlands? Today these early Cornish paintings may look easy on the eye, but one hundred years ago they were at the cutting edge of contemporary art. Wallis had chosen to exhibit paintings representing a major new movement in British art.

Most of the artists included in the 1894 exhibition, with a few exceptions, were British, but they had studied their craft on the continent, particularly in Paris. In the French capital, students from a wide range of countries and backgrounds could enrol in an 'atelier', gathering together in a master artist's studio to draw and paint while receiving direction and criticism. A more informal type of art tuition offered in Paris was the opportunity to visit historic collections at the Louvre, major exhibitions at the Luxembourg, as well as contemporary work in commercial galleries. Students would have had the opportunity to see exhibitions of work by Impressionist and Post-Impressionist[2] artists and absorb their modern approach to painting technique and subject matter. One further forum was the Parisian café where like-minded artistic people gathered and all forms of art: painting, sculpture, drama, dance, philosophy and music were discussed.

From this range of metropolitan-based art studies came, somewhat ironically, a commitment to travelling beyond the city to paint in the open air. Artists developed interests in 'unspoiled' rural life as well as in light and atmospherics. They rejected high levels of painterly finish, finding them an inadequate way of conveying what they, as artists, felt and saw. Artists' colonies sprung up on the continent and before long Cornwall, with its mild weather, clear light, remoteness and rustic lifestyle, became a real draw for artists who wanted to paint out in the open. There, they found a range of new subjects.

Even today, it would be unusual for a gallery in one region to focus on the art of another. The reason for the exhibition of Cornish art in Nottingham might remain a puzzle but for news reports from the opening of the exhibition where artist T.C. Gotch said he believed that Wallis had been 'prompted by Mr Arnesby Brown'[3] to put together the exhibition. John Arnesby Brown had been a student at the Nottingham School of Art before moving on to study at the respected Herkomer Art School, Bushey, run by portrait and social realist painter Hubert von Herkomer. Many students at the Herkomer Art School moved on to Cornwall and in 1889 Arnesby Brown travelled to St Ives for the first time, painting and meeting there artists such as Stanhope Alexander Forbes and Adrian Stokes.

Whether the suggestion of a young artist was reason enough to spark Wallis' interest, the Art Director would also have been aware of the growing success of Cornish artists and the notice their paintings were gaining. Cornish art was making a stir at the annual Summer Exhibitions held at the Royal Academy of Arts in London, the most prestigious exhibiting venue in England and the best forum for the artists to make sales. Stanhope Forbes' *A Fish Sale on a Cornish Beach*, painted in the open air on the beach at Newlyn and exhibited at the Royal Academy in 1885 was the first Cornish colony work to receive critical and public acclaim. Subsequently the Chantrey Trustees had acquired paintings for

1. Contemporary reports and reviews quote different totals but 234 pictures are listed in the published catalogue.
2. Artists such as Seurat, Gauguin, Cézanne and Van Gogh although the term Post-Impressionist was not used until 1910 when Roger Fry exhibited 'Manet and the Post-Impressionists' in London.
3. *Express*, 29 September 1894, Nottingham City Museums and Galleries Archives Press Cuttings.

the nation by Frank Bramley and Adrian Stokes in 1888, and Henry Tuke in 1889 and 1894.[4] Many of the new provincial public galleries had acquired work by a wide range of Cornish artists, whilst wealthy private collectors, such as Henry Tate and George McCulloch made enthusiastic purchases.

Wallis was keen to show major work at the 1894 Nottingham exhibition and the loan of Frank Bramley's *A Hopeless Dawn* was considered a coup, but he failed to borrow Stanhope Forbes' *Off to the Fishing Ground*, which had already been promised to an exhibition of marine painting at Birmingham Art Gallery, curated by Harry Wallis' brother Whitworth. The Birmingham exhibition certainly gave Harry Wallis some problems in bringing the Nottingham exhibition together, suggesting that perhaps the brothers did not discuss work matters and potential programming clashes. It also resulted in a slight spat, with Whitworth Wallis writing to the *Nottingham Guardian* to challenge Henry Blackburn's assertion in his opening speech that the Nottingham exhibition was 'educational', while the Birmingham exhibition merely showed 'work of a popular kind'![5]

Bringing Cornwall to Nottingham: How the exhibition was put together

The first official mention of the exhibition of Cornish painters appears in the Castle Museum Committee minutes of a meeting held on 6 June 1894, just three months ahead of the exhibition's late September opening: 'Mr Wallis suggested that the Autumn Exhibition should consist of Works by Cornish Painters forming the Newlyn and St Ives Brotherhood. Resolved that this be agreed to and that Mr Wallis be authorised to make the necessary arrangements.'[6] Planning and negotiations must have begun well before this, with correspondence from artists in the museum archives dating from early April 1894, some mentioning a visit made by Wallis to St Ives,[7] presumably some time in March. It is no surprise then that just one month later, at the July committee meeting, Wallis was able to report of '103 pictures having been promised by Public Galleries, Private Lenders and Artists, about forty painters being represented.'[8]

The museum archives hold many letters, some routine, some fascinating, as loans of pictures were negotiated. Although the museum archives are one-sided, holding correspondence from artists and other lenders rather than letters sent out from the museum, much interesting information may be gleaned from them.

Wallis was clearly very specific about wanting good, recent work from the artists and he named pictures in at least some of his requests. He was intent on displaying the very best work he could obtain and the resulting exhibition was made up in the main of large scale, high impact, 'exhibition' work. Wallis' original intention was to fill only the Long Gallery with Cornish work but in the end most of the first-floor galleries were dedicated to the exhibition. A transcription of Wallis's original approach to artists shows that initially he requested three to four works from them[9] but he accepted more pictures and made further requests later on as he became clearer about the pictures he had secured to fill the museum galleries. In the end some artists were represented by ten pictures or more.

An innovation of the 1894 exhibition was that Wallis intended to display each individual's work together and to make a clear visual space between each artist's work: Dorothy Webb Robinson writes 'I understood you to say that you would hang every artist's pictures together and that your galleries permit that they should be well hung.' This was a progressive proposition and would have been a welcome contrast to the very crowded hangs of the Royal Academy Summer Shows and the Paris Salon. The kind of display Nottingham was offering meant that an artist's work could be better appreciated by the viewer. There would be far less vying for space and battling against contrasting scale or colour scheme.

4. The Chantrey Bequest paintings, purchased for the nation, are now held in the Tate collection.
5. *Nottingham Guardian*, 3 October 1894, Nottingham City Museums and Galleries Archives Press Cuttings.
6. Castle Museum Committee Minutes, 6 June 1894.
7. For example, a letter from Ernest R Fox dated 15 April 1894: 'As I do not live at St Ives I had not the pleasure of seeing you when you were in Cornwall, but Mr Arnesby Brown suggested that I should write to you ...'
8. Castle Museum Committee Minutes, 4 July 1894.
9. 'I am desired to ask whether you are willing to co-operate in the proposed exhibition by contributing three or four important works ...' Transcribed letter, Nottingham City Museums and Galleries Archives.

Borough of Nottingham.
Museum & Art Gallery,
The Castle,
Nottingham.

It is proposed to hold in the principle Gallery of this Museum, in the coming Autumn, an Exhibition of pictures by artists painting in Cornwall, who form the school generally known as the Newlyn and St. Ives Brotherhood.

I am desired to ask whether you are willing to co-operate in the proposed Exhibition by contributing three or four important works; should you however, not have in your possession any pictures — suitable for the above proposal, will you kindly give me the names and addresses of the owners of such works you would wish to be represented by.

The pictures of each painter will be hung together with a space between each work, and all expenses of carriage packing etc. will be defrayed by the Museum Committee.

To ensure the success of the proposed Exhibition, the Committee wish to point out, that it is very important that each artist should — promise to contribute, or assist in obtaining the loan of his best work.

Trusting you will be able to favour me with an early reply.

I have
the honour to be

Your obedient servant
Harry Wallis
Art Director.

Transcribed letter from Harry Wallis to Cornish artists
Nottingham City Museums and Galleries Archives

This modern approach to display was appreciated by the artists and commented on favourably by reviewers although the running order in the catalogue shows that displaying artist's works together was not completely achieved.

It is no surprise that Wallis' proposal of a large-scale, professional exhibition in a public gallery was supported by the Cornish artists. It would act as a riposte and corrective to an exhibition held at Dowdeswells,[10] London in December 1890, where the pictures had not been representative of the high quality of work being created in Cornwall. The exhibition was slated by critics and at the Nottingham exhibition opening luncheon, St Ives artist W.H.Y. Titcomb described the Dowdeswells' exhibition as 'a frost' for the Cornish artists.[11]

However, the archive letters show that there was some initial scepticism from artists about participating in the exhibition and sending their best work. For example, established artist T.C. Gotch writes: 'I have never had the good fortune to sell a picture at Nottingham and one has to think about that ... I can let you have 1. *The Portrait of Mrs Cooke*, 2. *Sharing Fish*. I must decide later about *My Crown and Sceptre* and *A Golden Dream*.'[12] In the end Gotch exhibited eight works, including the show-stopping *My Crown and Sceptre*. He was also one of the key speakers at the exhibition opening luncheon. Some private collectors were reluctant lenders too, Henry Tate wrote: 'I cannot lend any more pictures this year. I have now three lots out and find those who come long distances to see my pictures are much disappointed when they cannot see them.'[13]

Selling the work they submitted to the exhibition was important to most of the artists; several priced their work when agreeing to lend it and the Nottingham Museum Committee was seen as a potential purchaser. The Cornish exhibition fell between two types of exhibition in the Nottingham programme, which had previously included shows of historic items, often borrowed from one private collector, then there were selling exhibitions, in spring work by local artists was shown and in autumn, an exhibition of 'Modern Paintings'. For the Castle Museum Committee, the idea of selling art did not seem at odds with the idea of educating through art.[14] Nottingham Castle Museum and Art Gallery had opened to great acclaim in 1878 as the first publicly-funded (i.e. local authority) museum and art gallery outside London and was established with a strong educational and egalitarian agenda, albeit one heavily concerned with improving design and therefore commercial success, particularly in the town's lace trade. The catalogue of the 1894 Cornish exhibition shows that opening hours and admission charges at the museum were geared towards universal access. The museum opened 10am–9pm Monday to Friday and 10am–9.30pm on Saturdays. Admission was free Monday to Thursday and 1d on Saturday. On Friday admission was 6d, possibly to create one 'quieter' day but this would also have priced out working people and stratified visits from the moneyed classes for one day each week.

As well as contacting artists, Wallis secured loans from regional public galleries that had already purchased Cornish work: Birmingham Art Gallery; Walker Art Gallery, Liverpool; Manchester City Art Gallery; Leeds Art Gallery; Peel Park Museum, Salford; Atkinson Art Gallery, Southport and the Dudley Corporation Art Gallery. Dudley's reason for being unable to lend a work by Henry Harewood Robinson gives an insight into how public galleries were developing their collections: 'It is a recent gift to the Gallery and has not been seen by the public and as it is particularly desirable to induce further gifts for the gallery we have decided to exhibit it in a conspicuous place at our forthcoming Autumn exhibition ...'[15]

Many private collectors also contributed to the exhibition and Wallis collected together paintings from across the country. Given the difficulties the curators have had in tracking down work for the 2015 exhibition, it is some comfort that even in 1894, after just ten years of exhibitions and sales, artists had lost track of their work and Wallis sought help from the Fine Art and General Insurance Company Limited in tracing paintings, to no avail.[16]

10. Messrs Dowdeswell & Dowdeswell's gallery in New Bond Street.
11. Record of the exhibition opening speech, *Nottingham Guardian*, 29 September 1894 held in the Nottingham City Museums and Galleries Archives.
12. Letter dated 27 May 1894, T.C. Gotch, Nottingham City Museums and Galleries Archives.
13. Letter dated 9 July 1894, Nottingham City Museums and Galleries Archives.
14. In contrast to the Manchester Art Treasures Exhibition held in 1857, for example, where there was 'everything to see and nothing to sell'.
15. Letter dated 10 August 1894, Dudley Corporation Art Gallery, Nottingham City Museums and Galleries Archives.
16. Letter dated 5 July 1894, Fine Art and General Insurance Company Limited, Cannon Street, London: 'With reference to previous correspondence I have been instructed to send one of my inspectors in all the principal dealers in London to find out if possible whether they can help us in finding any pictures by the Newlyn School, the present whereabouts of which are unknown to the artists.'

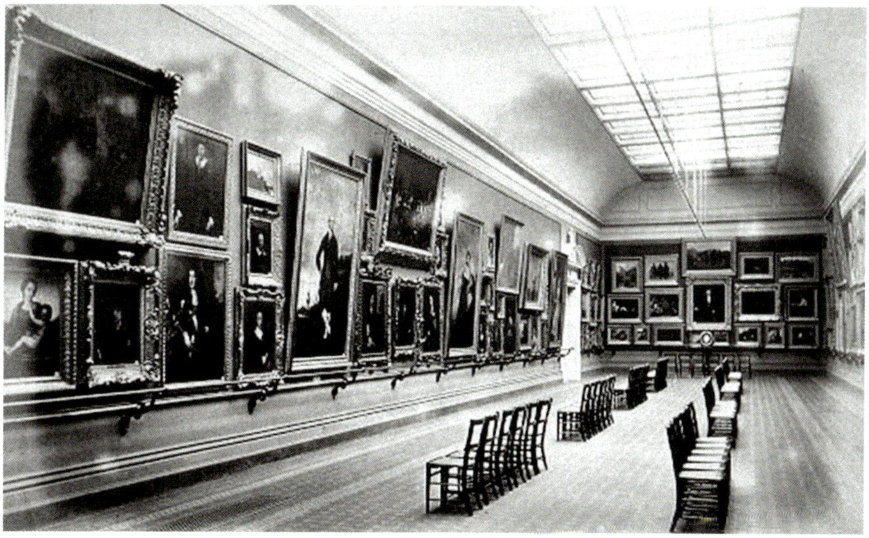

Crowded hang in the Long Gallery at Nottingham Castle (date unknown)
Nottingham City Museums and Galleries Archives

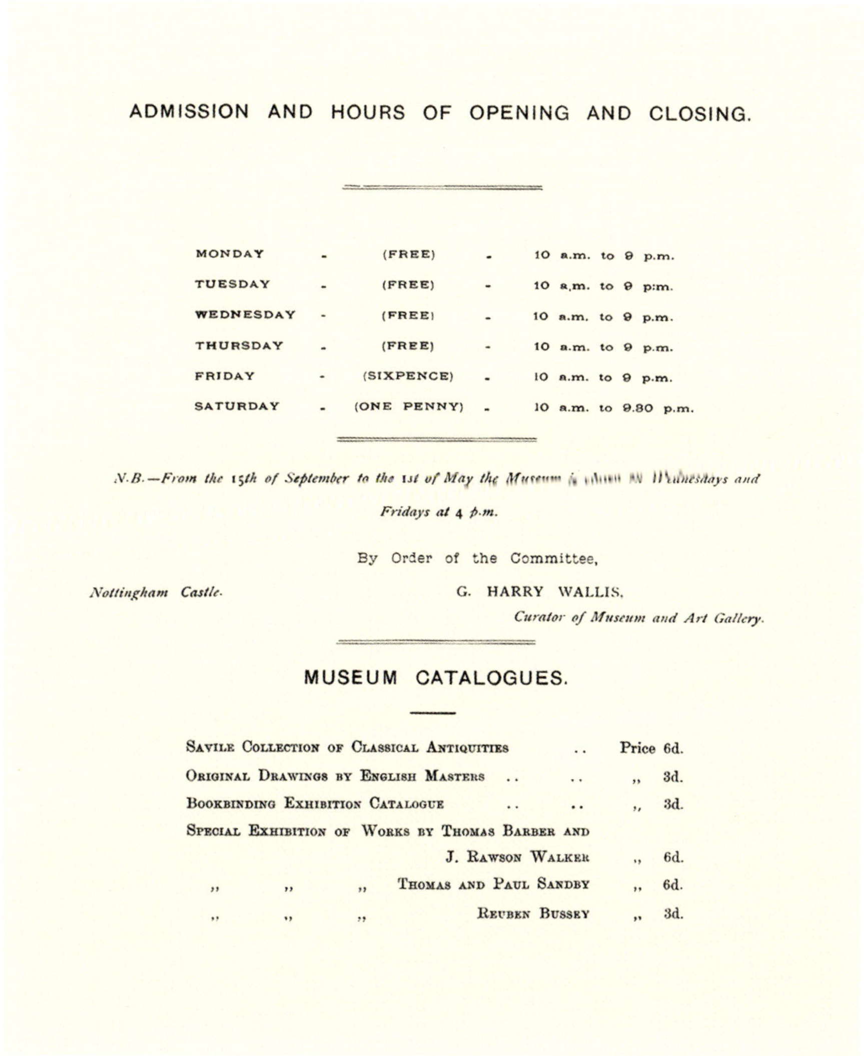

ADMISSION AND HOURS OF OPENING AND CLOSING.

MONDAY	-	(FREE)	-	10 a.m. to 9 p.m.
TUESDAY	-	(FREE)	-	10 a.m. to 9 p.m.
WEDNESDAY	-	(FREE)	-	10 a.m. to 9 p.m.
THURSDAY	-	(FREE)	-	10 a.m. to 9 p.m.
FRIDAY	-	(SIXPENCE)	-	10 a.m. to 9 p.m.
SATURDAY	-	(ONE PENNY)	-	10 a.m. to 9.30 p.m.

N.B.—From the 15th of September to the 1st of May the Museum is closed on Wednesdays and Fridays at 4 p.m.

By Order of the Committee,

Nottingham Castle. G. HARRY WALLIS,
Curator of Museum and Art Gallery.

MUSEUM CATALOGUES.

Savile Collection of Classical Antiquities	..	Price 6d.
Original Drawings by English Masters ..	..	„ 3d.
Bookbinding Exhibition Catalogue ..	..	„ 3d.
Special Exhibition of Works by Thomas Barber and J. Rawson Walker		„ 6d.
„ „ „ Thomas and Paul Sandby		„ 6d.
„ „ „ Reuben Bussey		„ 3d.

Details of admission to the Castle Museum and Art Gallery from the 1894 catalogue
Nottingham City Museums and Galleries Archives

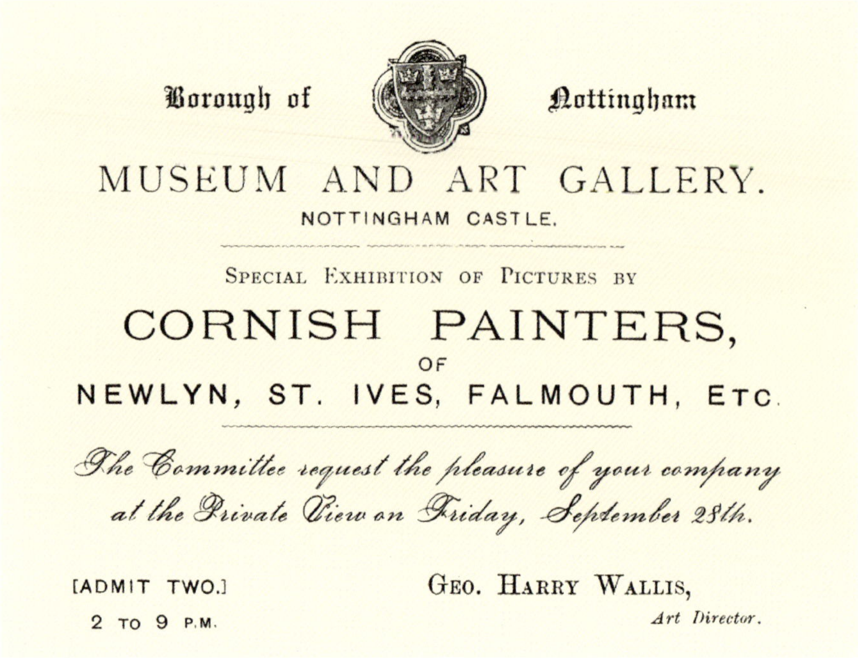

Borough of Nottingham

MUSEUM AND ART GALLERY.

NOTTINGHAM CASTLE.

SPECIAL EXHIBITION OF PICTURES BY

CORNISH PAINTERS,

OF

NEWLYN, ST. IVES, FALMOUTH, ETC.

The Committee request the pleasure of your company at the Private View on Friday, September 28th.

[ADMIT TWO.]

2 TO 9 P.M.

GEO. HARRY WALLIS,

Art Director.

Invitation to the private view of 'Pictures by Cornish Painters'

Nottingham City Museums and Galleries Archives

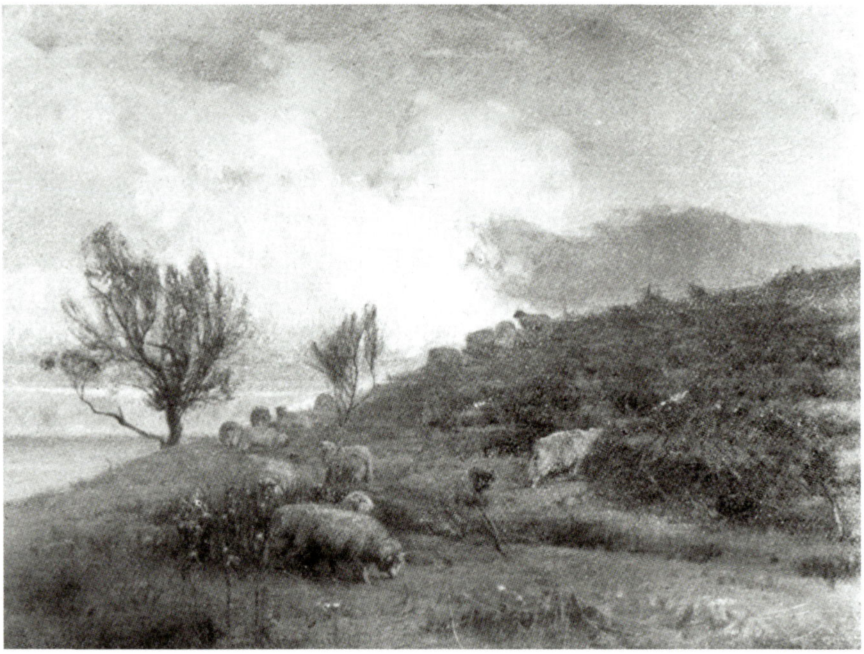

John Arnesby Brown

The Hillside

from the 1894 exhibition catalogue

In terms of the practical organisation of the exhibition, the concerns of 1894 will be recognised by curators, technicians, lending organisations and artists today. Crates were sent to Dudley but were the wrong size; a painting packed and sent by the framers and dealers, James Lanham, in Cornwall, was damaged in transit; Mr Albert Smith sent particular instructions that 'he expects the picture and frame returning to him (after the exhibition) in the same condition as when received. He makes this an obligation as the frames get so knocked about at exhibition.'[17]

Paintings arrived from across Britain, others were brought over from Paris, Vienna and Chicago.

Problems, stresses and strains notwithstanding, the exhibition was installed and ready to open as scheduled on Saturday 29 September 1894 with the private view and opening luncheon taking place on Friday 28 September 1894. The impressive space of the 40-metre Long Gallery was filled with large oil paintings and as promised, artists' pictures were grouped together as far as possible; two more galleries were filled with oils and watercolours. Cornwall had come to Nottingham.

The Exhibition caused a great amount of interest, and attracted visitors from all parts of the country...

Frustratingly, the Castle archives do not hold records for the number of visitors who came to the exhibition, nor have visitor comments survived. However the Annual Report of the Castle Museum Committee records that:

> *The most important of the Special Exhibitions was that of the works of painters who have settled at Newlyn, St Ives, and Falmouth, etc and now generally called the 'Cornish Painters'. It was the first time that so thoroughly a representative collection of these works had been brought together in a public gallery, and the exhibition created not only a local but a world-wide interest. The press, both English and Foreign, considered the Exhibition a remarkable one.*[18]

One of Nottingham's best-known artists, Laura Knight, aged 17 at the time of the Cornish exhibition and finding Nottingham 'aesthetically a desert', later wrote.

> *The most important exhibition I had seen at the Castle was one of the Newlyn School, then at the peak of its fame. My favourite picture then was Frank Bramley's Hopeless Dawn. Tears came into my eyes, I thought it so wonderful. There was also a little grey picture of Newlyn Bridge by Stanhope Forbes; I did not know anyone could paint like that.*[19]

The museum archives hold extensive press cuttings for the exhibition. Wallis understood the importance of marketing and press releases must have been first sent out in June 1894 as notices about the exhibition began to appear in newspapers and journals in Nottingham and beyond around then. *The Globe*, for example noted that 'a thoroughly representative show is promised',[20] the *Lady's Pictorial* commented that the Cornish artists had two of the most accomplished of women painters in their ranks,[21] while the *Western Daily Press* wrote 'it is very creditable that a provincial town has been able to organise an exhibition which would certainly have attracted great attention in London ...'[22]

In fact a recurring theme within the press coverage is a noting of the rise in quality of exhibitions across the country thanks to the establishment of public regional art galleries, presenting a challenge to the dominance of the London exhibiting calendar: 'each great provincial exhibition which we visit brings home to us with surer and surer conviction, that the era of centralization is over and the epoch of local interest, local organisation, local patriotism commenced ...'[23]

17. Letter dated 10 July 1894, Studio and Fine Art Galleries, Bradford, on behalf of Mr Albert Smith, Nottingham City Museums and Galleries Archives.
18. *Annual Report of the Castle Museum Committee for the year ending 31 March 1895.*
19. *Oil Paint and Grease Paint: Autobiography of Laura Knight*, Harmondsworth 1941 (1936). Knight later became part of a second wave of Cornish art colonists, settling in Lamorna.
20. *The Globe*, 6 August 1894, Nottingham City Museums and Galleries Archives Press Cuttings.
21. *Lady's Pictorial*, 28 July 1894, Nottingham City Museums and Galleries Archives Press Cuttings.
22. *Western Daily Press*, 7 August 1894, Nottingham City Museums and Galleries Archives Press Cuttings.

Another theme is the educational remit of galleries in the regions. On the day of the exhibition's public opening, the *Daily Telegraph* wrote:

> *A new departure of much interest has been taken at the autumn exhibition of the Nottingham Castle Art Gallery for some time past the aim and purpose of the able art director Mr G.H. Wallis – whose brother holds a like position in Birmingham – has been to give a series of exhibitions that, being more or less exclusively illustrative of a particular school or locality, shall have a more definite educational value than the omnium gatherum collections usually found in the provinces ...*[24]

And the *Guardian* commented:

> *This is not wholly an appeal to Nottingham. A phase of pictorial art which has by its strength made itself known throughout the whole of England and engaged the keenest attention of foreign nations, is for the first time well housed and exhibited, and there is no doubt that connoisseurs from all parts will come to look at these works of artistic genius. Perhaps it is best that such an exhibition should be held in such a central town as Nottingham. Far removed from the subjects of the works, it is known that the Corporation of Nottingham, in dedicating its Castle to the purpose of high art, has only the wish to encourage art for art's sake.*

They continue:

> *There can be no question that the old relation of the private patronage of art is undergoing a change; and if the English are to maintain as a nation, a high place in the domain of pictorial art, artists must look also to the collective efforts of the great municipalities as well as to private patronage for letting their works be widely known.*[25]

Whether it was his intention or not, in bringing a serious and comprehensive exhibition of contemporary Cornish art to Nottingham Castle Museum and Art Gallery, Wallis had managed to bring to the fore debates around national art, national identity, patriotism and the validity of art in the provinces!

Focusing on the content of the exhibition, there was praise by reviewers for the chance to see a substantial body of high quality work by such an important group of artists. It was felt that since the Dowdeswells exhibition, Cornish artists had developed their use of colour and shrugged off early mannerisms. The landscape paintings were praised by many and the *Guardian* stumbled to express their response to some of the works:

> *It is difficult to describe in words that effect which a painter's imagination adds to his faithful rendering of the world around him; the word 'poetic' means so much and so little; but it appeals to the higher feelings of the spectator ...*[26]

Many critics gave extensive reviews of specific paintings in the exhibition and these are detailed in the catalogue section.

After the show was over

The Special Exhibition of Cornish Art closed on 5 January 1895. The archive correspondence details the return and receipt of many of the works. Wallis was again required to cope with a range of requests from the artists, for example, on 1 January 1895, exhibiting artist Fred Hall wrote 'Will you please send my picture *Adversity* to Messrs Cole Brothers, as early as convenient. I shall be much obliged if you will let me know what condition the frame is in whether it is fit to hang on the walls of a funeral house...'. Frank Bramley was concerned that his picture was dirty and asked for it to be washed down with a clean rag and cold water

23. *Sunday Times*, 16 September 1894, Nottingham City Museums and Galleries Archives Press Cuttings.
24. *Daily Telegraph*, 29 September 1894, Nottingham City Museums and Galleries Archives.
25. *Nottingham Guardian*, 8 September 1894, Nottingham City Museums and Galleries Archives.
26. *Nottingham Guardian*, 4 October 1894, Nottingham City Museums and Galleries Archives.

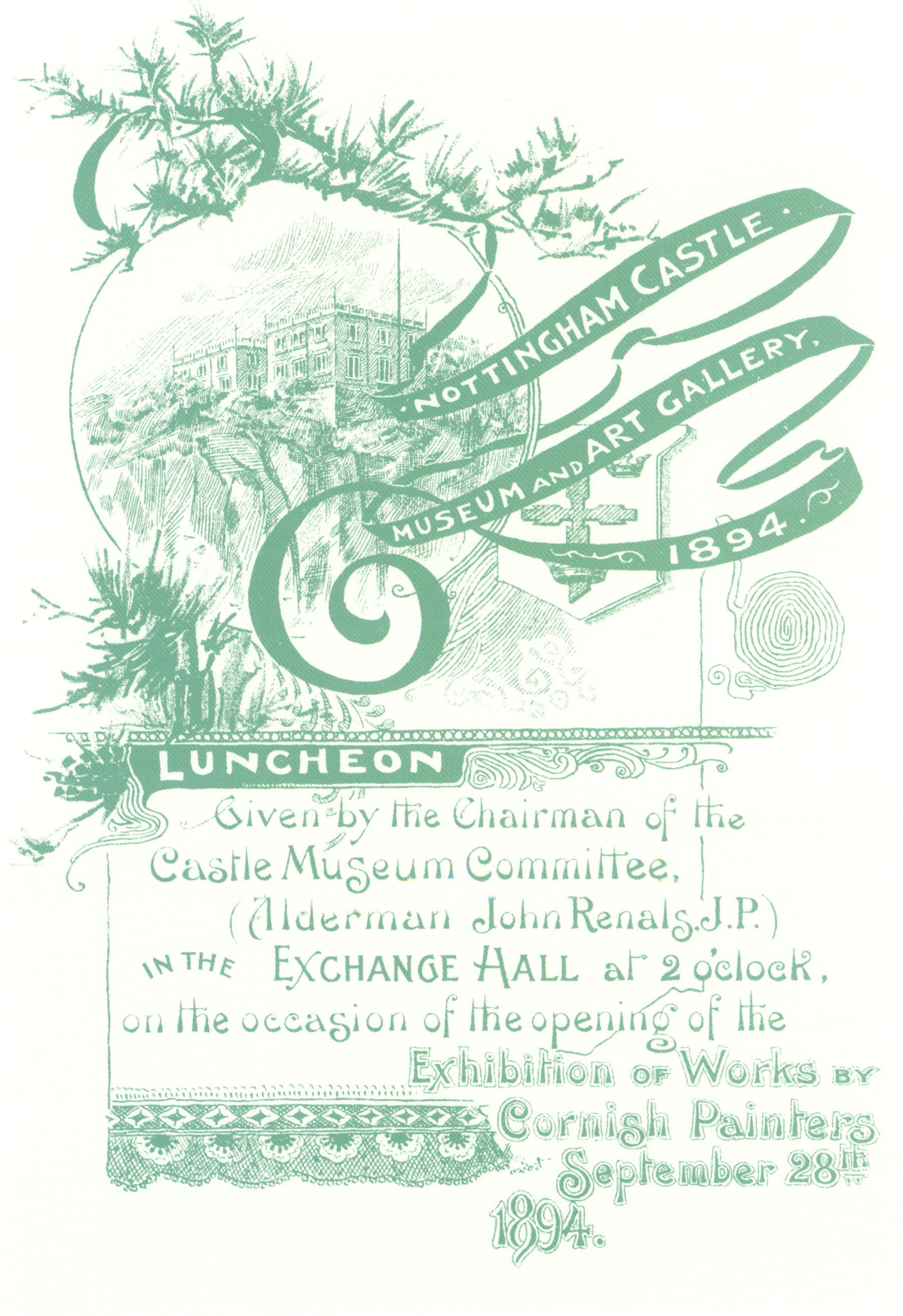

Menu card for the opening lunch of the exhibition
Nottingham City Museums and Galleries Archives

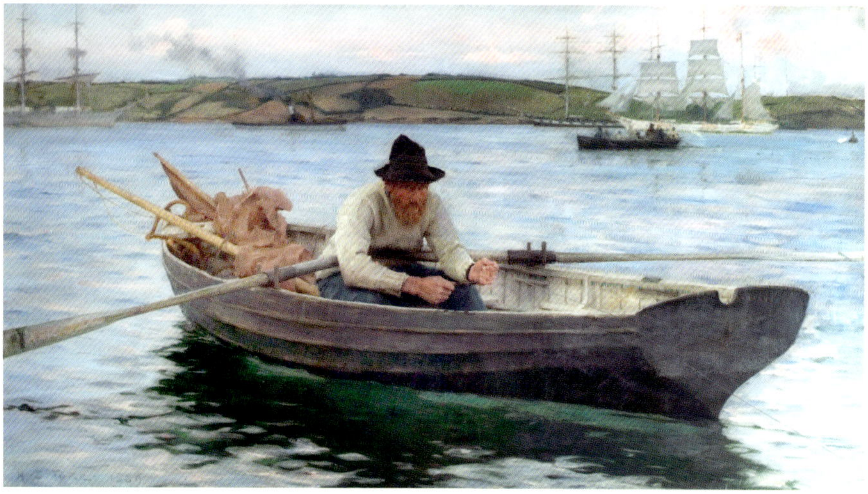

Henry Scott Tuke
The Fisherman
c.1888–9 • oil on canvas • 116 x 198 cm
Nottingham City Museums and Galleries

(a suggestion that would strike fear in the hearts of today's curators and conservators). Mary Bell was sending her works on to an exhibition in Canada while Henry Rheam commented 'It is rather disappointing that so few pictures have been sold out of such a good exhibition'.[27]

In fact records suggest that only two pictures were sold directly from the original exhibition and these were bought by the Nottingham Museum Committee. They visited the exhibition as a group and drew up a list with a view to purchasing 'one or two' works. The Committee minutes of 19 November 1894 resolve 'that the Art Director communicate with the following artists as to the lowest price they will take for their works viz: H.S. Tuke, W.H. Titcomb, C.G. Morris, A. Brown, A. Chevallier Tayler, J. Noble Barlow, Arthur Meade.' This makes it seem as if obtaining a painting at the lowest price was the main driver and indeed there was serious haggling over the final price. Eventually the two artists whose work had been selected, had to wait until March for payment perhaps an indication that even in these early years the Committee had to barter and plan carefully in order to acquire art for the collection.

Henry Scott Tuke's *The Fisherman* was one of the works that was acquired. From an asking price of £315 he reduced the price by £100 and then was asked to drop by another £15. W.H.Y. Titcomb's *Old Sea Dogs* was also selected for purchase. From an original price of £250 he dropped it right down to £100 in the altruistic expectation that the money saved would allow the purchase of a further work from another artist. He maintained a sense of humour over the delay in payment: 'fortunately I can wait til March for the money. Should the Committee care to ask me to accept an extra fifty pounds I should not refuse, but this is by way of a joke.'[28]

Wallis had hoped to buy Gotch's *My Crown and Sceptre* and two works by Walter Langley but this was not agreed by the Committee. S.M. Laurence's offer of *The Setting Sun* for £200, a reduction to the Committee of £300, was not taken up. Arnesby Brown had hoped that his painting *The Hillside* would be bought for the Nottingham Collection but was stoical when it wasn't, feeling that his local background went against him.[29] Two years on, in 1896, Marianne Stokes' *Childhood's Treasures* was bought from lender W.A. Michael who had been keen to sell at the time of the 1894 exhibition.

The three paintings that were acquired by the Museum and Art Gallery from the 1894 exhibition have stood the test of time, are still popular with visitors to the

27. Nottingham City Museums and Galleries Archives.
28. Letter from W.H.Y. Titcomb, 30 January 1895, Nottingham City Museums and Galleries accession record NCM 1895-1.
29. The Nottingham collection now includes ten oils by Arnesby Brown. The first, a portrait, was acquired in 1899.

Castle and have been borrowed for numerous exhibitions around the country. While some paintings from the 1894 exhibition have found their way into public galleries and private collections, others have disappeared, although art historian and researcher David Tovey has done sterling work in tracking down pictures and tracing images.

Wallis does not seem to have attempted such a large-scale exhibition again, contemporary or historic. Perhaps this was because of financial limitations and time constraints, perhaps because the Castle's permanent collection of art was growing and the Long Gallery was needed to display it, or perhaps because art became 'too modern'. However, an autumn exhibition of 'Modern Paintings' became a regular element of the annual programme at the Castle and continues to this day in the form of the Nottingham Open.

In the provinces the autumn exhibitions were all remarkably strong ...

The 1894 exhibition of Cornish Art was a major event for the Castle and for the Cornish artists. It did not result in many sales but this was not Wallis' aim. It did refute the bad press from the Dowdeswells exhibition and consolidated the separate exhibition successes of the Cornish artists at home and abroad.

The exhibition took place as museums and galleries in the regions were gaining confidence and increasing their impact on the public and the press. This was not limited purely to industrial centres, in Cornwall, for example, the first Falmouth Art Gallery opened in June 1894 (just a few months before the Nottingham exhibition). There was a clarity then about the importance of art for all and the educational role museums and galleries could play. Paintings full of 'Cornish light' brought inspiration and pleasure to visitors to Nottingham Castle Museum and Art Gallery. The exhibition also introduced Parisian and continental artistic influences to a new audience long before Impressionist and Post-Impressionist paintings were exhibited in Britain and the idea of new art forms for a modern world gained currency.

CATALOGUE OF ARTISTS AND EXHIBITION LISTINGS

David Tovey

This catalogue includes all artists who participated in the 1894 Nottingham exhibition and lists the works that they showed there, giving their titles, medium, if other than oil, their owners, if already sold, and catalogue numbers. In many cases, reviews of those works are also included so as to provide an indication of the style of work featured and the reception that it received. These are particularly interesting where paintings have not been located and may prove most useful in identifying such works, should they come on to the market in the future. Where of particular interest, extracts from the correspondence from the artists to Harry Wallis, the Curator, are also included.

Those paintings included in the 2015 exhibition are also listed separately. This exhibition revisits the 1894 show, but does not aspire to match the quantity of pictures displayed to the public then. Original 1894 works have been included as far as possible, as have original contributing artists' works. Where we have not been able to trace or negotiate the loan of appropriate paintings, we have substituted a work that is representative of the artist at around the period of the 1894 exhibition.

The artists featured in the 1894 exhibition were largely those currently resident in the respective colonies of Newlyn, St Ives and Falmouth. Accordingly, artists such as John Brett and James Clarke Hook, who were fairly regular visitors to Cornwall and who were included in the 1902 Cornish Artists' exhibition at Whitechapel, were not invited on this occasion. Harry Wallis clearly spent some weeks down in West Cornwall going around the various studios, but there were some artists who were away at the time and some who were ill, and so he was not able to see their work and judge for himself what was of sufficient quality for the show. In such circumstances, where someone was not a regular London exhibitor, Wallis clearly relied to some degree on Arnesby Brown to confirm that an artist was of sufficient standing. For instance, Ernest Fox, whose studio at Marazion Wallis had missed, was included as Brown had told him to write direct to Wallis. William Eadie and Lowell Dyer, both of whom had been ill, were each included, albeit only one of the two works Dyer sent was hung. One or two artists, with relatively limited connections to Cornwall, such as Charles Bartlett and Trythall Rowe, who had heard about the show from friends in the colonies, managed to persuade Wallis to include them, but the archive also contains a letter from Emily Latham Greenfield, an artist of moderate ability from St Ives, whose pleas to be included fell on deaf ears. Two other artists, who had been labelled by the St Ives paper as St Ives painters when their 1894 Academy exhibits were reviewed – Theodore Cook and Martin Gwilt Jolley – were also not included, whilst mention has already been made of the surprising omission of William Ayerst Ingram. Apparently, only J.H.C. Millar, of the artists asked to contribute, decided not to do so.

During his enquiries, Wallis discovered that some individuals were keen collectors of Cornish art and, accordingly, it is clear that a number of works were included not because they were necessarily the best examples of an artist's output, but because they were readily available. For instance, the London barrister, W.A. Michael, contributed two works by each of Walter Langley and Marianne

Stokes and also an Arnesby Brown, but his offer to lend what he called in a letter dated 25 June 1894 'a very clever black and white, *Storm at The Lizard*' by Alfred Warne-Browne, which he had acquired from an exhibition in St Ives, was turned down, presumably as it was felt that a black and white work would not fit in. This resulted, surprisingly, in Warne-Browne, who had recently moved from St Ives to The Lizard, not being represented at all.

Messrs W&P Holroyd, from Huddersfield, also lent a number of works by different artists, including two by each of Fred Hall and Arthur North, and a Chevallier Tayler and a Julius Olsson. The inclusion of North, a Huddersfield-born artist, who had died prematurely after a very short association with Newlyn, was clearly at their suggestion.

Given the Birmingham connections of many of the Newlyn artists, it was not surprising that collectors based in that city were to the fore. David Hedges from Yardley, near Birmingham, lent two works by each of Edwin Harris and Walter Langley, a painting by Chevallier Tayler and one by William Wainwright. Given that Wainwright had left Newlyn by 1886, this must be the only reason why he was included in the exhibition. W.H. Starkey, who lived in Edgbaston, lent two works by each of Edwin Harris and Chevallier Tayler and also a work by Fred Hall, whilst other Birmingham lenders included J. Holder, G.H. Kenrick, A. Maschwitz, J.P. Phillips, F. Ryland, and C. Showell.

One fascinating distinction between the art colonies at Newlyn and St Ives that was highlighted by the response to Wallis' letters is that, in the main, Newlyn artists responded from their homes in Cornwall, but the St Ives colony had dispersed almost in its entirety, as artists sought novel subject matter elsewhere. Several artists had gone to France – Adrian and Marianne Stokes were in Longpré-les-corps-saints on the Somme, Sydney and Alexandrina Laurence were on the banks of the Seine at Vétheuil and Harry and Dorothy Robinson were staying at a hotel in Marlotte, Seine-et-Marne and painting in the Forest of Fontainebleau. Lowell Dyer was staying at the Hotel du Luxembourg in Laroche in Belgium. Jessie Davidson, having returned from the Continent, went up to Lennoxtown in Scotland. Julius Olsson was experiencing life in another of Britain's coastal art colonies in Walberswick, whereas Louis Grier was in Wells-by-the-Sea in Norfolk, hoping that some students would respond to his advertisement in *The Studio*. William Titcomb was at his recently inherited property in Wickersley in South Yorkshire, where he was painting the local steel works, Arthur Meade was in Dorchester, with his wife's family, and Emily Latham Greenfield was in the depths of Wales. Fred Milner had gone back to Cheltenham and Eardley Blomefield had returned to his native Mansfield. Greville Morris was initially in Bushey, possibly for further study, before joining Charles Bartlett at The Manor in Steventon, Berkshire, whilst Noble Barlow was in Broadway, Worcestershire and Trythall Rowe was painting in Tewkesbury. The Canadian, Mary Bell, was staying with her friend Edith Fuller in Croydon. Only Algernon Talmage, William Eadie and Edmund Fuller replied from St Ives. This unique snapshot of a typical summer's scattering of artists is most illuminating.

The catalogue for the 1894 exhibition was only compiled after the show had been hung and so the exhibits are listed in the order that they were displayed. This enables one to see which of an artist's contributions were hung together in the manner that the artists desired.

Whilst Wallis clearly suffered a number of disappointments that major works proved unobtainable, what he did manage to borrow still made for a mightily impressive exhibition. The sheer number of large paintings brought together made it an astonishing achievement logistically, so that there is little doubt that it can be called the greatest exhibition of Cornish art that there ever has been and ever will be.

BARLOW, John Noble RBA, ROI, RW

MANCHESTER 1861–1917 PENZANCE

Barlow was a St Ives landscape painter who, at the time of the Nottingham show, had only recently settled in the colony. Whilst he had studied in Paris, he had also, unusually for a Cornish artist, spent some years in America, even taking out American citizenship. He went on to become one of the leading landscape painters in the colony, strongly influenced by Constable, and was a highly regarded art teacher, with students seeking him out from both America and Australia.

Father upholsterer. Sixth of nine children. Born and brought up in Manchester.
c.1882: First period of study in Paris.
1883: Joined American friend, Sydney Burleigh, in Providence, Rhode Island.
1883–7: In America – studied further in New York.
1887: Founder member of Providence Art Club. Took out American citizenship.
1888–9: Further period of study in Paris at Académie Julian.
1889: Visits to Normandy and the Isle of Arran.
1891: Studied in Holland. Married American Elizabeth Johnstone from Pittsburgh in London.
1892: Settled in St Ives.
1893: First exhibit at RA.
1898: First started painting classes in St Ives, initially with Louis Grier and then on his own (students included Americans William Wendt and George Gardner Symons).
1899: Won medal at Paris Salon with *One Summer Night*.
1900: Invited to join American section at the Paris World Exposition and again medalled.
1901–3: Spent a considerable time in America trying to exploit his success.
1905: Held exhibition in Antwerp.
1906–14: Based in St Ives but also had studio in the Lamorna Valley. In demand as a teacher – students included Garstin Cox, Herbert George, Herbert Fitzherbert, the Californian Anna Althea Hills and the Australians, Franklin White and Rose Lowcay.
1917: Died in Penzance.

WALLIS CORRESPONDENCE

Barlow responded to Wallis (5 July 1894) from Broadway in Worcestershire, where he was based all summer, and commented, 'I regret very much that I cannot send more than three pictures to the Museum, as my other important works are owned by Americans.'

1894 EXHIBITS

- ***Summer Pastures*** [13]
- ***Late Afternoon, November*** [199]
- ***November*** [200]
- ***Moonrise*** (RA 1894) [201]

None of these have been located, partly because Barlow does not appear to have affixed labels or inscribed titles on to his frames. One of his works was shortlisted for possible acquisition by Nottingham Castle for its permanent collection.

***Nottingham Guardian*, 13 October 1894**: 'Mr Noble Barlow is another young artist who sees nature with poetic eyes, and tries to render what he has seen with his brush. *Moonrise*, which he exhibited in this year's Academy, is a peaceful scene, with a pale moon just above the horizon, reflected upon the blue waters of a winding river. *Late Afternoon, November*, gives us a sketch of marshland, covered with tussock grass, with a peep of the river in the centre, and fields spreading away in the distance, while glowing clouds in a pale blue sky, fading away to green, crown the whole. In his *November*, we also get the glow of clouds reflected in water. All three show an appreciation of beauty and a tender sentiment, which one gladly acknowledges ...

'Another good landscape by Mr Noble Barlow is *Summer Pastures*, where the great white clouds in a serenely blue sky cast their mighty shadows over the sunny fields and the trees, beneath which cattle are lying – a vigorous piece of work in greens and blues.'

BARTLETT, Charles William RWA

BRIDPORT, DORSET 1860–1940 HONOLULU

At the time of the Nottingham show, Bartlett was a London-based landscape and figure painter, who had visited St Ives in 1892-3. He later became a well-known woodblock print artist.

1860: Born in Bridport, Dorset and educated at Clifton College, Bristol.
1880s: Worked for several years for a metallurgy firm in Bristol, then studied at the RA Schools and in Paris (Académie Julian).
1889: On return to England, married Emily Tate, but she died in childbirth shortly afterwards.
1890–1: Overcome with grief, spent a year travelling through France and Italy with Frank Brangwyn.
1892–3: First mentioned in a St Ives context in December 1892 and over-wintered in the colony.
1893: Exhibited at RA *A Study in a Sail Loft*, and noted as a visitor to St Ives again in April/May.
1894–1917: No further connection with Cornwall.
1917: Eventually settled in Honolulu and is now recognised as one of the world's finest woodblock print artists in the Japanese ukiyo-e (floating world) style.

WALLIS CORRESPONDENCE

Bartlett was not originally invited to participate in the Nottingham exhibition, but when he heard about it from Greville Morris, who was staying with him in August 1894 in Berkshire, he wrote to Wallis declaring, 'I am a St Ives artist'.

1894 EXHIBITS

- ***Lombardy Poplars*** [131]
- ***Sunshine and Shadow*** [132]

BELL, Mary Alexandra PS, WIAC

DOUGLAS, ONTARIO 1864–1951 ALMONTE, ONTARIO

Mary Bell was a Canadian artist, who had married fellow St Ives resident, Charles Herbert Eastlake, in 1893. Working in a unique style, often in pastel, she delighted in decorative poetic landscapes and idealised studies of children or of mother and child relationships.

Father engineer. Spent early life in Almonte, Ontario and Carillon, Quebec.
1884–8: Studied in Montreal under Robert Harris and then at the New York Arts Students League under William Merritt Chase.
1888–9: Studied in Paris at Académie Julian and at Colarossi's and painted at Pont-Aven.
1889: Had great success at Paris Salon with *La Petite Malade, Basse-Bretagne*.
1889: Visited St Ives that September with fellow Canadian artist, Margaret Houghton.
1890–2: Back in Montreal, where taught at Victoria School of Art for a while.
1893: Returned to St Ives and met and married Charles Herbert Eastlake.
1893–8: Based in St Ives.
1898–1939: Travelled extensively, whilst based in London, and exhibited widely.
1939: Returned to Canada.
A number of her St Ives period works are held in Canadian public collections.

WALLIS CORRESPONDENCE

Wallis' initial letter had had to be forwarded to the Croydon address of Bell's long term friend, Edith Fuller, with whom she was then staying. Wallis had clearly asked for her RA exhibit of that year to be included, and she agreed in a letter dated 1 May 1894 to send this and a couple of others. At the end of the exhibition, she asked for all her pictures to be returned to St Ives, where she was then working.

1894 EXHIBITS

- ***Moonrise*** (RA 1894) [34]
- ***Firelight Fancies*** [35]
- ***Portrait*** [59]

None of these paintings have been located, albeit *Firelight Fancies* is illustrated in *Black and White* 1895 at p.113.

***Nottingham Evening Post*, 6 October 1894**: 'Moonrise over faintly gleaming water seems to a favourite study with many of these young artists. Miss Mary Bell, in her *Moonrise*, gives us one of the cleverest. A girl, leaning on a long stick, gazes at the white orb in a purple sky, seen through the trunks of trees, lighting up the dark water. It is an impressionist study of feeling. She also sends a good firelight effect in No. 35, in which a girl is telling a small child, night-gowned and with bare feet, what fairy tales may be found in the glowing coals.'

BLACKBURNE, Ernest Robert Ireland

CHESTER 1864–1947 POOLE, DORSET

Ireland Blackburne was a landscape painter, from a very wealthy and distinguished Cheshire family, who was based in Newlyn for over a decade, and exhibited eight times at the Royal Academy. On his marriage to the local vicar's daughter in 1898, he was described as 'a zealous church helper' and he also was a keen cricketer. His work is little known now, not only because his landscapes are a little sparse, but also because he seems to have given up painting shortly after his marriage following a significant inheritance.

The Ireland Blackburnes were Cheshire landowners, whose estates had been held since Norman times, and relatives of the artist held significant positions in politics, the Navy and the Church. His father, John (d.1884), was a wealthy Chester wine merchant.

1890: Settled in Newlyn and took part in the Cornish Artists show at Dowdeswells.
1891: Census records him lodging with Frederic Millard in the Newlyn home of Eliza Trahair.
1895: Participated in the opening exhibition of the Newlyn Art Gallery.
1898: Married Mildred Emily Perkins, the daughter of the vicar of Newlyn.
1900: Moved to Lilliput, Poole, Dorset but exhibited very little thereafter.
1902: Wessex scene featured in the Cornish Artists Exhibition at Whitechapel Art Gallery. Appears to have inherited significant funds from his uncle Vice Admiral Francis Richard Blackburne.[1]

WALLIS CORRESPONDENCE

Ireland Blackburne's letter to Wallis (received 11 July 1894) is most informative and suggests that he was enjoying appreciable success at the time. It was on headed paper, with the address 'The Belgrave Mansions, Grosvenor Gardens', presumably his London base, but this was crossed out, as he was writing from 'The Myrtles, Newlyn', where he had just arrived. It indicated that Wallis had suggested three works for inclusion in the show. Two of these, *The Song of the Seabirds* and *'Neath the Shadow of the Hill*, were available, but the third work requested, his 1894 RA exhibit, *Lengthening Shadows*, which had been considered one of the landscapes of the year, had been sold to Lord Overtown in Dumbartonshire, and his Lordship required it to be despatched to him as soon as the RA show was over. In suggesting alternatives, the artist commented, 'Most of my recent work has been sold without being exhibited and, in most cases, I should not care to ask for the loan of it yet.' However, in addition to a small work, *A Moorland Pool*, then with the art dealers, Macleans in the Haymarket, he also recommended *The Haunt of the Waterfowl*, which had been bought by Lady D'Arcy-Godolphin-Osborne of 2 Chesham Place, London, and her Ladyship duly agreed to lend this. The artist also indicated that his London agents were Blackburne and Johnstone, which was presumably a family connection. *Lengthening Shadows* is now owned by Glasgow Museums, but is in a poor state of repair.

1894 EXHIBITS

- ***The Haunt of the Waterfowl*** (Lady D'Arcy-Godolphin-Osborne) [182]
- ***'Neath the Shadow of the Hill*** [188]
- ***The Song of the Seabirds*** (RA 1892) [189]

None of these works have been located, although *The Song of the Seabirds* was sold by Phillips, London on 7 October 1997 and was illustrated in *Pall Mall Gazette's Pictures of 1892*. It was well regarded when it was exhibited on Show Day in Newlyn that year. '*The Song of the Seabirds* shows a stretch of wet sand and rippling sea with a flock of gulls circling in the air and gathered in groups on the sand. The picture is really a harmony in silver grey, as the sea, sky and shore are tinged with this soft and delicate tone. Mr Blackburne has the clean touch which is necessary when depicting a smooth sea-washed shore with little limped and glistening pools.'[2] However, none of Blackburne's works were mentioned in reviews of the Nottingham exhibition.

BOURDILLON, Francis Wright

MADRAS 1851–1924 LITTLE SODBURY, GLOUCESTERSHIRE

Frank Bourdillon was a Newlyn figure painter, who tackled an eclectic mix of subjects. In addition to attractive depictions of the local fisherfolk in similar vein to his Newlyn colleagues, he also produced Elizabethan costume dramas. Known to his close friends as 'Dilla', he was greatly liked in the artist community. However,

1. I am indebted once again to April Marjoram, the Exeter historian, for genealogical research on the Ireland Blackburne family.
2. *The Cornishman*, 24 March 1892.

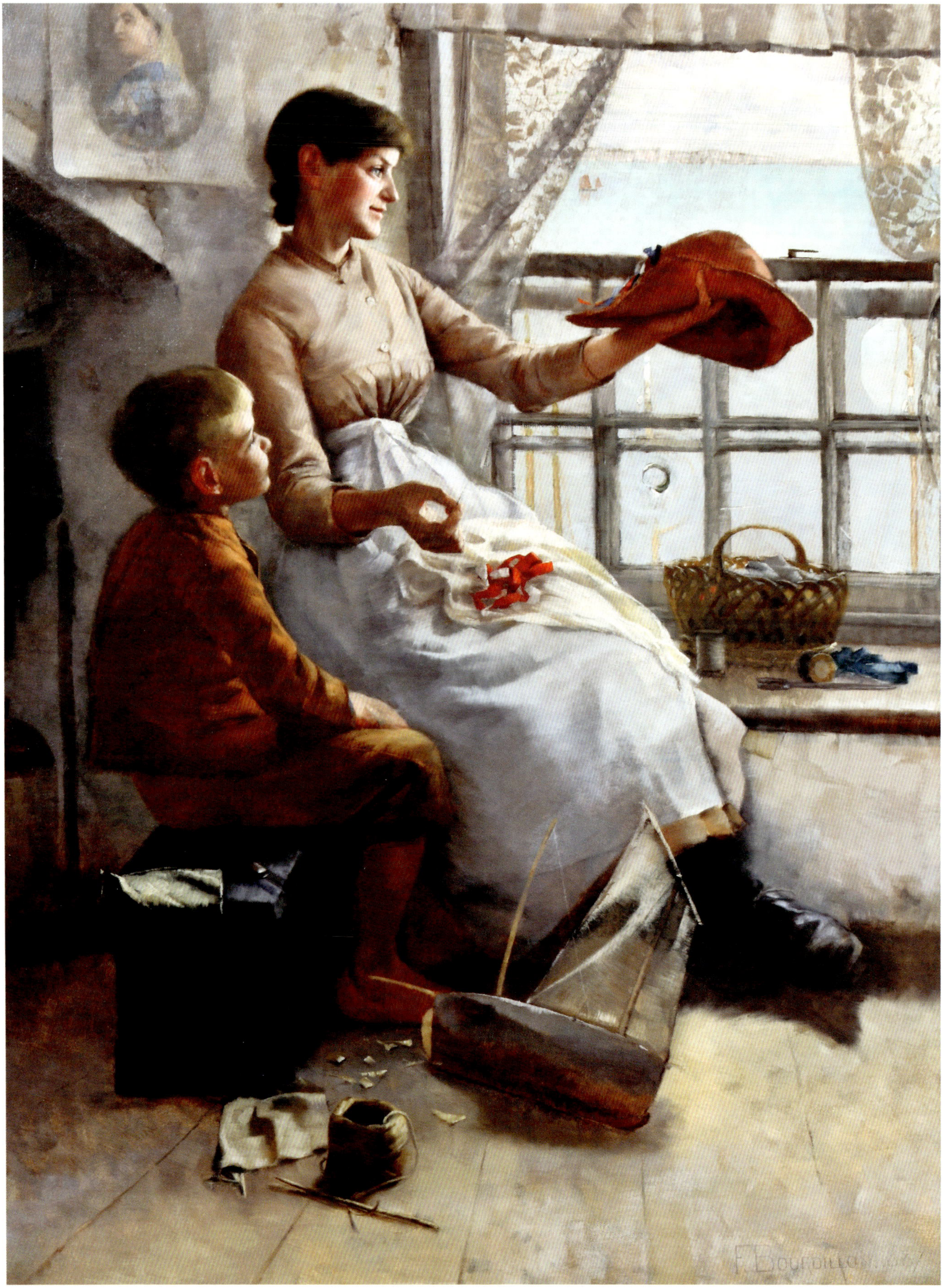

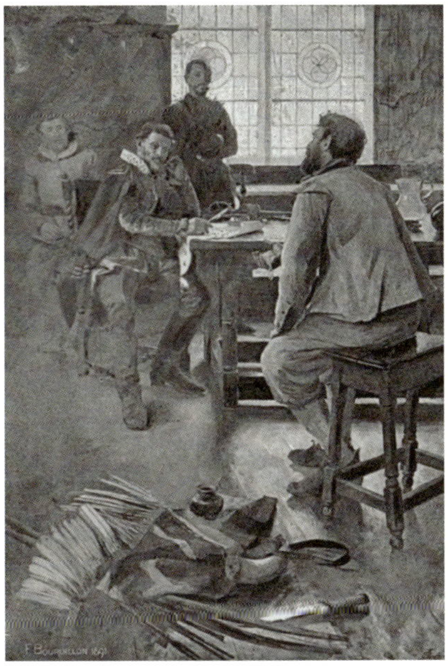

Francis Wright Bourdillon
From the Spanish Main
from the 1894 exhibition catalogue

by the time of the Nottingham show, he had already left Newlyn to become a missionary in India, leaving all his pictures behind. Accordingly, Bourdillon was not represented in the exhibition by his best works, but by those that his relations wanted to dispose of.

Father civil servant. Brought up in India and began working as a coffee planter.
1882: Studied at the Slade School of Art.
1883–4: Studied in Paris.
1885: Lived in Oxford.
1886: Worked at Polperro from May to December.
1887: Settled in Newlyn.
1889: Lived at Belle Vue House, Newlyn with Mrs Maddern, in the same house as Stanhope Forbes.
1890: Sold *On Bideford Sands*, one of his Elizabethan costume dramas, to the Art Gallery of New South Wales, Sydney. Participated in the Cornish Artists show at Dowdeswells.
1891: At time of Census, living at 35 Paul Hill, Newlyn with Mrs Roberts.
1892: Decided to become a CMS Missionary in Burdwan, India (1896–1901), where he married a fellow missionary, Kathleen Edwards.
1901: Due to ill health, they returned to England, and Frank took up a curacy in Ramsgate before becoming the Rector of Horton, Gloucestershire (1914–23).

WALLIS CORRESPONDENCE

Wallis had correspondence both with Chevallier Tayler, who was entrusted by Bourdillon with his business arrangements after his departure, and with Bourdillon's sister, Charlotte. Tayler, writing from Rosemellin, Newlyn, on 1 October 1894, forwarded to Wallis a list of prices that had been put on the works by the artist's sister, which included £600 for *On Board the 'Revenge'* and £400 for *From the Spanish Main*, and commented that he considered that these figures were far too high 'as he has, now, no opportunity for increasing his reputation'. On the other hand, *Across the Harbour* and *From a Newlyn Studio* were only priced at £7. After the show, the artist's sister asked for Nos 84, 85, 165 and 193 to be sent to the Spring Exhibition at Derby.

1894 EXHIBITS

- ***'Twas in '55'*** (J.M. Lowis) [15]
- ***From the Spanish Main*** (RA 1891) [49]
- ***The Haven where he would be*** [57]
- ***Across the Harbour*** [84]
- ***From a Newlyn Studio*** [85]
- ***Strayed*** (RA 1888) (Walter Roche) [122]
- ***The Only Survivor – October 1578*** (RA 1890) [165]
- ***The Bailiff's Daughter of Islington*** (RA 1886) [193]
- ***On Board the 'Revenge', 1591 'Sink me the ship, master gunner'*** (RA 1892) [209]

On Board the 'Revenge', 1591 is now owned by Exeter University and *Across the Harbour* is in a private collection. None of the other works have been located, although *The Bailiff's Daughter of Islington* was sold at Sotheby's, London on 10 March 2005. The lender, J.M. Lowis, lived at Alton, Hampshire, and Walter Roche in London.

***Nottingham Evening Post*, 6 October 1894**: 'Mr Frank Bourdillon's work is unequal but some of it makes one regret that he has now given up art and means to devote the rest of his life to missionary work in the East. Alone among the Newlyn men, although using that village and Cornish scenery as his background, he was fond of selecting subjects from stirring stories of the Elizabethan period … *On Board the 'Revenge', 1591*, full of the smoke of battle, illustrates Tennyson's

pl. 1 **Francis Wright Bourdillon**
The Jubilee Hat
1887 • oil on canvas • 92 x 67 cm
private collection, on loan to
Penlee House Gallery & Museum, Penzance

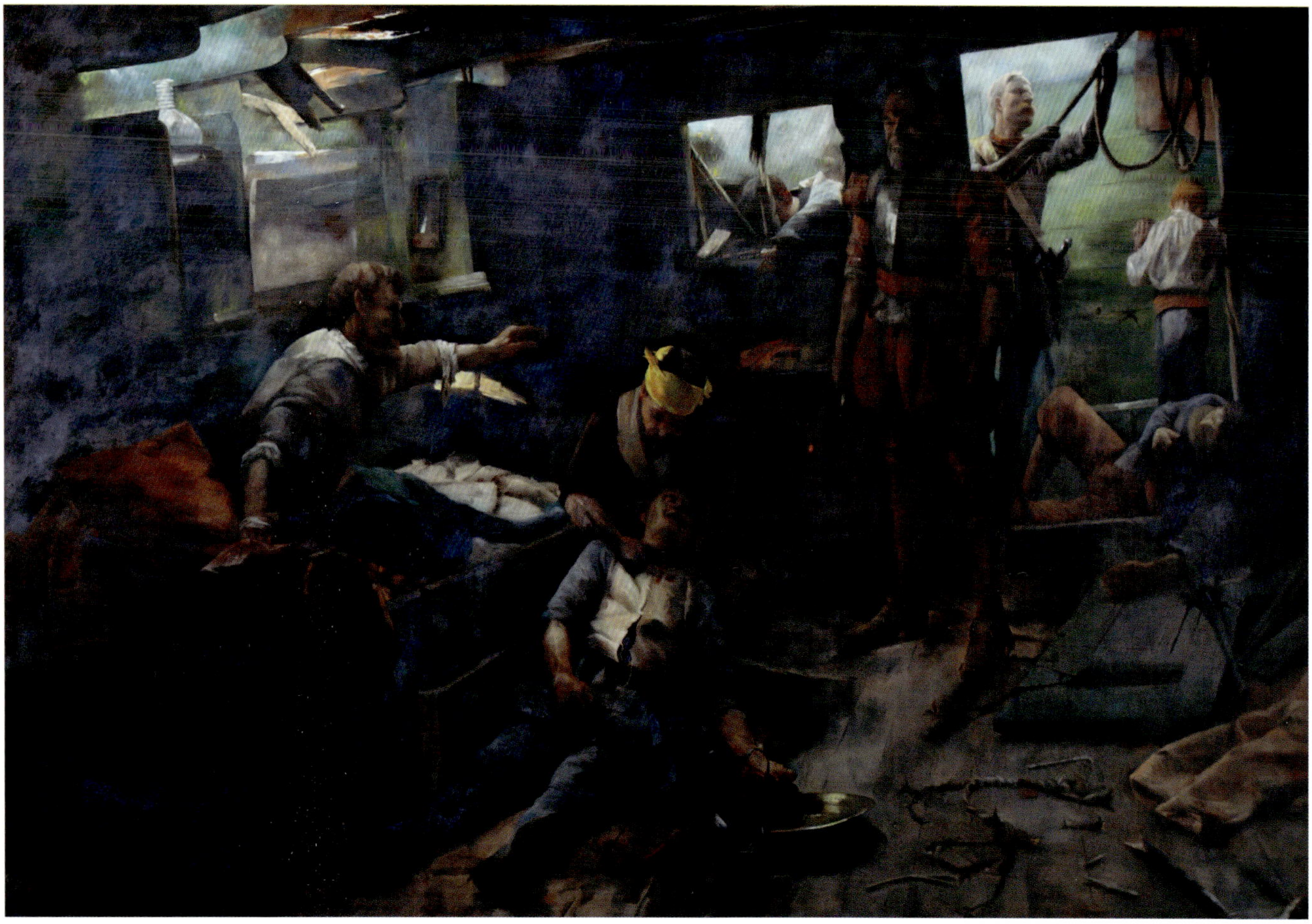

Francis Wright Bourdillon
On Board the 'Revenge', 1591
oil on canvas • 135 x 210 cm
University of Exeter, photograph © University of Exeter

pl. 2 **Francis Wright Bourdillon**
Across the Harbour
1892 • oil on canvas • 61 x 40 cm
private collection, photograph courtesy
Richard Green Gallery, London

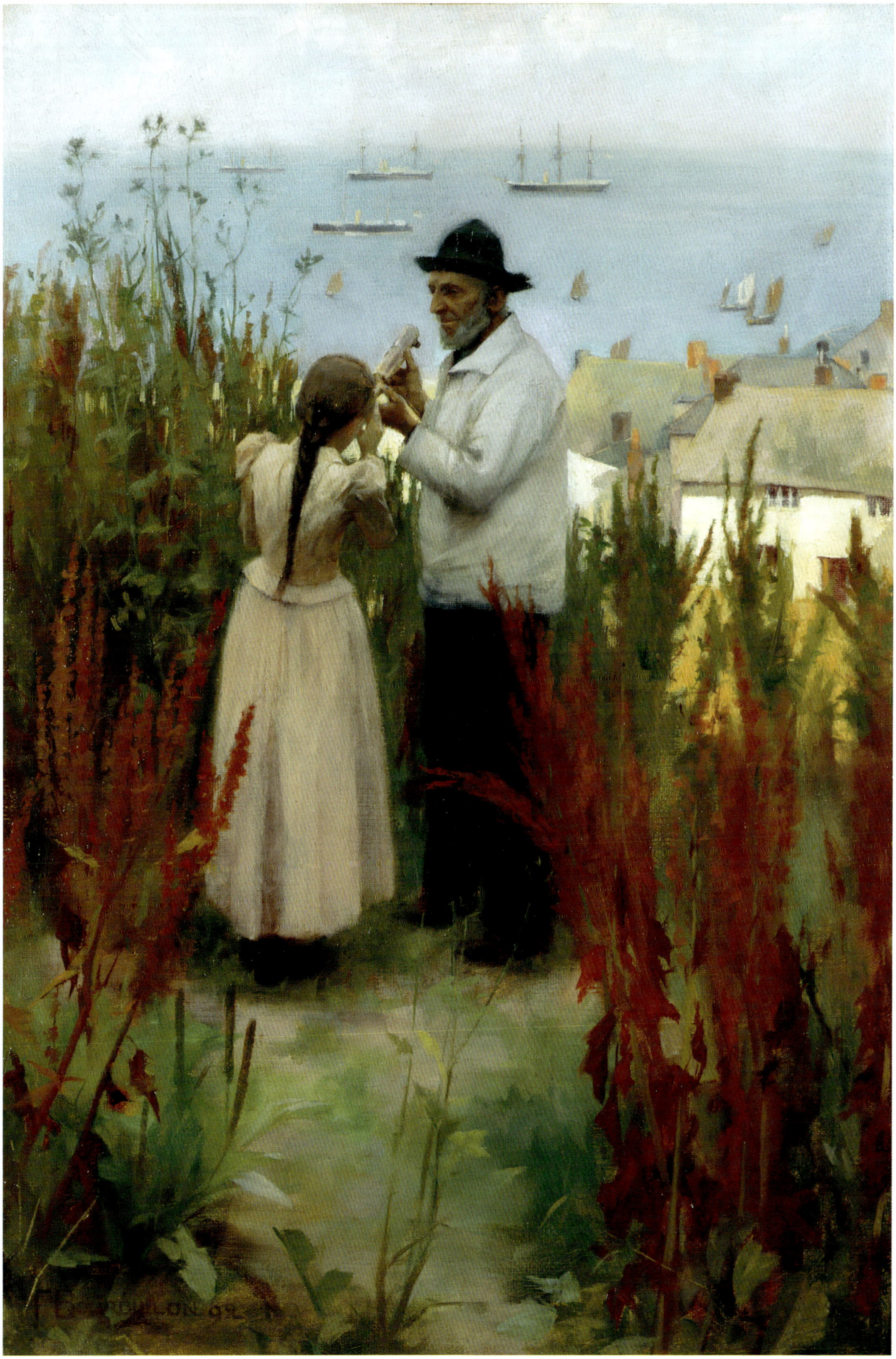

poem, with the brave Sir Richard Grenville, wounded to death, lying in his cabin and telling the master gunner to blow up the ship.'

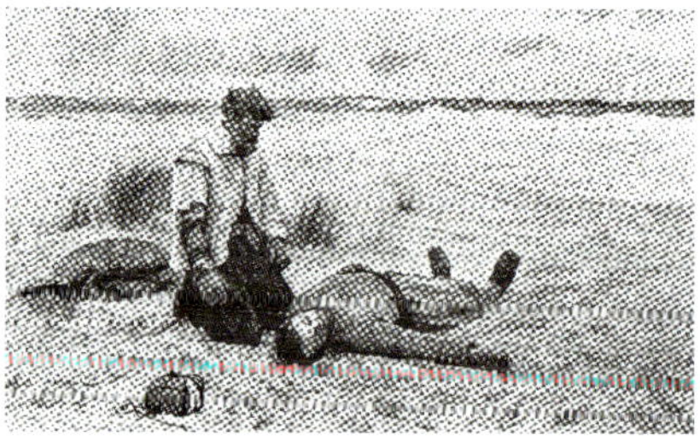

Francis Wright Bourdillon
The Only Survivor
from the 1894 exhibition catalogue

2015 EXHIBITS

Across the Harbour (pl. 2, private collection): This painting, dated 1892, depicts an old fisherman holding a telescope so that a young woman, probably his daughter, can view the ships anchored in Mounts Bay. They are standing in an overgrown garden on the hillside above Newlyn, and the rooftops of the houses of the village can be seen below.

The Jubilee Hat (pl. 1, private collection): This is now a well-known and popular painting, which depicts a young local woman making preparations for Queen Victoria's Golden Jubilee celebrations in Newlyn, as evidenced by the print stuck rather haphazardly on the wall. In order to see better whilst she is sewing a patriotic ribbon on to her hat, she has placed herself by the window, whilst her younger brother sits beside her, doing some repair work to his model fishing boat. However, he has stopped to admire his sister's handiwork. Their position gives the artist the ability to depict the view out of the window over Mounts Bay, on which, one day, it is suggested, the young boy will sail in a real fishing boat, such as the one depicted, with its attractive red sails reflected in the waters of the Bay. It is surprising, given the quality of this painting, that Bourdillon indicated that he felt compelled to produce his Elizabethan costume dramas 'as there are lots of clever fellows who do the village business so much better than I can'.[3]

BRAMLEY, Frank RA, NEAC

SIBSEY, LINCS 1857–1915 CHALFORD, GLOS

Frank Bramley was a leading Newlyn figure painter and, at the time of the 1894 Exhibition, he was at the zenith of his fame, having been, in 1888, the first Newlyn artist to have a work bought by the Chantrey Trustees. He had also sold other major works to leading colonial galleries and had recently been made an ARA. However, the year after the Nottingham Exhibition, he left the colony, and his career rather petered out.

Studied at Lincoln.
1880: Studied art in Antwerp under Verlat at same time as Edwin Harris (q.v.) and William Wainwright (q.v.).
1882–3: Visited Venice: brief visit to Brittany in the autumn of 1883, where linked up with Edwin Harris (q.v.) in Pont-Aven.
1884: Settled in Newlyn; regarded as a silent, modest, rather melancholy man; leading advocate of the 'square brush' technique.
1888: *A Hopeless Dawn* bought by the Chantrey Trustees for the nation; its success resulted in such bereavement scenes proliferating in the colony, and, after a while, critics began to lament such mournful subject matter.
1889–94: Whilst his subsequent paintings, into which he often introduced more symbolism, did not enjoy universal critical acclaim, he sold *Saved* (RA 1889) to Durban Art Gallery and *For of Such is the Kingdom of Heaven* (RA 1891) to Auckland: a number of paintings featured aged rustics, and displayed broader handling and an increasingly daring use of colour.
1890: Participated in the Cornish Artists show at Dowdeswells.
1892: Won medal at Paris Salon with *For of Such is the Kingdom of Heaven*.
1894: Elected ARA (RA 1911).
1895–1915: Moved to Droitwich in 1895 and then to Grasmere, his wife's family home, in 1900.

3. Letter from Frank Bourdillon to his sister, dated 29 October 1890.

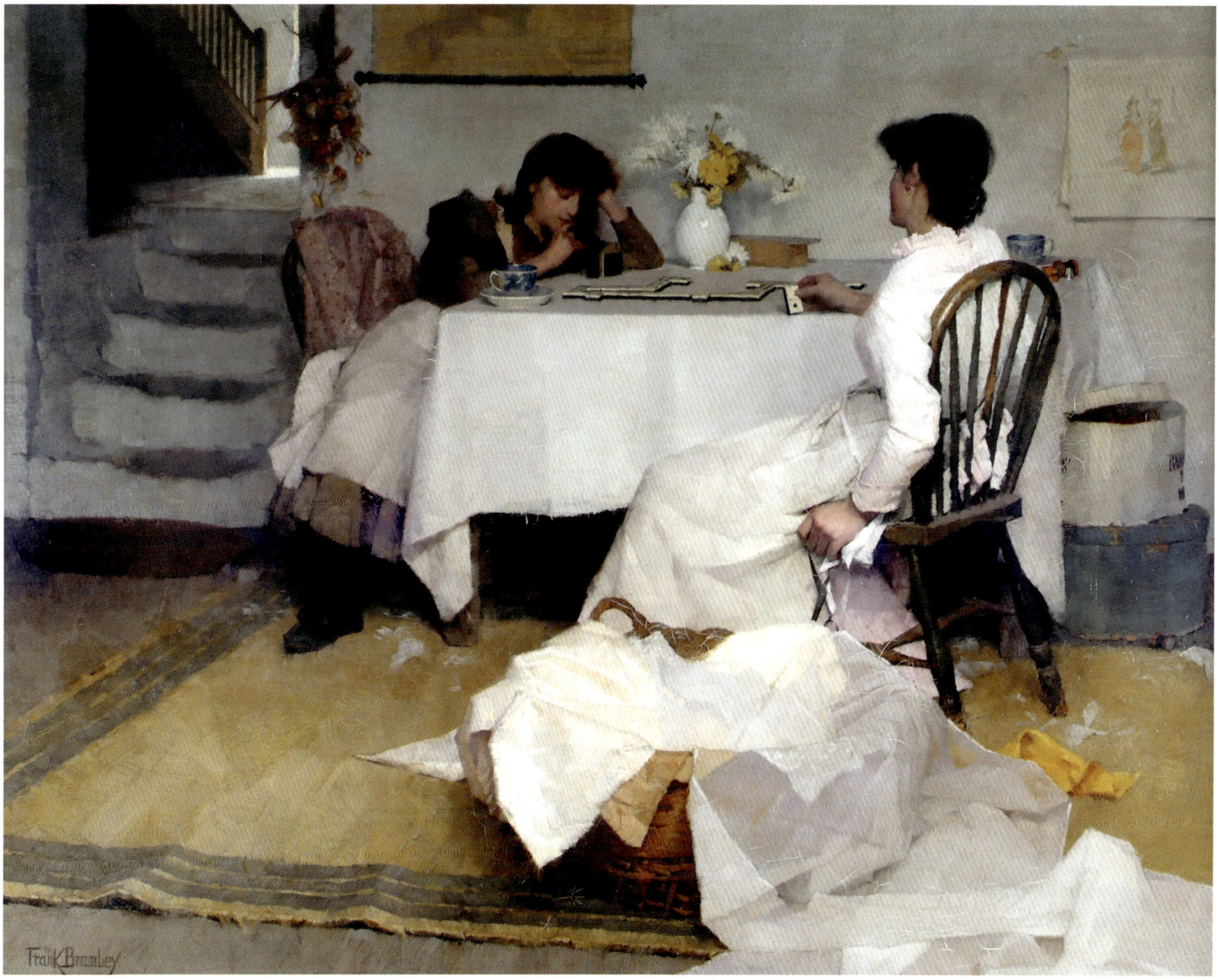

Frank Bramley
Domino!
1886 • oil on canvas • 69 x 112 cm
Crawford Art Gallery, Cork

WALLIS CORRESPONDENCE

Bramley indicated that he never managed to visit the exhibition, but recorded how his colleagues had all thought it a great success. Wallis had been particularly keen to show Bramley's painting *After Fifty Years*. However, Bramley had promised this first to Birmingham and then to Derby. Accordingly, it was not available for the Cornish Artists exhibition, but Wallis was still keen to get it for another Nottingham show in 1895. However, when it arrived, it had two cuts on it, which needed attention. Derby refused to pay the £50 demanded and Bramley agreed that Wallis' recommended restorers in Nottingham should do the remedial work. Having been to the industrial towns of Birmingham and Derby, Bramley was certain that the work would be very dirty and told Wallis to 'wash it with a clean rag and cold water and rub it gently dry with a silk handkerchief'.

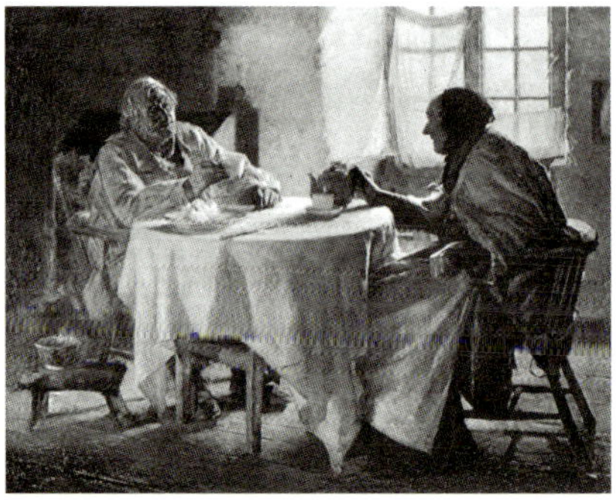

Frank Bramley
Old Memories
from the 1894 exhibition catalogue

1894 EXHIBITS

- ***Study of a Head*** (William Richardson) [104]
- ***Old Memories*** (RA 1892) (S.G. Holland) [172]
- ***A Hopeless Dawn*** (RA 1888) (Royal Academy) [173]
- ***Eyes and No Eyes*** (Merton Russell Cotes) [174]
- ***Domino!*** (RA 1886) [216]

Old Memories and *Study of a Head* have not been located. S.G. Holland was a Londoner, and William Richardson lived in Derby.

***Nottingham Guardian*, 13 October 1894**: 'The deliciously quiet, cool tones of this little picture [*Domino!*] are admirable and should be noted by everyone ... The painting of the accessories, the blue and white tea-cups, the bonnet boxes and scraps of stuff on the floor, the yellow and white chrysanthemums in the white vase, are all excellent.'

***The Nottingham Evening Post*, 6 October 1894**: '[*Old Memories* has] an effect of twilight coming through the window and contending with the firelight within. The fire glows upon the apron and white smock frock of the old woman and her husband, [who are] talking together of the happiness of their early days' whilst taking tea.'

2015 EXHIBITS

A Hopeless Dawn (pl. 3, Tate): The inclusion of this work in the 1894 exhibition was clearly considered a coup, and the catalogue contained the full wording of the piece by John Ruskin from which the title came. The *Nottingham Guardian* (6 October 1894) rated it as Bramley's best work ever. 'He may have painted other canvases in which his technical ability is shown to equal advantage, and in which his seizing of a particular effect or scheme of colour is equally worthy of praise, but the *Hopeless Dawn* beyond all this possesses that true and fine poetry which gives such an added delight to a good picture when anyone with imagination looks upon it. There is a dramatic power in it, which is not often found among these young Cornishmen; which, indeed, is not as a rule sought for by them.' Having described in detail the scene depicted, the reviewer concludes, 'This pathetic story Mr Bramley has told with great completeness and power, while the colour scheme, cool and sad, harmonising, as it does, so well with the picture, is an added beauty which crowns the whole.' Finally, the Ruskin quote was deemed to be 'one of the most beautiful that word-magician ever penned.'

Eyes and No Eyes (pl. 4, Penlee House Gallery & Museum): Dismissed by the *Art Journal* when it was first exhibited in 1887 as a 'good specimen of the dab and spot school', this painting is now considered to be Bramley's most appealing work, particularly the way in which he has captured the two girls laughing at

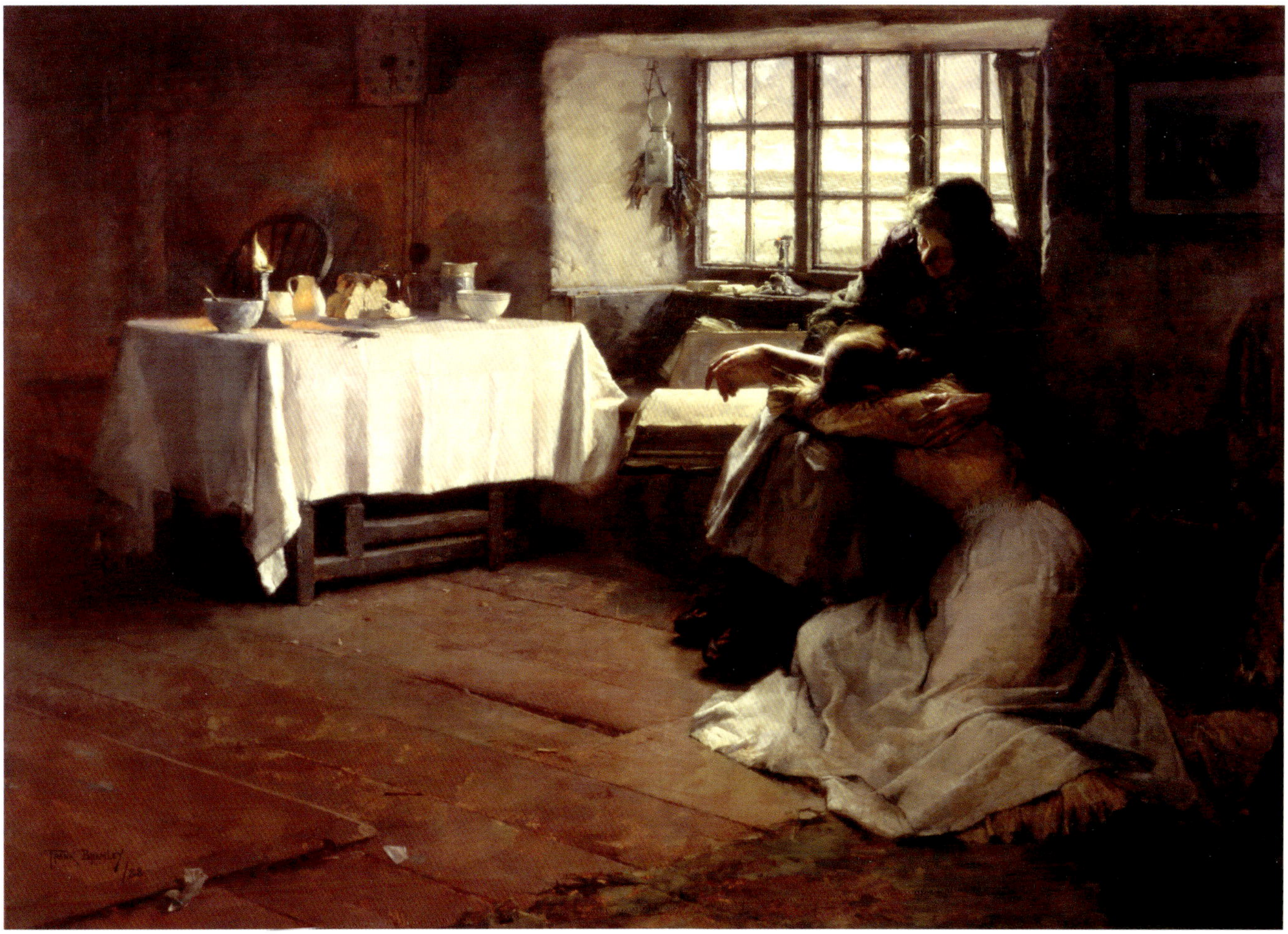

pl. 3 **Frank Bramley**
A Hopeless Dawn
1888 • oil on canvas • 122 x 167 cm

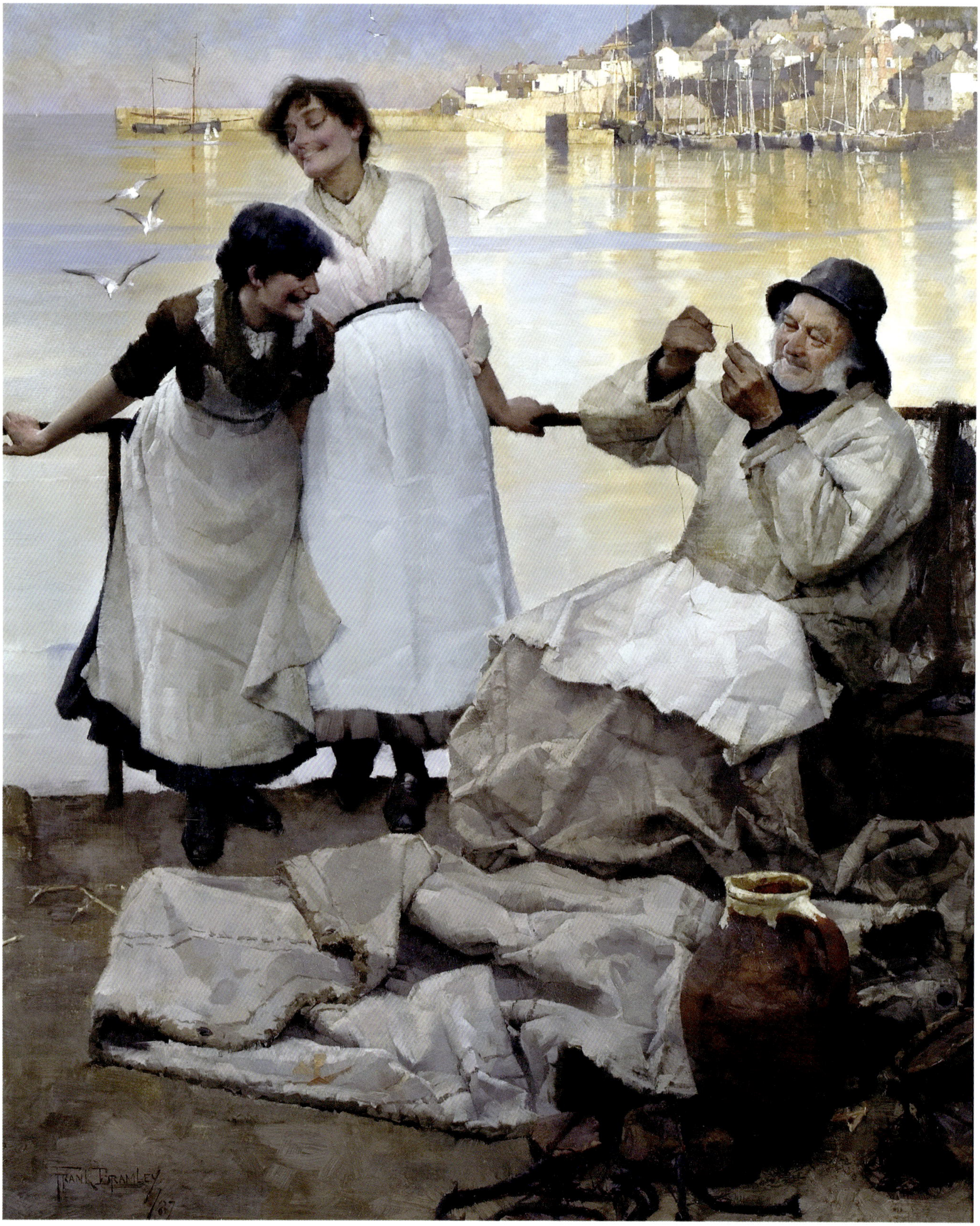

pl. 4 **Frank Bramley**
Eyes and No Eyes
1887 • oil on canvas • 114 x 92 cm
Penlee House Gallery & Museum

the difficulties being experienced by the old fisherman, as he tries to thread a needle, whilst mending his nets. It was a work also that was specifically referred to by William Titcomb in his speech at the opening of the Exhibition, for he considered it was a good example of an artist seeking to attain absolute truth of tone by posing his models and painting them in the exact background and surroundings which it was intended the picture should represent. He was quite certain that Bramley 'had posed the various figures in his picture sufficiently near to the sea to receive the reflections from the water'. The painting also displays Bramley's accomplished use of the square brush technique.

Victorian viewers would probably have recognised that the title was also that of a moral tale referred to by Dinah Mulock Craik in her 1884 book *Unsentimental Journey through Cornwall*, which she described as 'an old-fashioned story about two little children taking a walk; one seeing everything, and enjoying everything, and the other seeing nothing'.[4]

BROWN, Sir John Alfred Arnesby RA, RBA, RWA

NOTTINGHAM 1866–1955 HADDISCOE, NORFOLK

Arnesby Brown was one of the group of students from the Herkomer Art School, Bushey, who came down to St Ives in the late 1880s to study landscape painting out of doors with Adrian Stokes. He specialised in landscapes with animals, but also produced some marine work. He was the only Cornish artist with a Nottingham connection and the 1894 Exhibition resulted from discussions between him and Harry Wallis. Unsurprisingly, there was a great deal of interest in his exhibits in the local press. Brown, who divided his time between Norfolk and St Ives until 1910, went on to be hailed as the finest English landscape painter since Constable. He had three works bought by the Chantrey Trustees in 1901, 1910 and 1919, and sold works frequently to other national and international public collections. He was made an RA in 1915 (ARA 1903) and was knighted for his services to British art in 1939.

Father Nottingham wine merchant, with links to Nottingham Castle. Educated in Nottingham.
Late 1880s: Goalkeeper for Nottingham Forest.
1888: Studied art at Nottingham under Andrew McCallum.
1889–92: Studied at Herkomer Art School, Bushey.
1889: Unhappy with name John Brown; exhibited this year as Alfred J. Brown. First success at RA.
1889–90: Visits to St Ives.
1890: Participated in Cornish Artists' Exhibition at Dowdeswells in December.
1891: Began to use the name 'Arnesby Brown'.
1893–4: Shared Market Place Studio, St Ives with Sydney Laurence.
1894: Held an exhibition in July at his Midlands Chambers, Wheeler Gate studio in Nottingham.
1894–6: Based himself at Tregethas Farm, St Erth.
1896: Took a new Piazza Studios in St Ives. Lodged in Carbis Bay. Elected to RBA.
1896–1910: Tended to spend summers in Norfolk and winters in St Ives.
1911–55: Based in Norfolk; overwintered in Chelsea.

WALLIS CORRESPONDENCE

The Hillside was put on the short list of works to be considered for purchase for the permanent collection of Nottingham Castle. Brown's father, who would normally have been on the acquisition committee, stayed away from the meeting. Brown indicated that his Cornish colleagues felt that he had a good chance of having his work purchased, due to his involvement in the project, but although

4. See Mary O'Neill, *Cornwall's 'Fisherfolk': Art and Artifice*, Sansom & Co, Bristol, 2014, p. 47 and p. 144.

he reduced the offer price to £100, he was disappointed when it was not acquired, commenting rather bitterly that he knew 'what a drawback being a native of the town would be.' (Letter dated 10 December 1894)

1894 EXHIBITS

- ***Study for A Northerly Breeze*** (Walter Jevons) [113]
- ***The Grey of the Morning*** (W.A. Michael) [203]
- ***The Hillside*** [204]
- ***Lowland*** (RA 1892, Munich 1893) [205]

None of these works have been located. A poor image of *A Northerly Breeze*, a 'bright, strong marine', which was hung on the line at the RA that year, is reproduced in the *Black and White Handbook to the Royal Academy and New Gallery 1894* at p. 23.

***Nottingham Guardian*, 13 October 1894**: 'In last year's loan exhibition in these galleries, we noted a landscape by a young Nottingham artist that showed a poetic imagination and promised well for his future work. Mr Arnesby Brown's pictures in the present collection prove he is continuing his earnest work in the same path and that he can produce transcripts of Nature instinct with a true feeling for all that is beautiful in the sea, sky and earth, which it is his delight to paint.

'*The Hillside*, from this year's Academy, is a rendering of a bold sweep of high land, outlined against blue sea, and a sky filled with great purple and yellow-clouds, whilst the sheep are grazing amongst the gorse and bracken. It is an evening effect delicate in tone. Even better is *The Grey of the Morning*, lent by Mr W.A. Michael, a group of scotch firs and smaller undergrowth and bushes, with hilly country in the distance, and a glimpse of sea on the left. The great sun looms whitely in a pale pink and purple sky. The canvas shows real poetic quality.

'In *Lowland*, which was in the Academy two years ago, a dark lowering sky with heavy clouds is spread over the quiet corner of a wood, one bare, twisted trunk standing out against the greyness and the foreground filled with marshy land rustling with yellow and brown rushes. His study for *A Northerly Breeze* (in the last Academy and now at Birmingham) we like even better than the larger picture. It is fresh and true and really clever.'

2015 EXHIBITS

The Drinking Pool (pl. 5, Manchester City Galleries): At the time of the 1894 Exhibition, Arnesby Brown was working on this painting at Tregethas Farm, St Erth, which he used as his Cornish base in 1894–5. In a letter to Wallis from 'Tregethas Farm' dated 28 November 1894, he commented that he is 'busy studying cows which are to be the principal object of my "next"'. Cows were a popular subject at the time, as, in the age of the industrial revolution, with its noise and dirt, they signified the unsullied peace and quiet of the countryside. As with most work by St Ives landscapists, water is included to bring in reflections of light effects in the sky. It was exhibited at the RA in 1895 and was the first work bought from the artist for a public collection.

Sketch for 'The Two Piers' (pl. 6, Nottingham City Museums & Galleries): Brown produced a series of sketches of his subject before painting a major exhibition canvas. These were often brought to such a high standard of finish that he was prepared to exhibit them in their own right, as he did in the 1894 exhibition with his study for *A Northerly Breeze*. This sketch from Nottingham Castle's permanent collection relates to Brown's 1908 RA exhibit featuring the two piers in St Ives harbour. It is a good example of the St Ives artists' interest in evening light effects, and features reflections on both the sea and the cobbles of the pier.

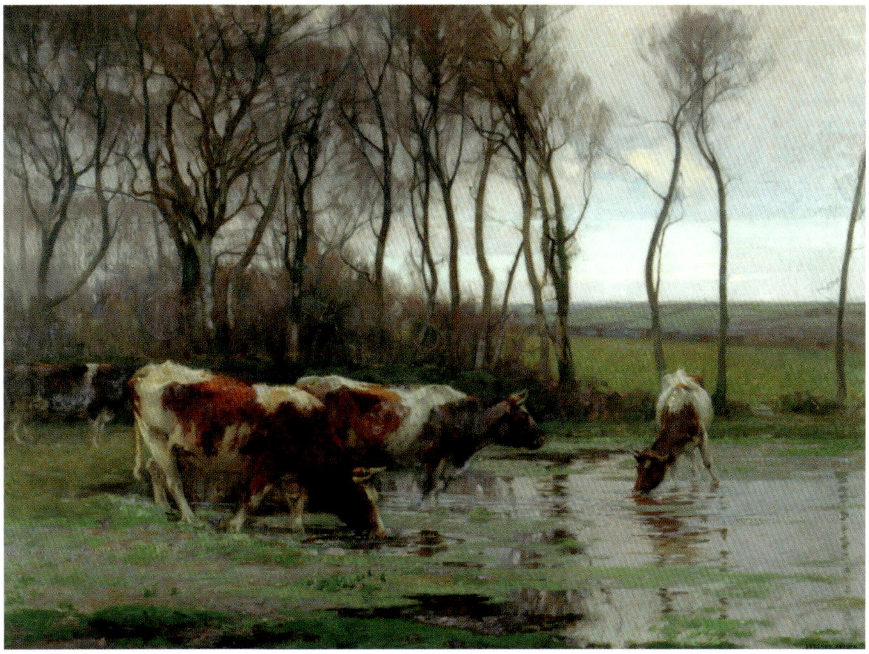

pl. 5 **John Arnesby Brown**
The Drinking Pool
1895 • oil on canvas • 128 x 165 cm
Manchester City Galleries; © The Artist's Estate

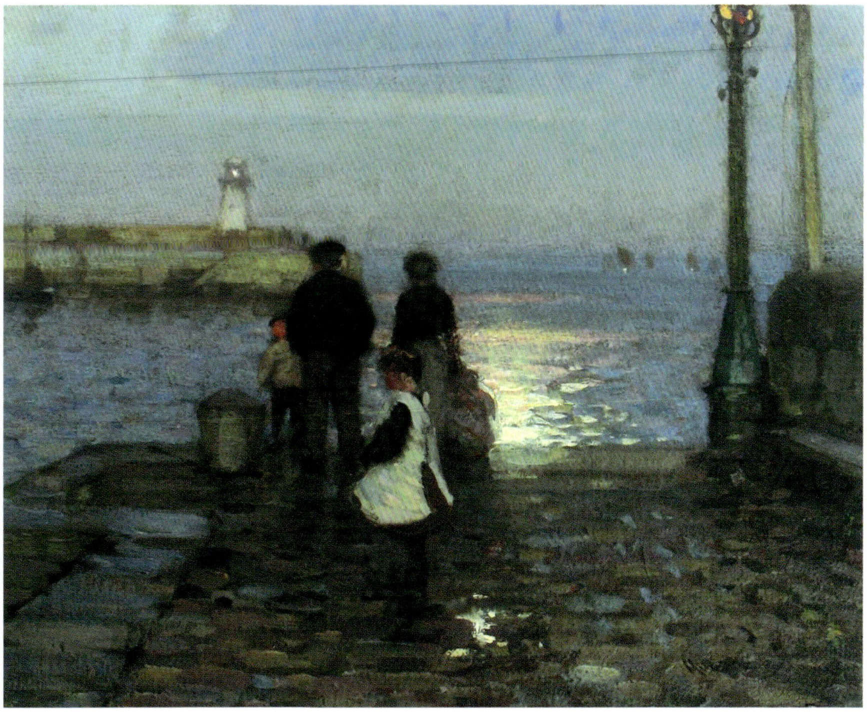

pl. 6 **John Arnesby Brown**
Sketch for 'The Two Piers'
oil on canvas • 30.5 x 37 cm
Nottingham City Museums and Galleries; © The Artist's Estate

CRAFT, Percy RBA

LONDON 1856–1934 LONDON

Percy Craft was a Newlyn figure painter, who also for some years had a studio in St Ives. A key figure in the Newlyn Artists' Theatrical group, he was well-liked. He had limited success with his art.

Studied at Heatherley's and the Slade School.
1882–5: Did series of illustrated articles on Cornish fishing subjects.
1885: Settled in Newlyn.
1888: Worked in St Ives on *Heva! Heva!* (Penlee House Gallery & Museum, Penzance), the first of his major works related to the pilchard fishing industry.
1890: Participated in the Cornish Artists show at Dowdeswells.
1890–98:Worked in both St Ives and Newlyn on typical Newlyn School subject-matter.
1899–1934: After a spell in Huntingdon, moved to London, where was involved with the running of the Royal British Colonial Society of Artists.

WALLIS CORRESPONDENCE

Craft did not reply to Wallis until 11 July, having been 'travelling about', and his correspondence in July and August comes from Burpham, Arundel. He had been sent a list of desired works by Wallis, but as he was away from home, he had difficulty recalling the precise addresses of the current owners. However, he confirmed that *Saturday* was with his frame-maker.

1894 EXHIBITS

- ***Saturday*** (RA 1891) [40]
- ***The Empty Chair*** (RA 1888) (Edmund Tautz) [41]
- ***The Only Son – The Return*** (John Aste) [52]

Craft indicated to Wallis that the copyright in *Saturday* was vested in Messrs Robinson & Co, Bristol. After being donated to Ramsgate Library by Dame Janet Harcourt-Wills, it was destroyed by fire in 2004. Neither of the other two works have been located. *The Only Son – The Return* was illustrated in *Pall Mall Gazette's Pictures of 1887* and *The Empty Chair* in Alice Meynell's article on the Newlyn

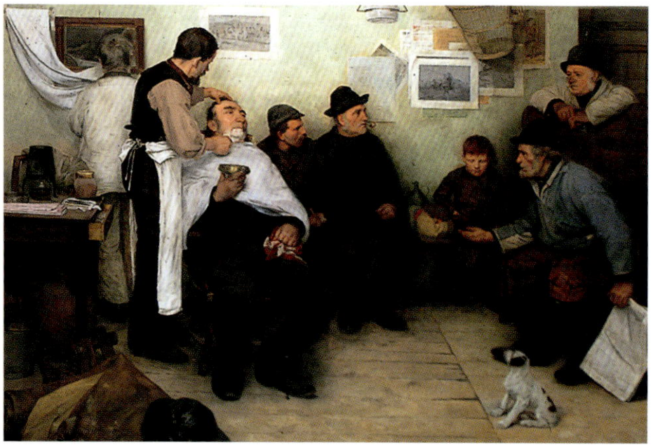

Percy Craft
Saturday aka ***The Barber's Shop***
1894 • oil on canvas • 111 x 162 cm
Kent County Council Libraries Registration and Archives

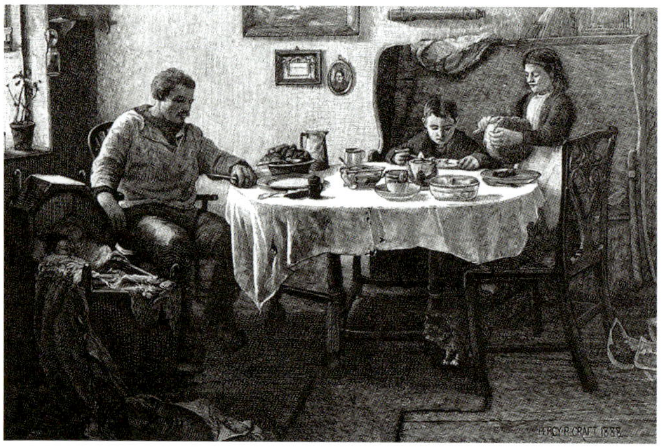

Percy Craft
The Empty Chair
from *The Art Journal*, 1889

artists in *The Art Journal* in 1889. None of the works were mentioned in the reviews. John Aste lived at South Norwood Hill and Edmund Tautz in London.

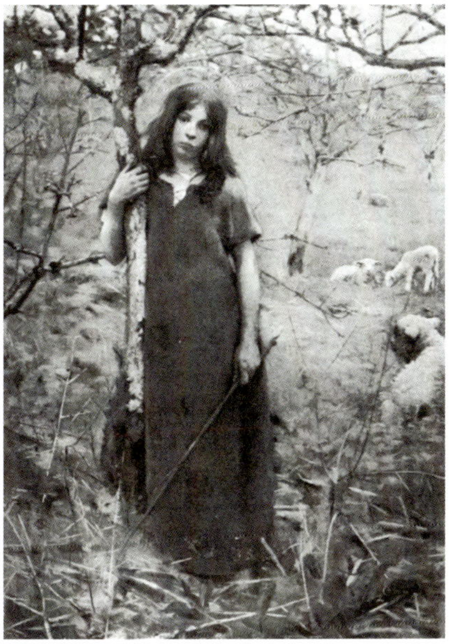

John da Costa
A Pastoral
from the 1894 exhibition catalogue

DA COSTA, John Henry Alphonse Frederick Francis ROI, RP

TEIGNMOUTH, DEVON 1866–1931 LONDON

Da Costa was a portrait and figure painter, who was based in Newlyn in the early 1890s. His work was considered to be ambitious, for he worked quickly and painted broadly, often with vivid colour. Whilst not all of his output was felt to be an unqualified success, he was considered technically accomplished and as 'one of the talented young artists who at any time may make a sudden spring much higher up the ladder of fame'.[5] As a well regarded violinist, with an expressive voice, he was also in demand at entertainments.

1880s: Studied in France for three years.
1890: Settled in Newlyn and contributed to Dowdeswell Exhibition that December.
1891: At time of Census, living at Cliff Castle Cottage in Belle Vue with Mary Josephine Da Costa, a widow (possibly his mother) from Metz, Germany, and Oscar M.J. Da Costa of the 21st Hussars from St Helier, Jersey.
1893: The studio that he constructed at North Corner for himself described as 'a palace'.
1895: Recorded in July as having left Newlyn for good, but still used a Newlyn exhibiting address the following year.
1904: Noted as running his own art school classes in Kensington, London, with the help of his Newlyn friend, Samuel Green Enderby.

1894 EXHIBIT

- ***A Pastoral*** (RA 1892) [180]

DAVIDSON, Jessie Young

EDINBURGH 1852–1904 UNKNOWN

Very little is known about this Scottish artist, except that, during her short exhibiting career, she was based in Liverpool and, in 1892–3, she had been involved briefly with the St Ives colony.

Father minister. Brought up in Edinburgh.
1885–92: Liverpool exhibiting address given during these years.
1892: First recorded in St Ives. Took part in Carnival Masquerade in February, exhibited on Show Day in March and had only success at the RA with *In the Shade*. Recorded again as a visitor between April and June.
1893: Took part in second Carnival Masquerade; listed as a visitor between May and July. No record of her exhibiting after the Nottingham exhibition.
1904: A relative has recorded her death as being in December.

WALLIS CORRESPONDENCE

Davidson was hard to contact as, having returned from the Continent, she had gone up to Lennoxtown in Scotland. Nevertheless, the catalogue gives her address as 'St Ives'.

5. *The Cornishman*, 4 April 1895.

1894 EXHIBIT

- *An Impromptu Skirt Dance* [33]

DETMOLD, Henry Edward

KINGSTON, SURREY 1854–1924 PARIS

Detmold was primarily a Newlyn-based figure painter, but also worked in St Ives. During his relatively brief time in Cornwall, he produced some important works, but as these have generally not been available for exhibitions, he is not as well known as he deserves to be.

One of eight children of German-born merchant, Julius Adolph Detmold. Educated at J.W. Tottenham's School, St Leonards.
1875–6: Studied at Académie Julian, Paris, and later at Atelier Carolus Duran.
Early 1880s: Also studied in Dusseldorf, Munich and Brussels.
1882: First exhibits at RA and Paris Salon.
1885: Arrived in Newlyn. Stayed with Stanhope Forbes at Belle Vue House.
1886: Joined NEAC.
1887: Worked in St Ives and suggested inter-colony cricket match.
1889: In late July, took lodgings for a few months in St Ives, at 7 Bellair Terrace.
1890: In St Ives again, from July; became founder member of St Ives Arts Club in August. Exhibited St Ives work at Dowdeswells exhibition in December.
1891: Married Julia Lane (b. 1863) in Mensthe & Moselle, France.
1892: Sold his St Ives scene *A Peaceful Evening* to Leeds Art Gallery. Moved to Hastings, then *c.*1898 to St Leonards, then *c.*1900 to Paris.
1893: Held one-man show at Castle Hotel Assembly Rooms, Hastings.
1902: Last known exhibit.
1924: Died in Paris, and buried in the Père Lachaise cemetery.

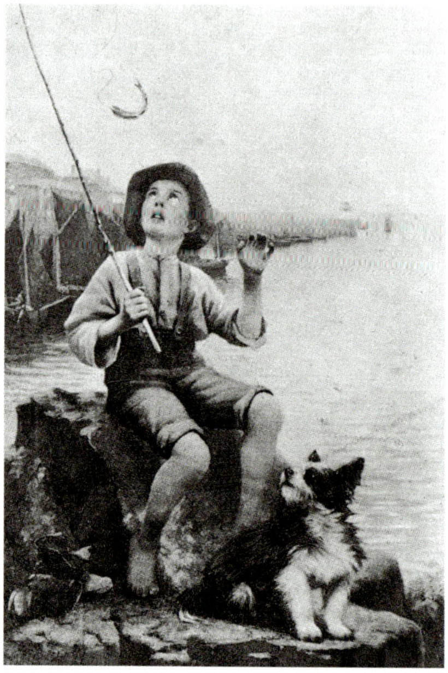

Henry Detmold
Hooked, Not Landed

WALLIS CORRESPONDENCE

Detmold wrote to Wallis initially from 'Sunny Bank', St Helen's Down, Hastings on 29 July 1894. He initially recommended two works that had been bought by Hastings locals – *Boys Spearing for Flat Fish*, which had been shown at the ROI in 1892, which was owned by Harry Coghill of Coghurst Hall, and *After Many Days* (RA 1893), which was owned by Major MacDonald of Meadow Bank, St Leonards. Clearly, the latter was not willing to lend. He also mentioned *Waiting for the Boats* (RA 1887), owned by Alexander Miller of Putney Hill, and two unsold works, *Loading the Nets* and *Waiting*. He indicated that the latter, which depicts a girl sitting on a rock, with a dog beside her, had been painted at St Ives, but then withdrew it from consideration, as he remembered that he had promised it to Manchester. Another work that he referred to was *The Departure of the Herring Fleet*, which was then at Colnaghis. In the end, the group of his work got together was rather different.

During the show, in early October, he wrote to Wallis from Amsterdam, asking if he could send a copy of the catalogue to Algiers, as he was going to be spending the winter there.

1894 EXHIBITS

- ***Boys Spearing for Flat Fish*** (Harry Coghill) [26]
- ***Hooked, Not Landed*** (RA 1890) [27]
- ***Loading Nets*** [28]
- ***A Peaceful Evening*** (Leeds AG) [29]

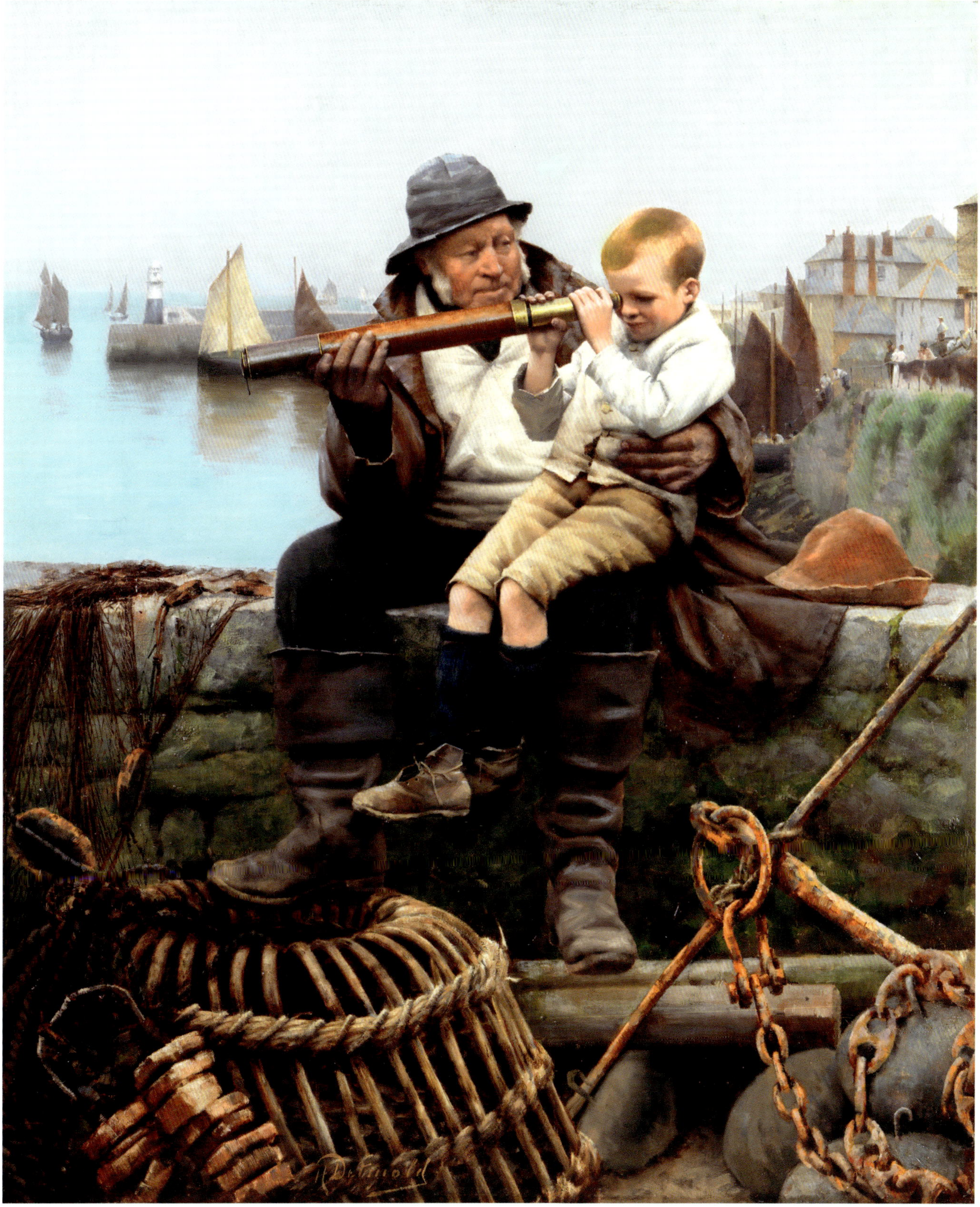

pl. 7 **Henry Detmold**
A Glimpse of Future Seas
oil on canvas • 102 x 82 cm
private collection, image courtesy Messum's

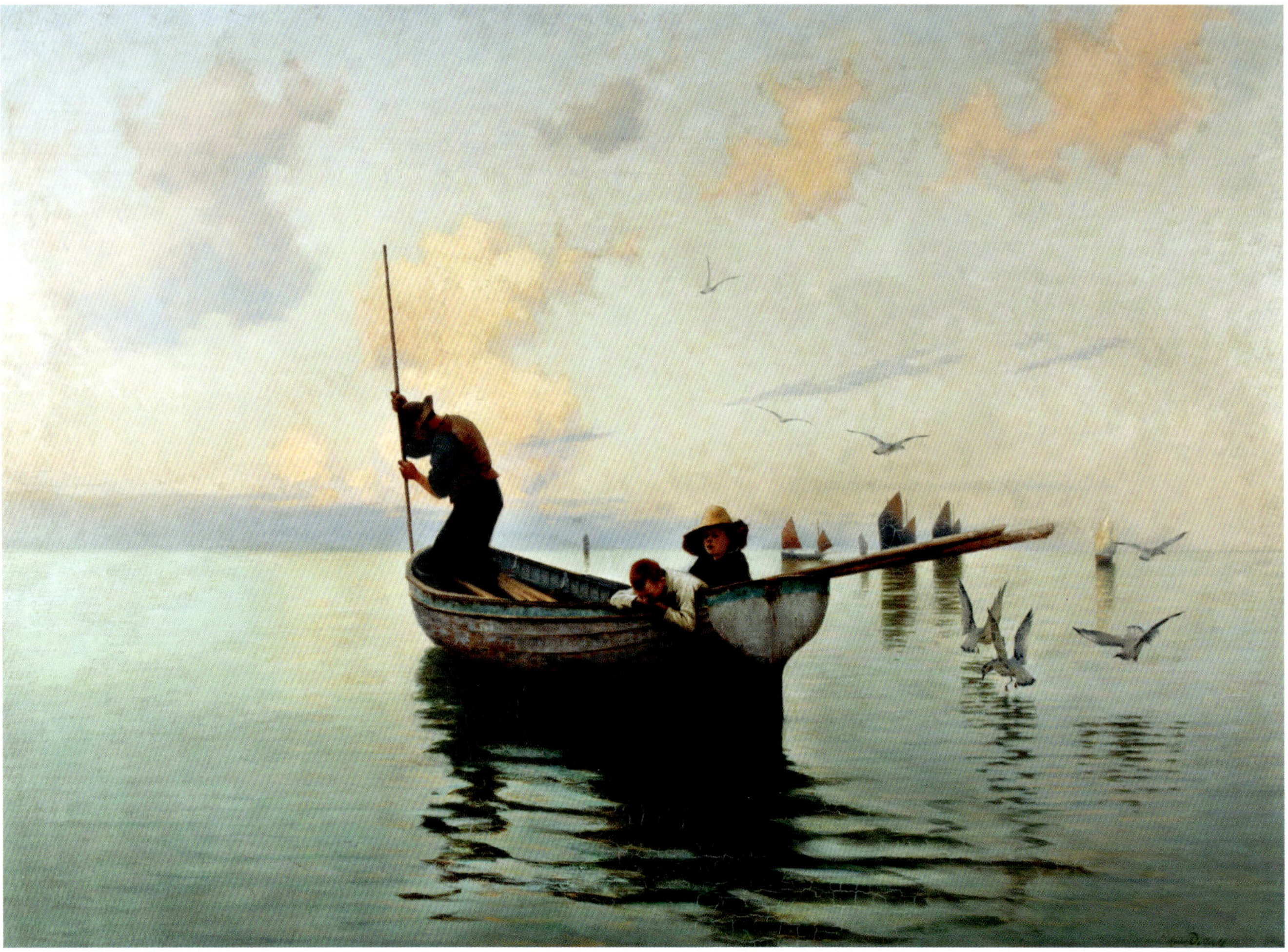

pl. 8 **Henry Detmold**
Spearing
oil on canvas • 152 x 203 cm
Manchester City Galleries

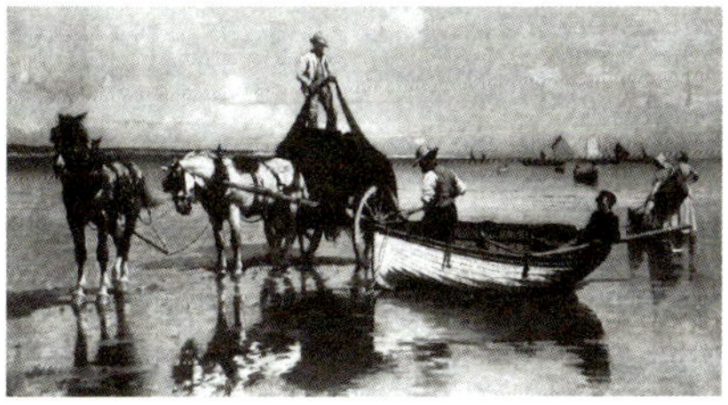

Henry Detmold
Loading Nets

- ***Spearing*** (RA 1892) [30]
- ***A Glimpse of Future Seas*** (RA 1889, Chicago 1893) [31]

The first four exhibits have not been located, Leeds having disposed of *A Peaceful Evening* in 1938. *Loading Nets* was exhibited previously at the first Anglo-Australian Society exhibition in 1890 and at Glasgow in 1892.

***Nottingham Evening Post*, 6 October 1894**: 'Mr Henry Detmold's six pictures are grouped together at the end of the first room. His work is rather unequal, and his colour is apt to become black in places, but at his best, as in *A Peaceful Evening* and *Loading Nets*, which gives a clever rendering of the reflection of a cart and two horses upon wet sand, he gives us good qualities of lighting and colour, and a picturesque arrangement of figures.'

2015 EXHIBITS

A Glimpse of Future Seas (pl. 7, private collection): This work was Detmold's most successful painting. It was exhibited at the Royal Academy in 1889, the Paris Exposition Universelle of 1889 and was also the front cover illustration of *The Graphic* on Saturday 19 October 1889. Later, it was selected for the Chicago World Columbian Exhibition of 1893, where it won a medal, and for the Societé des Beaux-Arts Exhibition in Nice in 1901–2. Set in Newlyn, the subject was a version of a common theme, which highlighted how successive generations were attracted by the sea-faring life. This implied a contentment with their lot that was comforting to the middle class spectator. The painting reveals the use of the 'square brush' technique and its concentration on tonalities makes it an archetypal Newlyn School work.

Spearing (pl. 8, Manchester City Galleries): This atmospheric painting was exhibited at the Royal Academy in 1892.

DICKSON, William

ALNMOUTH, NORTHUMBERLAND 1866–1933 NEWBURY, BERKSHIRE

The landscape and marine painter, William Dickson, is another artist about whom little is known, but he was based in St Ives between 1891–4.

Father solicitor; grandfather Clerk of the Peace for Northumberland. Educated in Harrogate.
1883: First exhibit at RA.
1889: Married Hetty Pallister in Scarborough.
1891: In Census, living at 25 Fitzroy Road, St Pancras. In July, lodged with his wife at Barnoon Villa, St Ives for a few weeks.
1892: Took part in Show Day and the Carnival Masquerade in March.
1893: Living in the newly built 'Godrevy House' by the Porthminster Hotel. Involved in the second Carnival Masquerade in February.
1894: Left St Ives and moved to Tadley, Basingstoke. Continued to exhibit until 1908.
1911: Still living at Tadley. No children.

1894 EXHIBIT

- ***Wild, wide and open to the Air*** [39]

This work was called *Wide, Wild and Open to the Sea* when shown at the RA in 1894 and was later brought by Brighton Art Gallery. It is currently unexhibitable, as is a similar painting, showing horses at the edge of a marsh, entitled *The Close of a Weary Day* (RA 1897), owned by Worcester Art Gallery.

***Nottingham Evening Post*, 6 October 1894**: 'One of the broadest, breeziest pictures in the exhibition is No. 39, by Mr W. Dickson, *Wild, wide and open to the air*, a bold piece of painting which we had intended to speak about sooner. Two horses, white and brown, are standing in the shallow water of a great marsh, bristling with brown reeds – over them is a fine sky, with rain falling in the distance, and the blue sea on the dim horizon. The canvas well expresses a great wind-swept open space, and we shall look for future work by this artist with great interest.'

DYER, Lowell

POSSIBLY BOSTON, MASSACHUSETTS 1856–1939 ST IVES, CORNWALL

Dyer was an American-born artist, who lived in St Ives for over 50 years. He was better known for his wit than his art. He later showed a predilection for paintings of young women or children as angels, often imbued with a heavy symbolism.

Father Reverend Oliver Dyer of Brooklyn, who became a Swedenborgian minister in Mount Vernon, New York.
1880s: Studied art in Paris under Gerome at the Beaux Arts and at Académie Julian. Also studied in Venice, where developed an admiration for the Italian Old Masters.
1888: First visited St Ives and returned to settle the following year.
1890: Participated in Cornish Artists' Exhibition at Dowdeswells in December.
1893–4: President of St Ives Arts Club.
1899: Started painting angels, of which an example is owned by Victoria Art Gallery, Bath.

WALLIS CORRESPONDENCE

Dyer was ill when Wallis came down to St Ives and so was unable to show him any of his work. Accordingly, he wrote on 17 April 1894 from his home, 2 Richmond Terrace, St Ives, indicating that Arnesby Brown should have mentioned his name to Wallis and asking to be included. However, in July 1894, writing from Hotel du Luxembourg, Laroche, Belgium, he indicated that he had only two pictures available, which he had left at Lanhams, the shop in St Ives that catered for the majority of the artists' needs. Both appear to have gone to Nottingham, but only one was hung. After the exhibition ended, Wallis was happy to keep both works at Nottingham for a while.

1894 EXHIBIT

- ***A Woodland Path*** [107]

The painting was not reviewed and its whereabouts are unknown.

EADIE, William

PAISLEY 1846–1926 ISLINGTON, LONDON

The Scottish portrait and domestic genre painter, William Eadie, was one of the initial three settlers of the St Ives colony in 1885. However, his background was

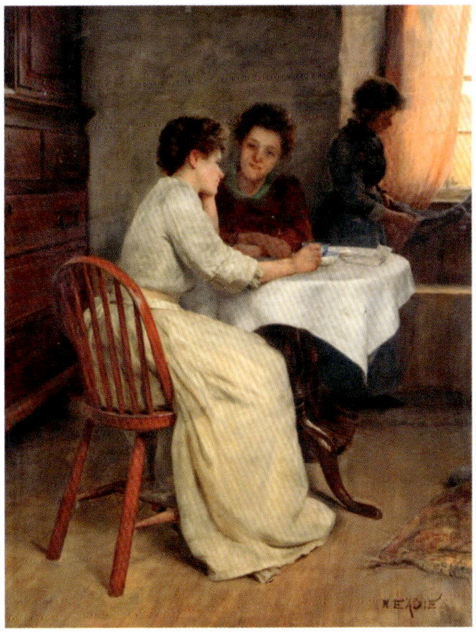

William Eadie
What Shall the Answer Be?
1891 • oil on canvas • 109 x 82 cm
Paisley Museum, Renfrewshire Council

very different from the other early colonists, for he was older, had a large family and had not trained in France.

Father silk dyer. Brought up in Paisley and initially studied at Paisley School of Arts (1868).
1871: First exhibit at RA. Now living in St John's Wood.
1880: Married in Glasgow.
1885: Moved to St Ives. Fifth child born in 1886.
1890: Founder member of St Ives Arts Club in August. Participated in Cornish Artists' Exhibition at Dowdeswells in December.
1896: Ceased exhibiting but continued painting.
1902: Moved to Islington. Wife died 1906.

WALLIS CORRESPONDENCE

Eadie did not respond to Wallis until 29 August 1894, blaming his dilatoriness on a long illness that meant that he had not been able to attend to his affairs. The list of four paintings that he sent to Wallis were not the ones that he would have chosen ideally, but he felt that they would be 'representative in a way'. Only three were hung.

1894 EXHIBITS

- ***Teazing the 'Mag'*** [58]
- ***Off to the Fishing*** [64]
- ***What shall the Answer be?*** (RA 1894) (John Eadie) [202]

John Eadie, a relation of the artist, lived in Paisley. *What shall the Answer be?*, which showed a girl opening a letter from a suitor, was originally exhibited on Show Day in St Ives in 1891, but was not hung at the Royal Academy until 1894. It is now owned by Renfrewshire Council. The other two works have not been located. None of Eadie's exhibits were specifically referred to in reviews.

2015 EXHIBITS

'Where there's Life, there's Hope' (pl. 9, Penlee House Gallery & Museum): There seems little doubt that Eadie's first choice for the Nottingham exhibition, if available, would have been this painting. When shown in Glasgow in 1893 it was priced at £300, a figure some five times higher than any other work that he exhibited there, and so he clearly considered it to be his masterpiece.

The lengthy commentary on this work published after it was first exhibited on Show Day 1890 is worth reproducing (below) not merely for its description of the picture itself but as an example of the way that the Victorians loved to interpret pictures of this sort:

St Ives Weekly Summary, 5 April 1890: Mr Eadie's Academy Picture is a large interior entitled *'Where there's Life, there's Hope'*. It depicts a scene – but too familiar to most of us – where a loved little one is lying dangerously ill. The grey light of the winter's day pours into the dwelling room of the fisherman's cottage and falls upon the kneeling figures of father and mother, who full of grief and care, are leaning over the cradle of their sick child, anxiously watching the ebb and flow of that young life most dear to them – so lately given; so soon perchance to be taken. In the foreground stands a venerable dame – a striking figure, full of singular power, and of that tranquil composure in times of trial, born only of three score and ten. She, by gesture of extended arm and slightly raised hand, is emphasizing those words of comfort which give the picture its title; and as we take our leave of this sympathetic scene, we, too, instinctively hope that all may be yet well with the child, and that its life may be spared. This cleverly-painted

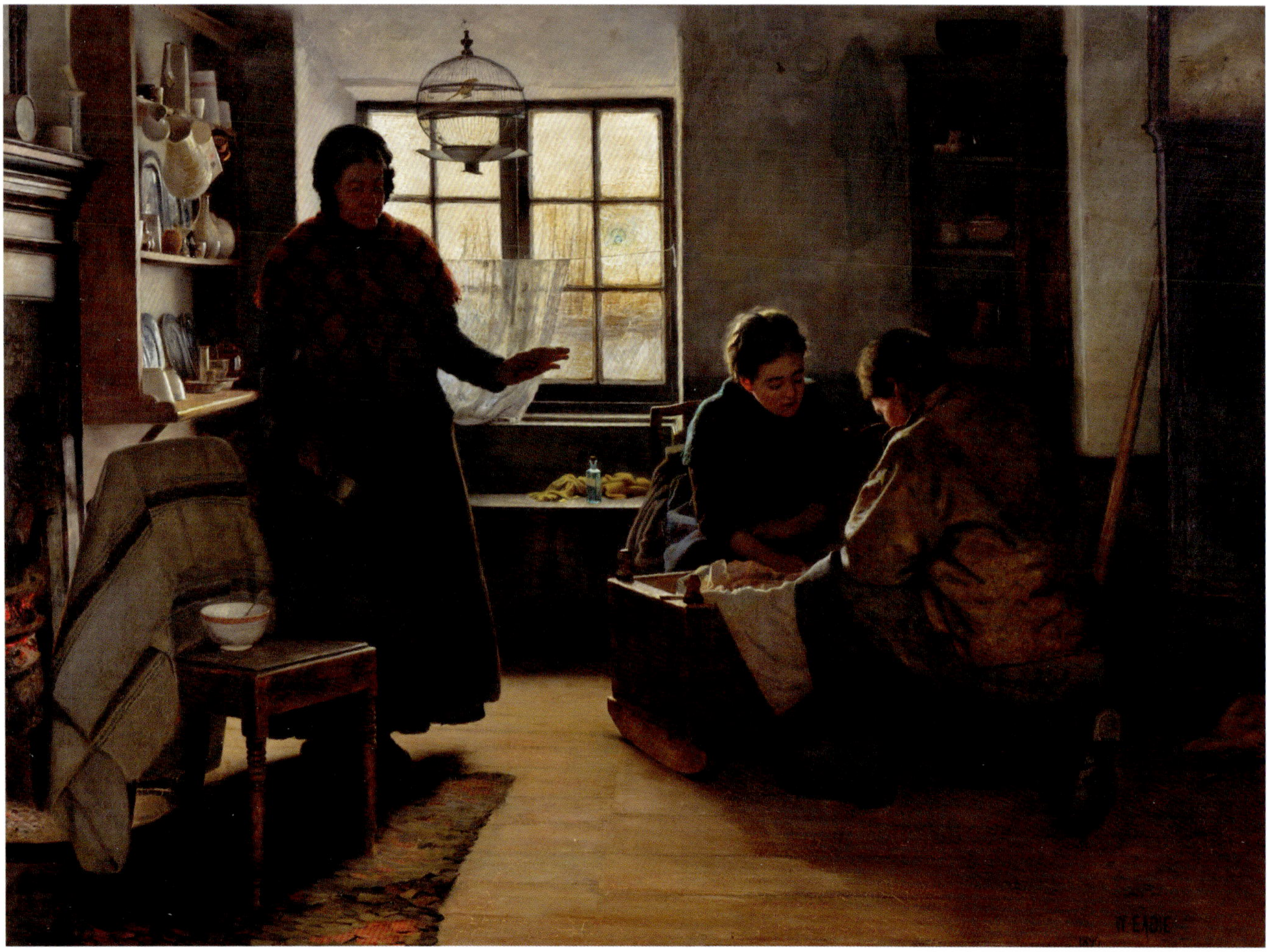

pl. 9 **William Eadie**
Where There's Life, There's Hope
1890 • oil on canvas • 127 x 168 cm
Penlee House Gallery & Museum

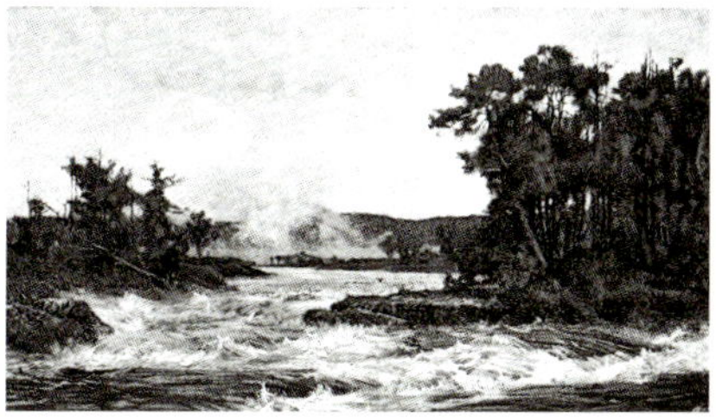

Alfred East
A Frosty Sunset
from the 1894 exhibition catalogue

picture is full of careful workmanship and of a realism so great that one seems to feel the warmth of the fire, to be able to touch the blanket airing before it, and to appreciate oneself the cleanliness and order of the sick room. We heartily congratulate Mr Eadie on his great success, whilst we feel sure that his important work will be one of the Popular Pictures of the coming Art Season.

EAST, Sir Alfred RA, PRBA, RE, RI

KETTERING 1844–1913 LONDON

Alfred East, who was a late starter as an artist, nevertheless achieved an extraordinary level of commercial success as a landscape painter, due to a business brain and an outgoing personality. He called Cornwall 'the county of my love', and was a regular visitor to St Ives throughout his career. Like Adrian Stokes and the other St Ives landscapists, he aimed to produce mood pieces to stimulate poetic thoughts. He won an extraordinary range of honours during his life and was knighted in 1910, but his reputation has never been as high since his death.

The youngest of a family of eleven children of a Kettering bootmaker, East was educated locally.
1859–79: Involved in family footwear manufacturing business in Kettering.
1879-82: Attended the School of Art in Glasgow before continuing his studies in Paris first at the École des Beaux Arts and then at Académie Julian under Fleury and Bougereau.
1882: Worked in the art colony at Barbizon.
1883: Settled in London and first exhibited at the RA. Also made an RBA and an RE.
1887: Visited Cornwall and contributed 37 paintings of Cornwall to an exhibition, held jointly with Ayerst Ingram and Thomas Gotch, at the Fine Art Society ('FAS') in April 1888.
1888: Attended Adrian Stokes' Chantrey Supper in St Ives in August.
1889: Sent by FAS to Japan; exhibition of his Japanese paintings at FAS in March 1890.
1890: Participated in Cornish Artists' Exhibition at Dowdeswells in December.
1890–4: Regular visitor to Lelant and St Ives, with several Cornish subjects hung at the RA.
1895: Exhibition at FAS – *English landscapes illustrating the effects from dawn to moonrise.*
1895–1913: Continued to visit Cornwall with regularity, whilst winning international renown.

WALLIS CORRESPONDENCE

East communicated with Wallis from 4 Grove End Road, St John's Wood. His significant presence at the exhibition will reflect his keen business sense and organisational skills. However, his principal recommendation, *An Angry Dawn*, painted at Lelant, which was owned by major collector, George McCulloch, and which had recently won an award at Chicago, proved unavailable. He also mentioned some watercolours of Hayle and Lelant but these were not included.

1894 EXHIBITS

- ***The Poultry Farm*** (Chas Showell) [18]
- ***An Autumn After-glow*** (RA 1887) (Dudley) [43]
- ***Reedy Mere and Sunlit Hills*** (RA 1891) (Fred Ryland) [44]
- ***Dawn – Trevethor Park near Lelant*** (M. Tomkinson J.P.) [45]
- ***Autumn 'The morning trembles o'er the sky, And, unperceived, unfolds the spreading day'*** (Manchester) [46]

- ***Hemmingford Abbey on the Ouse*** (John Lancaster) [47]
- ***A Frosty Sunset*** [48]
- ***A Cornish Wood*** [70]
- ***The Lonely Road*** [151]
- ***A Dewy Morning*** [158]

In addition to the two works already in public collections by 1894, *Reedy Mere and Sunlit Hills* is now owned by Birmingham Art Gallery and *The Lonely Road* by the Alfred East Gallery, Kettering. None of the other works have been located. Chas Showell lived in Edgbaston, Birmingham, Fred Ryland at Harborne, near Birmingham, John Lancaster in Rugby and M. Tomkinson at Franche Hall, Kidderminster.

Nottingham Guardian, 13 October 1894: 'It will, perhaps, cause surprise to some that Mr Wallis has included Mr Alfred East among the Cornish painters. Certainly, he has once or twice dwelt there for a short period, painting around Hayle and Lelant, but he is far from making his permanent home there from one end of the year to the other. Judged by his work, however, he is in complete sympathy with the landscape artists of the Duchy, although he has made his name elsewhere. Certainly, the seven or eight canvasses by which he is represented form an important feature in this section of the exhibition. The more important ones are hung together and form a fine glow of mellow colour and light upon the water. We should have liked to have seen one of his Japanese pictures here and his *Hayle from Lelant* but some of his very best works have been brought together for our pleasure, and enable one to judge of his power of imagination in depicting landscapes. Indeed, his *Autumn Afterglow*, lent by the Corporation of Dudley, displays him at his very best. The marshy pool, wrapped around with reeds, the foliage of the trees glowing with all shades of red, brown and purple, intensified by the red afterglow of the sun, stands silent and palely blue, while light clouds wander across the round white moon, set in a sky of delicate tones. The whole glows with delightful colour and mirrors that poetic and pathetic side of Nature, which is most strongly felt at the breaking of day or the falling of night.

'In *Reedy Mere and Sunlit Hills*, lent by Mr Fred Ryland, the artist again gives us a glow of light, with pine trees and undergrowth flushing red in the sunset, contrasting with the delicate blue of the rush grown mere, and the hills, snow-capped in the distance, towards which the swans are flying. *Dawn*, lent by Mr Tomlinson, as the title denotes, is a fine rendering of that mysterious hour when life begins to wake again upon this earth. The grey morning light floods the whole picture. A wild duck flies up from the reeds about the pool, while the trees loom greyly in the half light. Two thin, bare trunks are outlined gracefully against the morning sky. The scene is one in Trevethor Park, near Lelant, looking towards the open and cultivated country. A golden glow fills *Autumn*, lent by the City of Manchester, in which the dead and dying leaves are showered down upon the banks of a still pool, white in the distance where the light falls upon it; in all ways, a beautiful effect truly given.'

2015 EXHIBIT

The Lonely Road (pl. 10, Kettering Borough Council, Alfred East Gallery): East's landscape style was felt to be influenced by the Barbizon school but, like Adrian Stokes, Ernest Waterlow and other Edwardians, he hoped to develop a new great British school of landscape painting and so he tended to emphasise more his debt to the Norwich school and Constable. Fervently believing in an acute observation of the beauties of nature, which could only be achieved by sketching *en plein air*, East nevertheless considered it the duty of the artist to communicate the feelings that nature inspired in him. This led to a move away from strict realism to a more poetic vision. Frequently, as demonstrated by the paintings in the Nottingham Exhibition, the titles of works gave no indication of the whereabouts of the subject, but simply gave the time of day or the season or the light effect depicted.

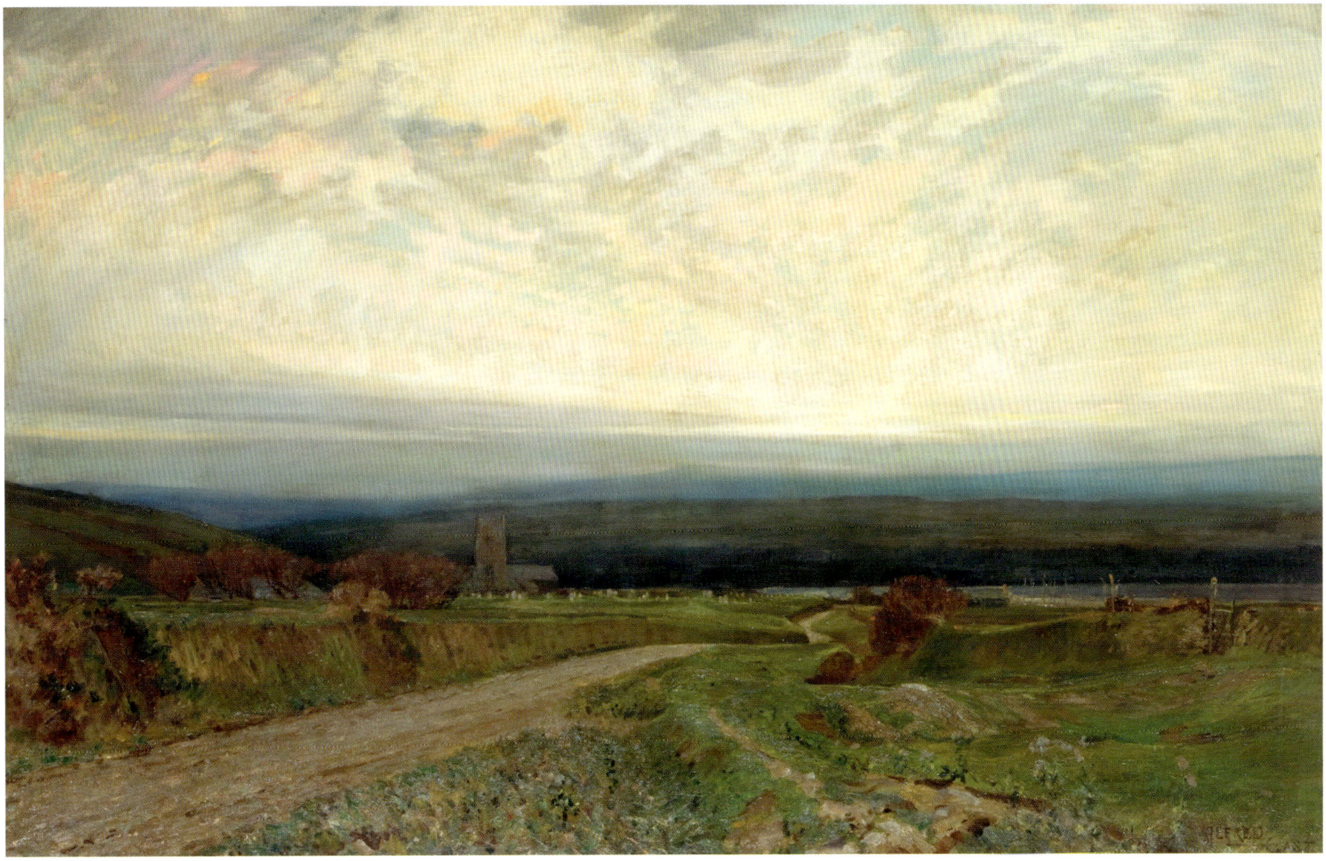

pl. 10 **Alfred East**
The Lonely Road
1890 • oil on canvas • 120 x 180 cm
Kettering Borough Council, Alfred East Art Gallery

These paintings sought to capture the essence of the English countryside in all its moods as the seasons changed, and so precise topography was of subsidiary relevance. Decorative design also came to play a key role in compositions. In 1895, East held an exhibition at the Fine Art Society of 95 such works, entitled 'English landscapes illustrating the effects from dawn to moonrise'. In his Prefatory Note, R. Jope-Slade commented that an East landscape was best described as 'a monument to an exquisite moment.'

With this interest in mood pieces, East indicated that often the descriptive lines of a poem would remain with him, awaiting the time and occasion when he could embody these imaginings into a scene or moment witnessed.[6] In the case of *The Lonely Road*, East indicated that the inspiration had been the words 'The lonely road that everyone must travel passes through the churchyard onto the eternal dawn'.[7] The church depicted is said to be St Uny, Lelant, albeit its setting is imaginary. The sky effect was commented upon favourably when it was shown at Nottingham, and an illustration of the work in East's book on landscape painting shows an attractive pink sky.[8] Accordingly, this painting may be another version of the scene.

The composition of this work also demonstrates East's view that, when the eye snatched at a general effect, it was the middle distance that it focuses on and that the rest was 'circumambient uncertainty'. Accordingly, he tended to place the heart of his subject (here the church) in the middle distance, leaving foregrounds hazy so that these did not detain or distract the eye from the central motif. This was in stark contrast to many landscapists, who painted objects in the foreground in elaborate detail, and used less definition as the subject receded.[9]

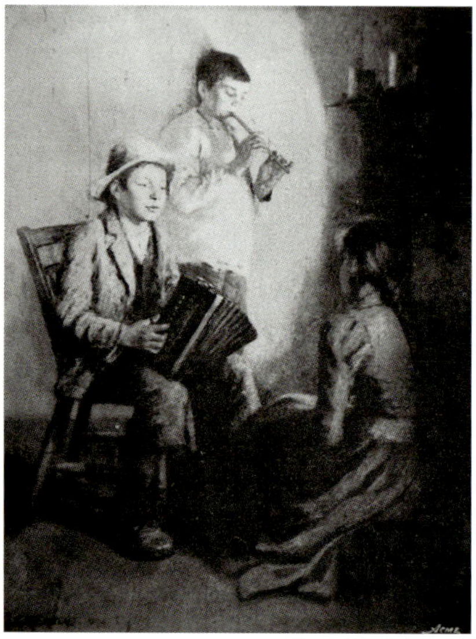

Charles Herbert Eastlake
A Duet
from *Royal Academy Pictures*, 1893

EASTLAKE, Charles Herbert RBA

WANDSWORTH, LONDON 1868–1940s CANADA

Charles Herbert Eastlake, the husband of Mary Bell (q.v.), developed into a leading figure in the St Ives landscape section, but two of his Nottingham exhibits were figure paintings, where he was not as accomplished.

Father, who was from Plymouth, was a Secretary to an MP.
1880s: Studied in Antwerp and Paris.
1889: First exhibited at RBA, where made member in 1895.
1892: Became member of St Ives Arts Club.
1893: Married Canadian, Mary Bell.
1894–8: Based in St Ives.
1899–1939: Based in London but travelled widely (Holland, Japan, New Zealand, Canada).
1939: Moved to Canada, where died.

WALLIS CORRESPONDENCE

Writing from St Ives in December 1894, Eastlake asked for his paintings to be returned to his London address, 17 Temperley Road, Balham.

1894 EXHIBITS

- ***A Duet*** (RA 1894) [116]
- ***November*** [117]
- ***Portrait*** [118]

None of these paintings have been located, albeit *A Duet* was sold by Bonhams,

6. See Prefatory Note by R Jope-Slade to 1895 Fine Art Society Exhibition.
7. Paul Johnson and Kenneth McConkey, *Alfred East: Lyrical Landscape Painter*, Sansom & Co, Bristol, 2009, p. 67.
8. Alfred East, *Landscape Painting in Oil Colour*, London, 1906, p. 67.
9. Ibid.

Bath in 2002 under the title *The Young Musicians*. It featured two young boys in jumpers, playing by the light of a fire, a flute and concertina, their sole audience being an attentive young girl, perhaps their sister.

EDWARDS, Sarah Harriette Mia

PONTNEWYDD, MONMOUTHSHIRE 1864–1931 HADDISCOE, NORFOLK

Mia Edwards was the girlfriend of Arnesby Brown, whom she married in 1896. They had met at the Herkomer Art School, Bushey. She went on to have a successful career as a figure painter, specializing in broadly painted studies of children, particularly in garden settings.

Father clergyman but died when she was 12. Educated in Cardiff.
1889: Studied at Herkomer Art School, Bushey.
1892: Portrait by Arnesby Brown exhibited at RA.
1893: Took part in Carnival Masquerade in St Ives in March. First exhibit at RA.
1895: Participated in St Ives Show Day.
1896: Married Arnesby Brown and spent most winters in St Ives until 1910.

1894 EXHIBIT

- ***'Once upon a Time'*** (RA 1893) [105]

This work has not been located and was not reviewed. However, an image of it is in the Brown archive at Norwich Castle Museum. It depicts a woman reading a story to a child.

FORBES, Elizabeth Adela (née Armstrong) RWS

ONTARIO, CANADA 1859–1912 NEWLYN

Elizabeth Forbes, the Canadian wife of Stanhope Forbes, was considered by many to be the leading female artist in England at this time. Her early style reflects the rustic naturalism of the Newlyn School, but she later specialised in more decorative figure paintings of children inspired by myth and poetry.

Father was civil servant. Studied at South Kensington in 1873, but mainly at the Art Students' League in New York under Chase (1878–81) and then in Munich (1882).
1882: Visited Pont-Aven and took lessons in etching from Mortimer Menpes.
1883: Elected as member of RWS; began to exhibit regularly at London galleries.
1884: Visited Zandvoort, Holland.
1885: Moved to Newlyn.
1886: Became engaged to Stanhope Forbes (q.v.) and painted that summer in St Ives.
1887–8: Returned to paint in St Ives with her American friend, Rosalie Gill.
1889: Married Stanhope Forbes; won medal at Paris World Exposition.
1890: Participated in the Cornish Artists show at Dowdeswells.
1893: Won medal at Chicago. After the birth of her son, Alec, she became more interested in works of fancy based on medieval folk-lore, Shakespearean plays and such-like, all imbued with poetic feeling and demonstrating a wide range of influences.
1899–1912: Assisted with Forbes Painting School and developed considerable reputation as leading female painter in England, exhibiting widely; represented in public collections worldwide.

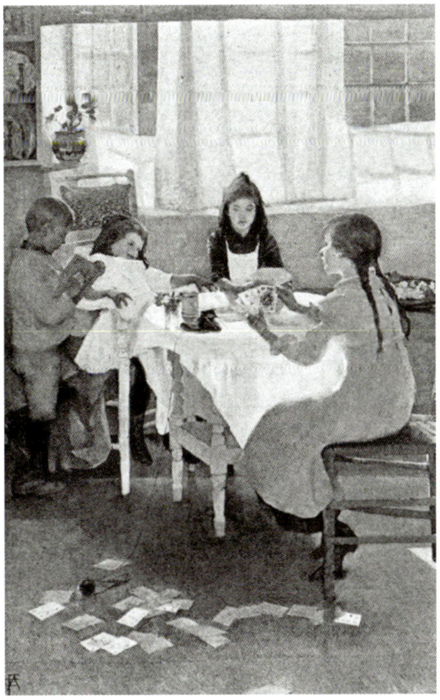

Elizabeth Forbes
A Game of Old Maid
from the 1894 exhibition catalogue

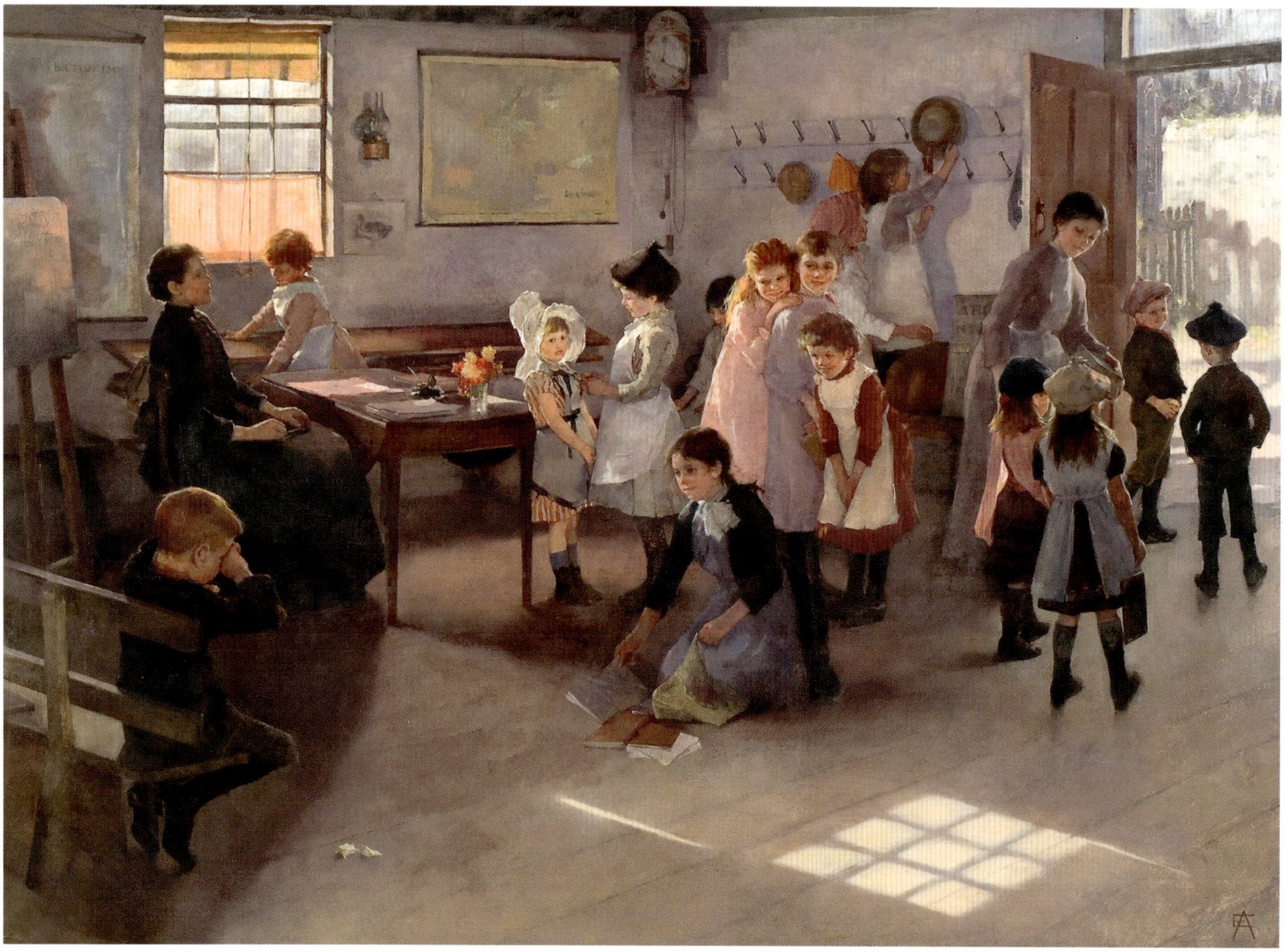

pl. 11 **Elizabeth Forbes**
School is Out
1889 • oil on canvas • 106 x 145 cm
Penlee House Gallery & Museum

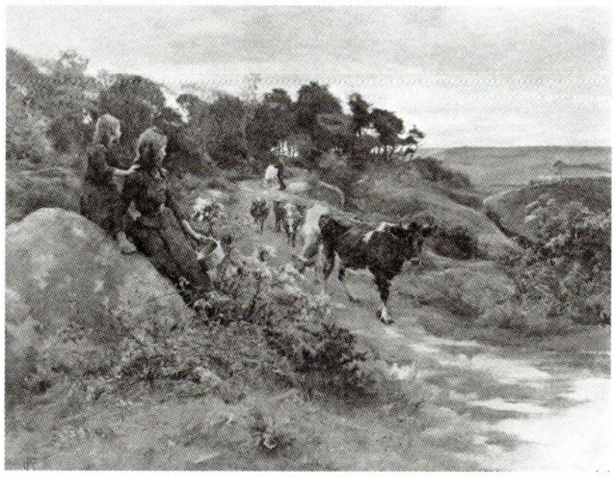

Elizabeth Forbes
Moorland Princesses
from the 1894 exhibition catalogue

1894 EXHIBITS

- ***Moorland Princesses*** (RA 1893) [20]
- ***A Game of Old Maid*** (RA 1891) [156]

Neither exhibit has been located, but the catalogue contained images of both. Forbes asked for both works to be sent on, after the exhibition, to the Atkinson Art Gallery, Southport.

***Nottingham Guardian*, 6 October 1894**: '[*Moorland Princesses*] ... filled with the most lovely autumnal colours ... delicate in feeling, delightful in colour, and is painted with technical power of a high order.'

2015 EXHIBIT

School is Out (pl. 11, Penlee House Gallery & Museum): This is one of Penlee House's most popular paintings. Although there are alternative suppositions, it is believed that the setting is Paul School and that the small boy crying is Richard Vivian Spargo, whose two elder sisters are the red-haired girls laughing at him. Particularly in the early years of the Cornish colonies, women artists tended to restrict themselves to painting women and children, possibly due to some unwillingness on the part of adult males to sit for a female artist. The work was painted in 1889, the year of Elizabeth Armstrong's marriage to Stanhope Forbes, and is the last major work by her to be signed with her maiden initials, 'EA': after marriage, she changed her monogram to 'EAF'.

FORBES, Stanhope Alexander RA

DUBLIN 1857–1947 NEWLYN

Stanhope Forbes was the leading figure in Cornish art from the time of his arrival in Newlyn in 1884 until his death in 1947. In particular, he was the figurehead of the Newlyn colony. Having challenged the establishment with his French inspired technique in the mid 1880s, he had been elected an Associate of the Royal Academy in 1892.

Father was railway manager; his influential mother, Juliette de Guise, was French. Studied at Lambeth School of Art under John Sparkes (1874–8), and then in 1880 at Bonnat's studio in Paris.
1881: Visited Brittany with H.H. La Thangue, working principally at Cancale; sold *A Street in Brittany* to the Walker Art Gallery, Liverpool.
1882–3: Based for several months each year in Quimperlé.
1884: First visited Newlyn, and had huge success at the Royal Academy in 1885 with *A Fish Sale on a Cornish Beach*, now regarded as the seminal work of the Newlyn School.
1886: *Off to the Fishing Grounds* acquired by the Walker Art Gallery, Liverpool; became engaged to Elizabeth Armstrong (q.v.); worked in St Ives during the summer and autumn.
1889: Married Elizabeth after the sale of *The Health of the Bride* to Henry Tate; medal at the Paris World Exposition for his St Ives work *Une famille de nomads*.
1890: Participated in the Cornish Artists show at Dowdeswells.
1891: Won gold medal at the Paris Salon with *The Village Philharmonic*.
1891–1912: Produced a succession of highly regarded large scale figure paintings of the local populace, which are in public collections around the world; further medals at international exhibitions, including one at the Paris Salon in 1900 for *The Forge*.

1899: Set up, with his wife, Elizabeth, the Forbes School of Painting, which attracted new young talent to the colony.
1910: Made Royal Academician (ARA 1892).

WALLIS CORRESPONDENCE

Forbes' work was in such demand at the time that it was difficult to secure the paintings most desired. Forbes had promised *Off to the Fishing Grounds* (RA 1886 – Liverpool) and *The Lighthouse* (RA 1892 – Manchester) to the contemporaneous Birmingham Marine Exhibition. A letter in the archive from Henry Tate, refusing to lend a work, as he did not wish to disappoint visitors coming a long way to see his collection, was presumably in response to a request for the loan of *The Health of the Bride* (RA 1889). Wallis had also tried to borrow *By Order of the Court* (RA 1890 – now National Museums, Liverpool) but its owner, Sharpley Bainbridge of Lincoln, refused to lend it, as he had hardly had the chance to have it on his own walls since he had purchased it and had just completed a rehang to fit it in. However, he did lend *Grey Rocks and Grey Mullet*. *Forging the Anchor* was clearly another choice of Wallis', given the attention that it had received recently, and Forbes was glad that major collector, George McCulloch, had agreed to lend this, but the frame had suffered some damage whilst it had been at the Paris Salon. Forbes reiterated, more than once, that it was essential that the painting be sent to London for its frame to be restored at Forbes' expense before it was returned to McCulloch, who was most irate at paintings being returned to him damaged. McCulloch was such an important patron of art at this time, that it was not sensible to upset him.

Forbes, who wrote from Trewarveneth, was not able to make the opening of the exhibition and, when asked rather late in the day to write something on the Cornish artists for the catalogue, recommended Norman Garstin. However, the time-scale was too tight for anything to be included.

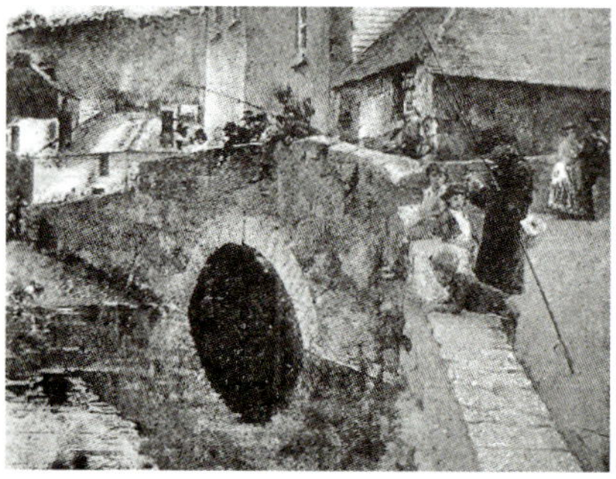

Stanhope Forbes
The Bridge
from *Pall Mall Gazette's Pictures of the Year*

1894 EXHIBITS

- ***The Bridge*** (John Maddocks) [7]
- ***Grey Rocks and Grey Mullet*** (RA 1892) (Sharpley Bainbridge) [8]
- ***The Village Philharmonic*** (Birmingham) (RA 1888, Gold Medal Paris Salon 1891) [207]
- ***Forging the Anchor*** (RA 1892) (George McCulloch) [208]

For *Forging the Anchor*, Forbes had to eschew his principles of painting on the spot, as he found the grime and smoke of the foundry impossible to work in. Accordingly, he re-created the scene in his studio. The painting is now owned by Colchester Art Gallery but was not borrowed for the 2015 exhibition as it is too large to fit into Penlee House Gallery, Penzance. The whereabouts of the two small oils are not known, albeit images have been located. John Maddocks lived in Bradford.

***The Sketch*, 1 August 1894** [a note about the forthcoming exhibition]: 'Mr Stanhope Forbes is, as it were by right, the chief of this little band. His, at any rate, has been the foremost personality of the Cornish School. From the very first, he showed evidence of an acute observation, of a breadth of style and a sense of atmosphere which were at the time very rare indeed among any English painters. He began by painting small canvases, and we must confess that it is at this period of his career that we like him best. In these smaller efforts, he showed himself the possessor, in addition to these other qualities, of a tenderness and a sense of soft colour – particularly in silver greys –which were very attractive and engrossing.

'Success flew to crown his ambition and from that time forth, Mr Stanhope Forbes ARA seems to have dealt exclusively with canvases of a portly acreage. His subjects are now cast upon a grandiose and important scale: so far that the old tenderness and minute care, which once belonged to his pictures, appear to have been so diluted and beaten out that the most that we have to admire now

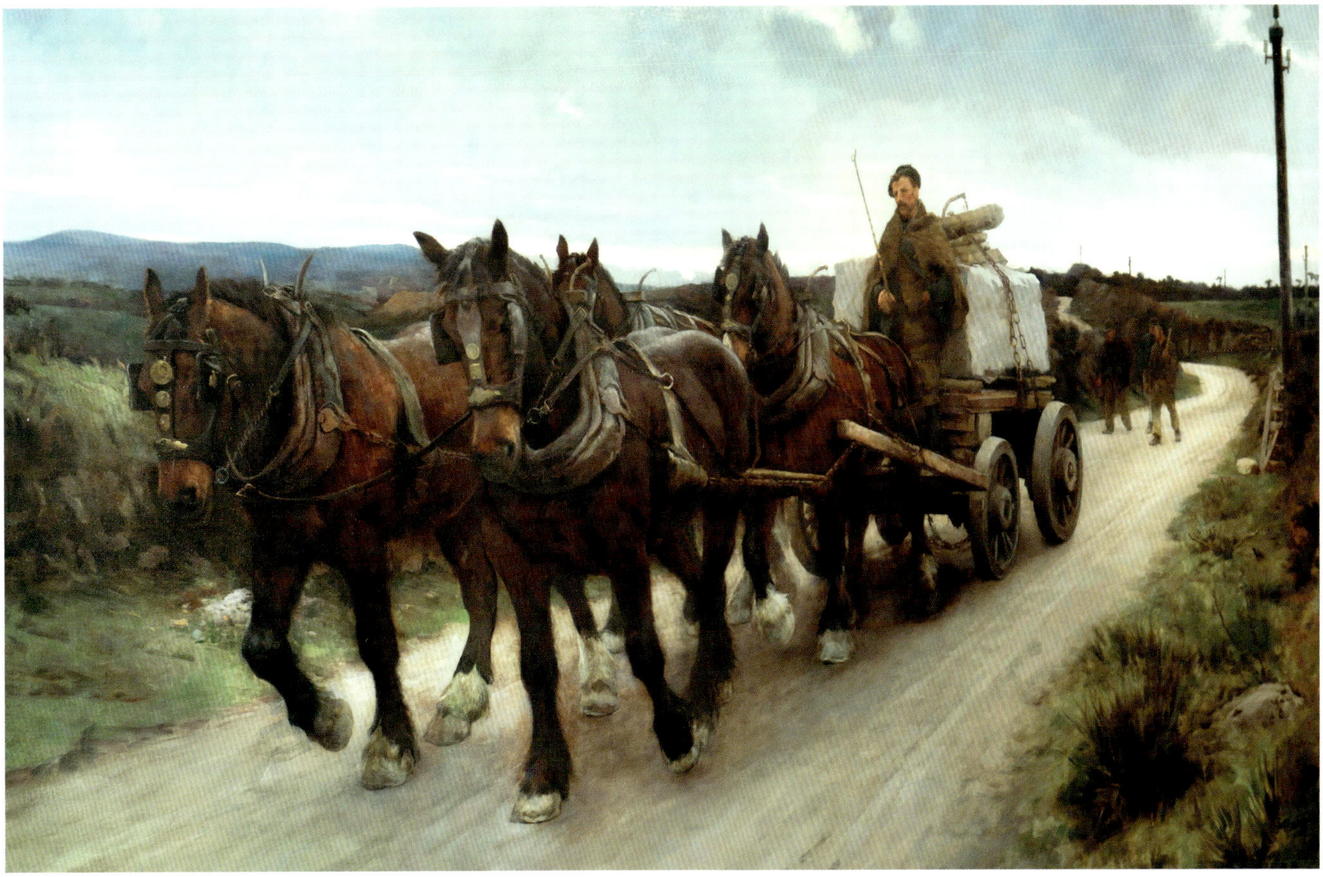

pl. 12 **Stanhope Forbes**
The Quarry Team
1894 • oil on canvas • 152 x 244 cm
private collection, image courtesy Newlyn School Gallery; © Artist's Estate/Bridgeman Art Library

is the cunning craftsmanship, the extraordinary patience, the solemnity and responsibility of achievement, the breadth and solid squareness of style, which, after all, remain to this very clever artist.'

Nottingham Guardian, 6 October 1894: 'Mr Stanhope A Forbes, who with Mr Frank Bramley shares the leadership of the Newlyn section of the exhibition, is well represented by four works, two large ones and two smaller. The one which will probably attract the most attention is *Forging the Anchor*, lent by Mr McCulloch, which the French Government recently and vainly attempted to purchase for the Luxembourg Gallery. In this remarkably fine and vigorous piece of painting, we can study the Newlyn method of work, and the motives that suggested the work in one of the very best examples that the school has yet produced. What has attracted the painter to this subject is the glow of the molten metal and the blaze of light from the furnaces, as it affects the figures of the brawny blacksmiths at work in what would otherwise be almost total darkness, for the light of day only filters through a small window, a distant door and a few holes in the roof... One can almost hear the ring of the blows and feel the heat radiating from the glowing mass. The canvas displays technical ability of high order and is filled with a true realism, while the general tone and the glow of grimy muscles in the firelight, is worthy of all praise.'

After describing the scene in *The Village Philharmonic* and indicating that the contest between the two small oil lamps and the light of the dying day from the window was well handled, the reviewer concluded 'The grave and serious manner in which these fishermen and lads are attacking the business in hand and the way in which the elders handle their instruments is most admirably rendered, whilst the absolute painting itself is as strong and effective as anything Mr Forbes has yet done.'

Grey Rocks and Grey Mullet was a Breton subject, whilst *The Bridge* was an early painting and depicted 'the old grey stone bridge over the small brook which divides Newlyn from Penzance, seen on a typical Cornish "grey day".' Numerous figures, mainly children, were included in the scene, some fishing. 'Nothing exciting or dramatic in the subject, all quiet in tone, but pleasing perfectly, owing to the truth contained in this rendering of cool daylight upon every-day village life.'

The Bridge was one of two paintings that the young Nottingham art student, Laura Johnson (later Knight), was impressed by, commenting, 'I did not know anyone could paint like that.'[10]

2015 EXHIBIT

The Quarry Team (pl. 12, private collection): This large painting, depicting a team of four heavy horses pulling a wagon loaded with a large block of granite on a country road near Sheffield, Paul, Penzance, was exhibited at the Royal Academy in 1894, the year of the Nottingham show. The *Leeds Mercury*, when reviewing the Academy exhibition, commented, 'Mr Stanhope Forbes' *Quarry Team* will scarcely fail to attract the most casual loiterer. It is a vigorous bit of work, much on the scale of his *Forging the Anchor*, which brought the artist into more distinct prominence than his earlier and more refined work. There is a distinct touch of French realism in this work, and, at the same time, in the widespread landscape and the soft tones of evening, there is a suggestion of the more poetic French School.'[11]

FORTESCUE, William Banks RBSA

BIRMINGHAM 1850–1924 ST IVES

Fortescue was one of the 'Birmingham Boys', who played a major role in the early years of the Newlyn colony. He specialized in archetypal Newlyn School genre scenes, before moving to St Ives in 1896 for the rest of his career. A fine cellist.

10. Laura Knight, *Oil Paint and Grease Paint*, London and New York, 1936, p. 65.
11. *Leeds Mercury*, 21 May 1894.

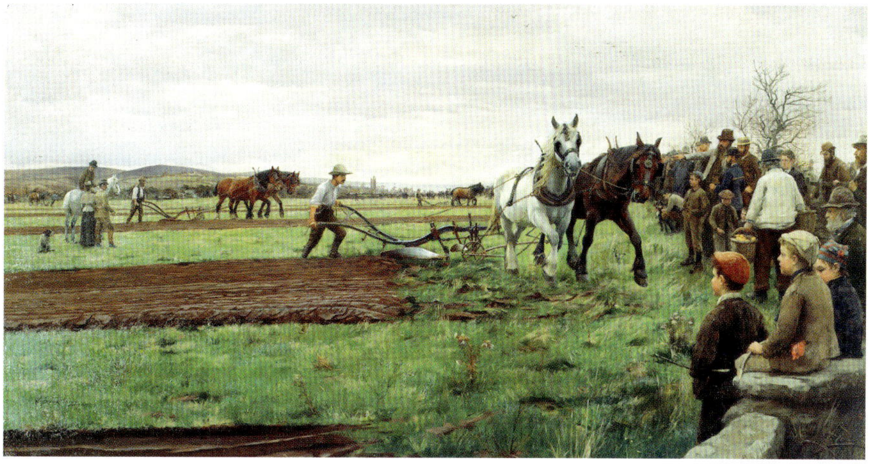

William Banks Fortescue
A Ploughing Match, Cornwall
1891 • oil on canvas • 102 x 183 cm
private collection, image courtesy Christies

Eldest child of a Birmingham wine merchant; started as engineering designer in Birmingham before deciding to become an artist.
1880: First exhibited at the RBA.
Early 1880s: Studied at Académie Julian under J.P. Laurens, and c.1884 in Venice.
1885: First visited Newlyn in December, when stayed with Forbes at 'Bellevue'.
1885–96: Integral figure in Newlyn colony, living first in Newlyn and then in Paul.
1890: Participated in the Cornish Artists show at Dowdeswells.
1896: Moved to St Ives and lived in Trelyon Cottage, just outside the town, designed by fellow artist, Edmund Fuller (q.v.). This was his home for the rest of his life.
1898: Elected member of RBSA.
1924: Memorial Exhibition at Plymouth Museum and Art Gallery.

WALLIS CORRESPONDENCE

Fortescue, writing from Paul, initially suggested another of his RA exhibits, *Harvest Festival in a Cornish Fishing Village* (RA 1890), then in his possession, rather than *A Ploughing Match*.

1894 EXHIBITS

- ***The Fish Fag*** (Southport) [153]
- ***A Ploughing Match, Cornwall*** (RA 1891) [154]
- ***Lent Lilies*** (T.B. Bolitho) [155]
- ***February*** (RA 1893) [178]

T.B. Bolitho was the local Penzance M.P., who lived at Trewidden. Fortescue's contributions to the exhibition were not reviewed.

2015 EXHIBITS

The Fish Fag (pl. 14, The Atkinson, Southport): When Fortescue first lodged with Stanhope Forbes at Bellevue, Newlyn, with Mrs Maddern, he clearly was most impressed with Forbes' *A Fish Sale on a Cornish Beach*, as this painting, which he exhibited at the RBA in 1886, owes much to Forbes' work. Fortescue is stated to be living in Southport at this time and the picture was acquired by a Mr E.J. Rimmer and donated to the Atkinson Art Gallery in Southport in 1888. It is interesting

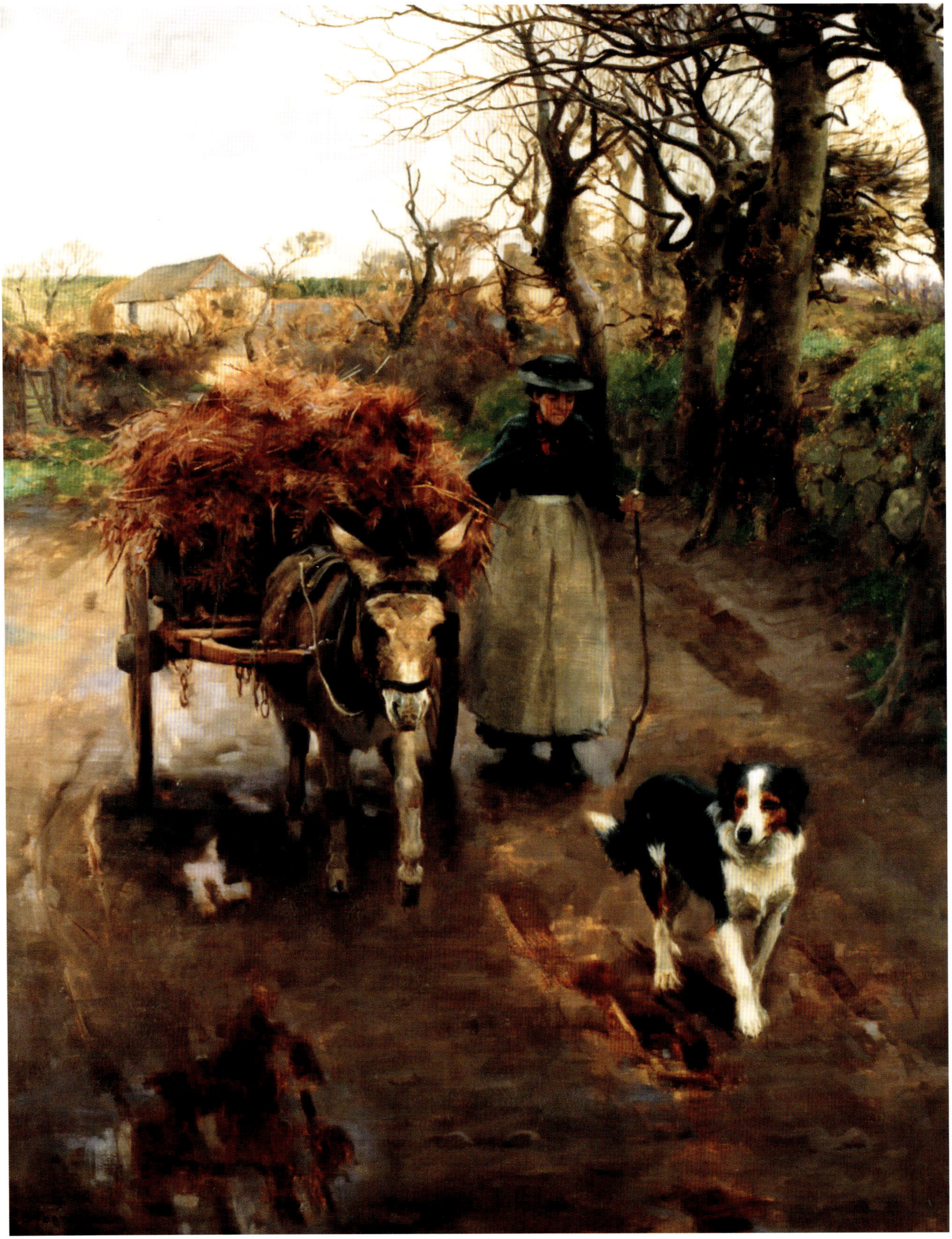

pl. 13 **William Banks Fortescue**
February
1893 • oil on canvas • 91.5 x 71 cm
Bowerman Charitable Trust

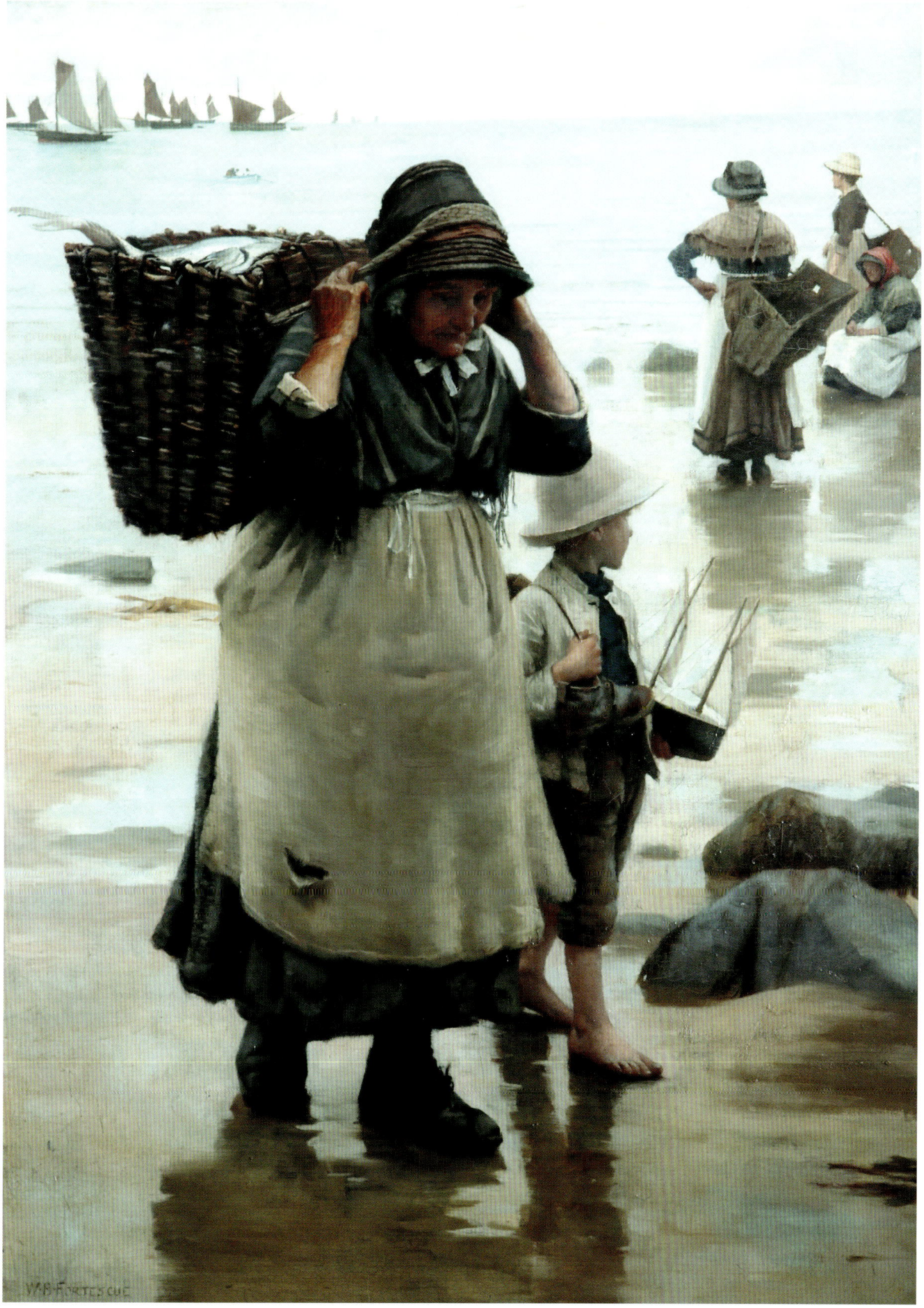

pl. 14 **William Banks Fortescue**
The Fish Fag
oil on canvas • 110 x 85 cm
The Atkinson, Southport

that, for the 1902 Whitechapel Exhibition by the Cornish Artists, Fortescue still selected this as his major work.

February (pl. 13, Bowerman Charitable Trust): This painting, which was exhibited at the Royal Academy in 1893, depicts a woman bringing home a cart-load of bracken from the moors.[12] Whilst a pernicious weed, it had many beneficial uses, such as for fertiliser, weed control, animal bedding, insect repellent, seed treatment and biofuel. The woman, however, looks a little glum, as it has been a wet, cold and windy day on the moors. Her dog, though, is still jaunty.

FOX, John Ernest Ravescroft NEAC

DORCHESTER, DORSET 1862–1940 WHERWELL, ANDOVER

Despite exhibiting quite extensively, with a number of his works being in public collections, little is known about the landscape painter, Ernest Fox. However, although he spent most of his career living with his parents in Kent, he was based for a while in Marazion, Cornwall, in the early 1890s.

Father clergyman.
1881: Living at home in Hastings and noted as a landscape artist.
1883: First exhibited, with Teddington, Middlesex address.
1886: Exhibiting address given as Strood, Kent, until 1891, when becomes Wingham, Dover, his parents' home for at least the next twenty years.
1888: Made member of NEAC.
1890: Exhibited with Cornish Artists at Dowdeswells.
1891: In Census, boarding at 25 Fore Street, Marazion with Eliza Symons.
1894–1917: Left Cornwall in September 1894, to return to Wingham, Dover.
1917: Last exhibiting address in Hythe.

WALLIS CORRESPONDENCE

Fox, writing on 15 April 1894 from Glanville Cottage, Marazion, indicated that he had heard about the exhibition from his friends in St Ives and that Arnesby Brown had suggested that he wrote. He indicated that he had not been sending works to exhibitions for a few years, but had previously had work hung at Nottingham and been a member of NEAC. In a subsequent letter dated 12 September 1894, he asked Wallis to direct future correspondence to Wingham, Dover, as he did not expect to return to Cornwall just at present. However, he agreed with Wallis that it was better to put Marazion as his address in the catalogue.

1894 EXHIBITS

- ***St Michael's Mount – Autumn Evening*** [66]
- ***Off the Gurnard's Head*** [101]
- ***A Cornish Lane*** [102]
- ***Old Cliff Cottages, Marazion*** [109]
- ***An April Day*** [152]

Fox worked in both watercolour and oil and the medium of the works, other than the oil of St Michael's Mount, is not given.

***Nottingham Evening Post*, 6 October 1894**: 'Mr Ernest Fox sends, among others, a picturesque view of St Michael's Mount, seen on an autumn evening.' (This may be the work that he exhibited at the RA in 1895.)

12. When the painting was exhibited on Newlyn Show Day in 1893, the reviewer called the load '"quail" ferns'. *The Cornishman*, 30 March 1893.

FULLER, Edmund George RBA, RWA

BROMPTON, LONDON 1858–1940 PORTISHEAD, SOMERSET

On his death in 1940, Fuller was described as 'painter, architect, comic artist and metal worker' and he distinguished himself in all these disciplines, but it was as a marine artist that he achieved the highest renown. In addition to depicting tales of drama on the high seas, so beloved by the Victorians, he also produced seascapes and evocative depictions of St Ives harbour in various atmospheric conditions.

Father became a General; educated at Sandhurst.
1881: First started exhibiting.
1882: Married Emma Wing, a Suffolk girl, and lived initially in London.
1892: Took part in the St Ives Carnival Masquerade in March. Settled in 1 Barnoon Terrace. Took a large studio in a net loft on the harbour beach, which he retained for 30 years.
1893: First exhibit at RA. Began to gain reputation as a marine painter.
1895: Made a member of RBA.
1897: Held exhibition of 120 works in Porthmeor Studios, St Ives. Started to produce comic pieces which found favour as early postcards.
1897–1924: Still produced marine paintings, but was also a comic artist, metal-worker, graphic artist and architect. Left St Ives in 1924 for Portishead.

WALLIS CORRESPONDENCE

Writing from Barnoon, St Ives on 5 April 1894, Fuller thanked Wallis for his invitation to exhibit and said, 'I shall be very pleased to contribute the best work I have.'

1894 EXHIBITS

- ***Fish Sale, St Ives – Morning*** [15]
- ***Herrings Gigs at Moorings*** [16]
- ***Drifting Cloud Shadows*** [62]

None of these works, or images of them, have been located.

***Nottingham Guardian*, 13 October 1894**: 'Mr Edmund G. Fuller's *Herring Gigs at Moorings* deserves more than a passing word of praise. The long white boats lying at anchor on a pale blue sea, with the pier, lighthouse and the St Ives fishing fleet beyond, form a delicate scheme of colour, which is truly pleasant to look upon. We like this better than his *Fish Sale, St Ives – Morning*, a study in blues and greys. He also sends another blue sea, No. 62, *Drifting Cloud Shadows*, with a ship under full sail, which is sufficiently described in the title, and is undoubtedly good in colour.'

GARSTIN, Norman NEAC

CAHERCONLISH, CO. LIMERICK 1847–1926 PENZANCE

The Irishman, Norman Garstin, was a charming and witty member of the Newlyn figure painting brotherhood, but struggled to sell his work. However, he was highly regarded as an art critic and art teacher.

Father was a Colonel, who committed suicide in 1861. His mother was paralysed shortly after his birth and could not speak. Brought up in Ireland but educated in Jersey. Tried engineering and architecture, before being lured to the gold and

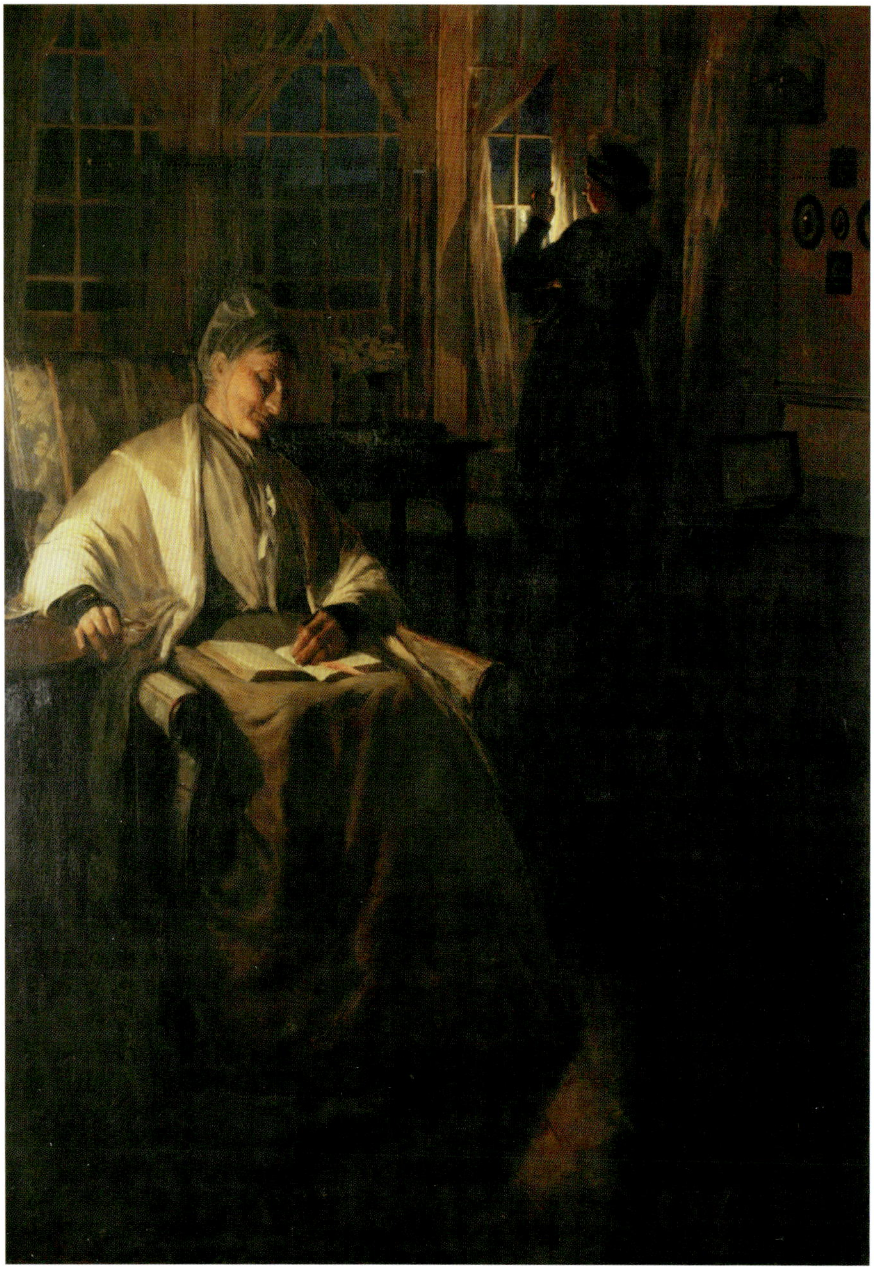

Norman Garstin
Her Signal
c.1892 • oil on canvas • 155.5 x 110.5 cm
Royal Institution of Cornwall/Royal Cornwall Museum

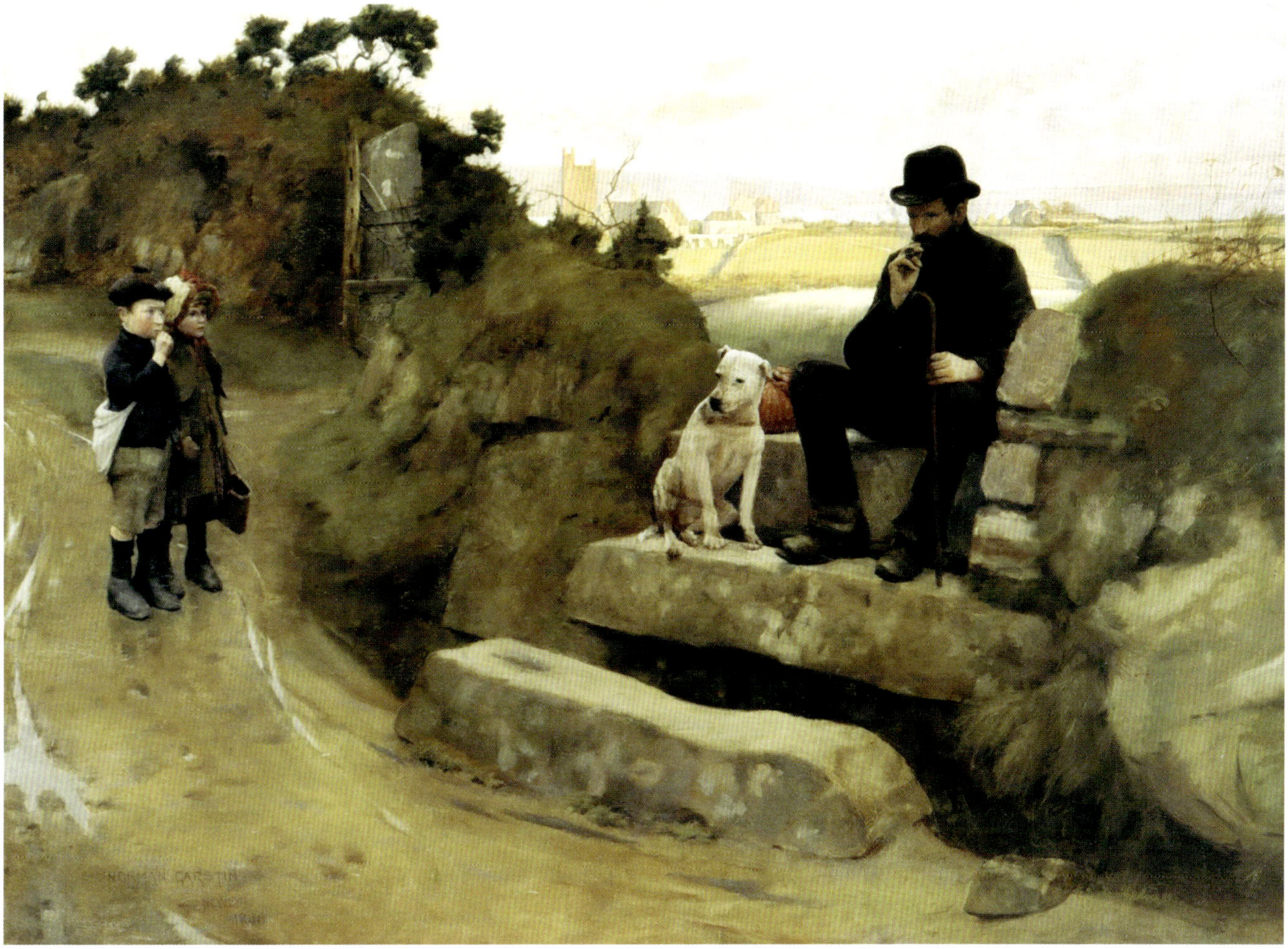

Norman Garstin
The Stranger
1890 • oil on canvas • 135 x 211 cm
Dublin City Gallery The Hugh Lane

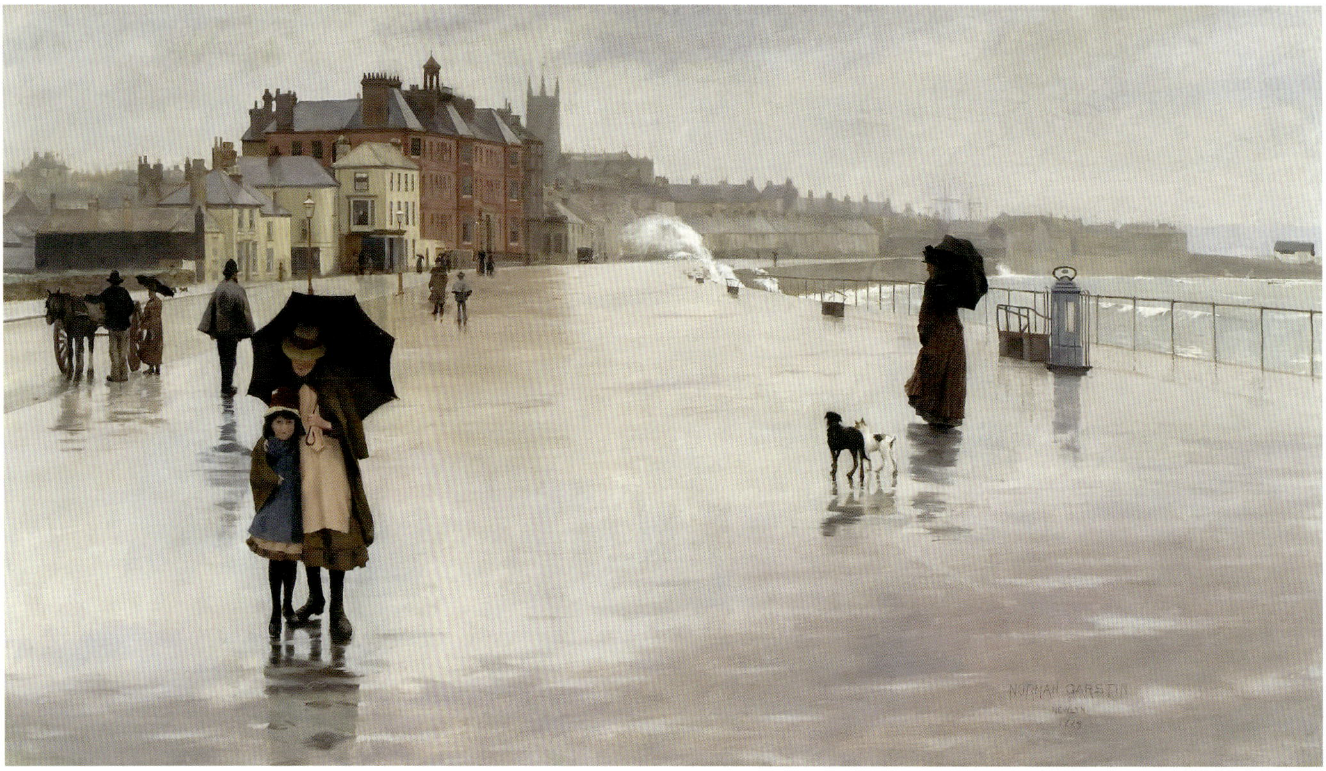

pl. 15 **Norman Garstin**
The Rain it Raineth Every Day, Penzance
1889 • oil on canvas • 95 x 164 cm
Penlee House Gallery & Museum

diamond fields of South Africa (1872–7). Finally, decided to study art, ironically having been blinded in one eye in a hunting accident.
1878-83: Studied in Antwerp under Verlat (1878–9) and in Paris under Carolus Duran (1880–3).
1882: Visited Quimperlé.
1884–5: Visited Italy, Tangier and Spain.
1886: Married and settled in Newlyn.
1890: Participated in the Cornish Artists show at Dowdeswells.
1889–1926: Had little success with his paintings, but was well respected as an art critic and art teacher, often taking groups of students on study trips abroad.

1894 EXHIBITS

- ***A Cotillon*** [17]
- ***Progress and Poverty*** (RA 1888) (C Briggs) [24]
- ***The Rain it Raineth Every Day, Penzance*** [218]
- ***The Stranger*** (RA 1890) [219]
- ***Her Signal*** (RA 1892) (T.B. Bolitho) [220]
- ***Portrait of a Boy*** (RA 1893) [221]
- ***'To cheat surprise and prying eyes'*** [222]

The Rain it Raineth Every Day, Penzance is now owned by Penlee House Gallery & Museum, Penzance, *The Stranger* (135 x 211 cm) by Dublin City Gallery The Hugh Lane and *Her Signal* (155.5 x 110.5 cm) by the Royal Cornwall Museum, Truro. The latter, which has become rather dark with age, was felt by the *Nottingham Evening Post* (6 October 1894) to be 'a good interior with clever effect of double lighting'. The other exhibits have not been located, but contemporary illustrations give an indication of the subject matter of another three works. *Progress and Poverty* (112 x 89 cm), which was illustrated in *Academy Notes* in 1888, depicted a middle class lady playing a harp in a public house, and so the relevance of the title is a little obscure. Its owner, C. Briggs, lived in Bradford. *A Cotillon* (124 x 96 cm), which was illustrated in *Academy Notes* in 1892, was described in the *Nottingham Guardian*. It depicted 'a children's party, the room gay with lamps and Chinese lanterns, reflected in the polished floor. A small boy in a chef's costume stands hesitating to approach the group of girls farther up the room, whilst a lady standing playing at a piano smiles down upon him'. Accordingly, it probably depicted a typical Newlyn children's party, and the boy may well be Garstin's son, Crosbie, who became a well-known author

Portrait of a Boy (152 x 94 cm), which was illustrated in *Royal Academy Pictures* 1893, most certainly features Crosbie, but dressed up as an eighteenth-century swell, standing by a balustrade of a sea-side garden. This again may have been related to a typical artists' fancy dress party, but quite why Garstin felt that a portrait of such a subject, of such large dimensions, would appeal to anyone outside the family is unclear.

2015 EXHIBIT

The Rain it Raineth Every Day, Penzance (pl. 15, Penlee House Gallery & Museum): Given that this is one of the most popular paintings owned by Penlee House Gallery & Museum, it seems astonishing, firstly, that it was accepted but not hung at the Royal Academy in 1889, and, secondly, that Garstin never managed to sell it, when the initial asking price was only £75. Whilst the painting is often compared with Gustave Caillebotte's *Paris Street: Rainy Day* of 1877 (The Art Institute, Chicago), its sophisticated asymmetrical composition owes more to Garstin's interest in Japanese art. The St Ives modernist artist, Patrick Heron, who later became close friends with Garstin's daughter, Alethea, felt that in Garstin's work 'the *space between* the objects represented is already itself *a shape* of equal pictorial value to that of each object itself' and felt that 'this distinction alone places Garstin above the academic or the second-rate'.[13]

13. Patrick Heron and Michael Canney, *Norman and Alethea Garstin: Two Impressionists – Father and Daughter*, Penwith Society of Arts, 1978, introduction, p. 12.

GOTCH, Caroline Burland (née Yates)

LIVERPOOL 1854–1945 NEWLYN

Caroline Gotch, along with Elizabeth Forbes, was one of the few women artists in the Newlyn colony, and enjoyed some success initially with typical Newlyn School scenes, but her production of paintings dwindled in the mid-1890s.

Father wealthy landowner. Youngest of three daughters. Grew up at Lammermoor, near Sway, on the edge of the New Forest. Educated privately and in Switzerland and Germany.
1878–9: Studied at Heatherley's School of Art and the Slade School, where met Thomas Gotch.
1879: Visited Newlyn with her sister, Esther, and linked up there with Gotch.
1880: Studied at Académie Julian, Paris.
1881: Married Thomas on 31 August at St Peter's Church, Newlyn.
1882: Continued studies in France. Daughter, Phyllis, born in France in September.
1883: Spent July to October in Newlyn before going to Australia, returning in July 1884.
1886: In Newlyn between July and October.
1887: Settled in Newlyn.
1890: Founder member of St Ives Arts Club, as working in that colony that summer. Participated in the Cornish Artists show at Dowdeswells.

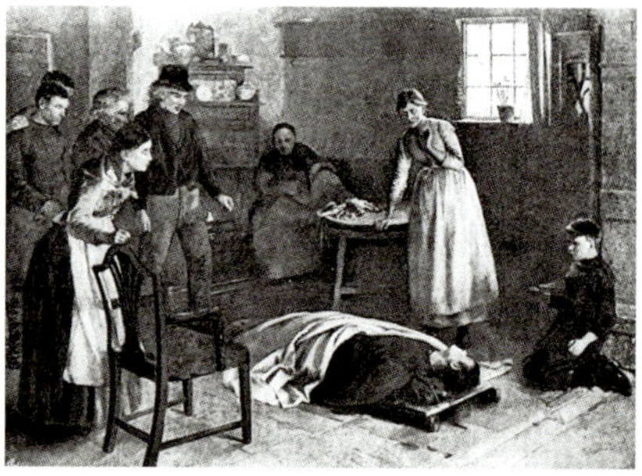

Caroline Gotch
In the Midst of Life we are in Death
from the 1894 exhibition catalogue

WALLIS CORRESPONDENCE

Thomas responded to Wallis on behalf of Caroline. He had clearly asked initially for *Motherhood*, *The Bard* and a work called *A Cosy Couple*, but Gotch indicated that the latter was unavailable as it had been 'sold in India'.

1894 EXHIBITS

- ***'In the Midst of Life we are in Death'*** (RA 1891) [50]
- ***The Bard*** (RA 1893) [51]
- ***Motherhood*** [217]

At the end of the exhibition, the three paintings were sent on to the public galleries in Sheffield, Derby and Southport respectively.

2015 EXHIBIT

Newlyn Old Pier and Gwavas Lake (pl. 16, private collection): This dates from 1879 and so was executed during Caroline's first visit to Newlyn, before the colony was formed and before her marriage.

GOTCH, Thomas Cooper RBA, NEAC, PRBC, RI, RP, VPRWA

KETTERING 1854–1931 LONDON

The Newlyn figure painter, Thomas Gotch, at the time of the Nottingham exhibition, had just made a fundamental change in his approach to painting, abandoning realism for imaginative symbolism. Thereafter, in the words of Norman Garstin, he 'remained true to his own conception of art as a revelation of beauty and a glimpse of nature touched and illuminated by imagination'.[14] He went on to produce a highly regarded and totally distinctive body of work.

14. Foreword to Catalogue for Cornish Artists' exhibition at Whitechapel, Spring 1902.

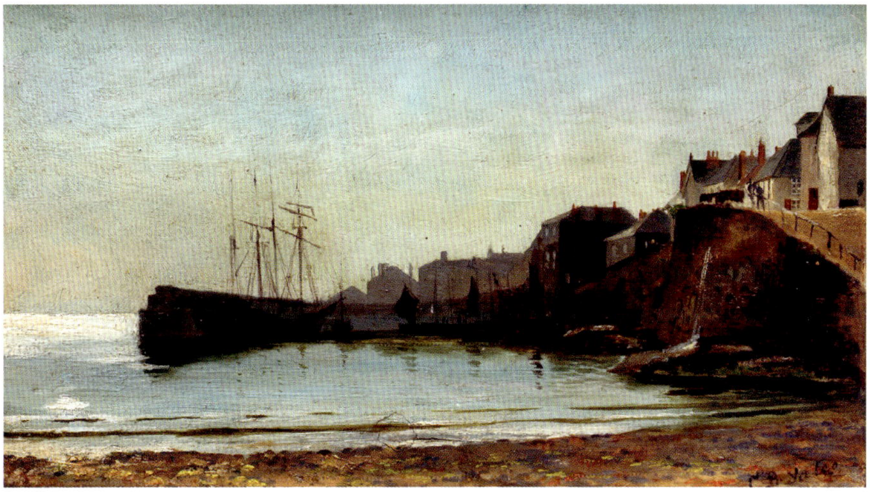

pl. 16 **Caroline Gotch**
Newlyn Old Pier and Gwavas Lake
c.1879 • oil on panel • 11 x 20.5 cm
The Gwavas Collection (private)

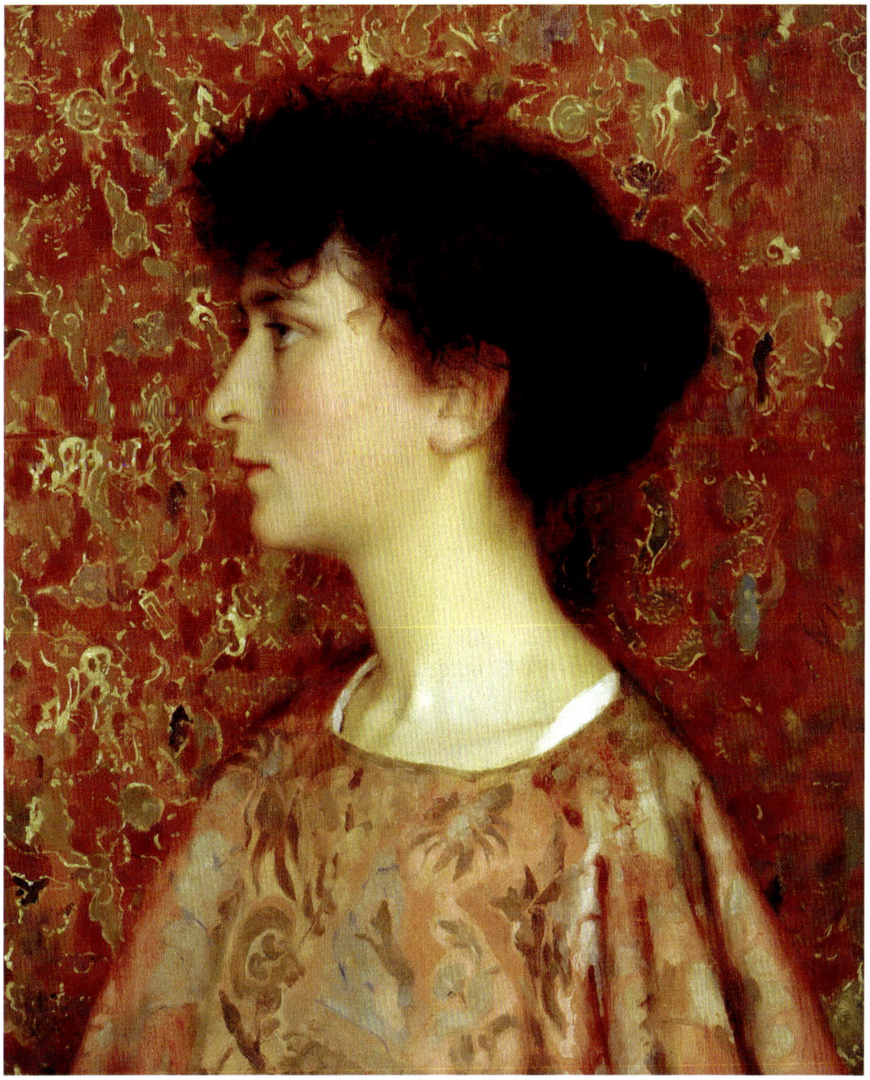

Thomas Cooper Gotch
Study of a Head
aka ***Study of a Young Woman***
oil on panel • 53 x 42.5 cm
Ferens Art Gallery: Hull Museums

Father was banker and boot and shoe manufacturer, but declared bankrupt in 1857. Studied at Heatherley's, London, at Antwerp under Verlat, at the Slade School and in Paris under Laurens (1876–80). Also took lessons in portraiture from Samuel Lawrence.
1879: Stayed the summer with Henry Tuke in Falmouth and visited Newlyn for first time.
1880: First exhibited at the Royal Academy.
1881: 31 August, married Caroline Burland Yates in Newlyn, later returned to Paris.
1882: Moved from Paris to Brolles.
1883: Spent July to October in Newlyn before going to Australia, returning in July 1884.
1885: Elected a member of SBA, but later fell out with Whistler.
1886: Involved in formation of New English Arts Club and Anglo-Australian Society of Artists; In Newlyn between July and October.
1887: Settled in Newlyn and, to begin with, produced realist paintings of the fisherfolk in a style influenced by his Newlyn School colleagues.
1887–90: Sold paintings to Dunedin, Christchurch, Sydney and Adelaide Art Galleries.
1888: Had joint exhibition of Cornish paintings at Fine Art Society with Alfred East and Ayerst Ingram.
1890: Founder member of St Ives Arts Club, as working in that colony that summer. Participated in the Cornish Artists show at Dowdeswells.
1893: Won medal at Chicago for *My Crown and Sceptre*.
1894: *The Child Enthroned* (RA 1894, Paris Salon – medal 1895) marked a new departure.
1896: *Alleluia* bought by the Chantrey Trustees; also medals in Paris and Berlin.
1900: *Heir to all the Ages* won medal at Paris World Exposition.
1900–8: Left Newlyn for a while and lived at Shottermill, Surrey; further successes at RA; sales to public galleries, including the National Gallery of South Africa, Cape Town.
1908: Settled back in Newlyn; produced paintings of pageants and night scenes.
1910: Retrospective at Laing Art Gallery, Newcastle, which acquired *Holy Motherhood*.
1912: Elected member of RI.
1913: Elected President of Royal British Colonial Society of Artists;
1916–31: Style less popular in post-War period, but series of retrospective exhibitions in Kettering, Bristol and Northampton; elected Vice-President of RWA.

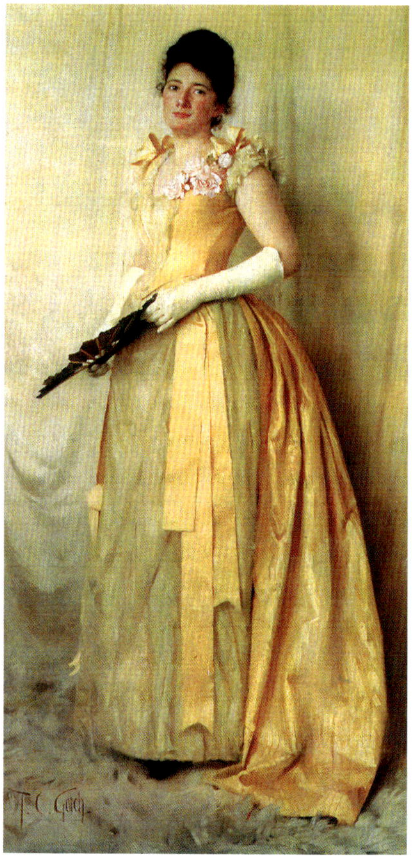

Thomas Cooper Gotch
Portrait of Mrs John Crooke
aka ***Lady in Gold***
1891 • oil on canvas • 193 x 99 cm
courtesy the Artist's Estate

WALLIS CORRESPONDENCE

In his initial letter to Wallis from The Malt-House, Newlyn, dated 27 May 1894, Gotch signified that he had had a number of applications from galleries for his paintings and, as he had 'never had the good fortune to sell a picture at Nottingham', he was clearly not inclined to lend his best unsold work. In particular, he wanted to think about *My Crown and Sceptre*, albeit, in the end, most probably having heard of some of his colleagues' choices, he lent it. *A Golden Dream* (now Harris Gallery, Preston) was another that he vacillated about sending, but, in this case, he decided not to. From those works that he had already sold, he mentioned as a possibility *Twixt Life and Death*, which had been acquired by leading collector, George McCulloch, but this loan was not forthcoming. Some months later, he offered one or two watercolours, but ended up sending four. The *Portrait of Mrs Crooke* came from an exhibition in Plymouth.

On 17 September 1894, Gotch responded to Wallis, having been one of a number of recipients of a telegram extending an invitation to the Opening Luncheon. Unfortunately, many of the artists, to whom these were addressed, were not in Cornwall at that juncture, and others were already otherwise engaged or felt that the cost of the long journey could not be justified. He commented, 'Had the distance been less or had we had a better year, there would have been a ready response to the invitation.' However, he agreed to make the journey himself to represent Newlyn, as he doubted that Stanhope Forbes could be persuaded to

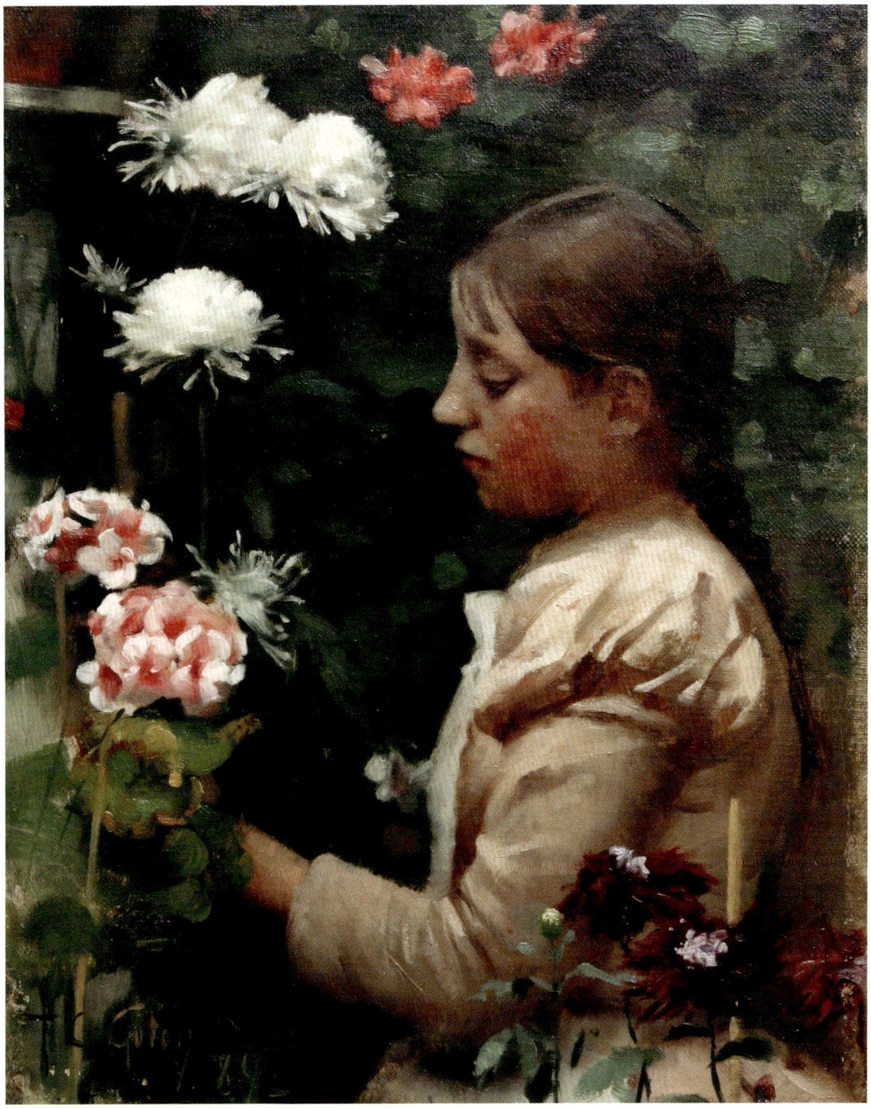

pl. 17 **Thomas Cooper Gotch**
Girl in a Cornish Garden
1889 • oil on canvas • 30 x 22.5 cm
private collection, on loan to
Penlee House Gallery & Museum

make the trip. He also indicated that he had gone over to St Ives and found the colony there 'dispersed'. However, James Lanham, whose shop catered for all the artists' needs in St Ives, had suggested that it might be worth contacting those artists, who were sketching in more northerly parts of England – namely, William Titcomb, who was at Wickersley in Yorkshire, Louis Grier who was at Wells-next-the-Sea in Norfolk, Julius Olsson, who was at Walberswick, Alfred East, who was at Stow-on-the-Wold, and Adrian Stokes, who was in Ross in Scotland. This was very helpful, as Titcomb, Grier and East did make it to the opening.

After the opening, Gotch wrote on 4 October 1894 to ask for copies of the reviews. He added, 'I need hardly say that we were all most gratified at the opening of the Exhibition; everything seemed to me to be admirably arranged, and carried out. I hope that it will prove a success as well from your point of view as from ours.'

Gotch indicated in a further letter dated 15 October 1894 that Wallis had written to both Stanhope Forbes and himself on 4 October – i.e. after the exhibition had actually opened – asking them if either was prepared to write a note on the history of the Cornish settlement for the catalogue. In turning down the invitation, having discussed the matter with Forbes, Gotch made a number of interesting points. 'For a variety of reasons, I think that we have had rather too much in the press in the way of hasty and erroneous conclusions. For instance, the dispersal of the so-called school over the continent after the Dowdeswell show, is very much exaggerated and, as far as I know, was not due to the failure of that show.'

This is a reference to a piece written by R Jope-Slade on the 1894 Royal Academy exhibition, which was included in *Black and White's Handbook to the Royal Academy and New Gallery 1894* and which was very cutting about the Dowdeswells show. Gotch added, 'I do not think that it would be wise for me to appear in print further on the subject of the Cornish painters, and I would rather see someone else's views.' He went on to recommend Norman Garstin as regards Newlyn, and Harry Robinson as regards St Ives. In the end, the timescale did not permit anything to be included.

1894 EXHIBITS

- ***My Crown and Sceptre*** (RA 1892) [12]
- ***Portrait of Mrs John Crooke*** (RA 1891) [42]
- ***A Blossom*** [75; watercolour]
- ***Study of a Child*** [76; watercolour]
- ***Portrait of a Lady*** [77; watercolour]
- ***Blue Hills Mine*** [78; watercolour]
- ***Study of a Head*** [120]
- ***Sharing Fish*** (RA 1891) [206]

Nottingham Guardian, 6 October 1894: '[*My Crown and Sceptre* is] probably the best thing this well-known artist has yet done ... The child's yellow hair is crowned with a bunch of scarlet ash berries, and in her left hand, she holds a green reed as a sceptre. The dress is yellow seen against an orange background, fleur-de-lise with gold. Her amber necklace, her pale pink sash, and the bunch of red berries that she holds in her lap, all harmonise with the frock and embroidery in this charming scheme of colour Mr Gotch has produced for our pleasure. As a piece of portraiture too the work has many good qualities and the picture would form a worthy addition to any Corporation Gallery.'

Regarded as Gotch's finest exhibit, and a medal winner at Chicago the previous year, the reviewer might have been hinting that Nottingham should acquire *My Crown and Sceptre*. And it was short-listed for purchase, but, ultimately, Nottingham Castle opted for other works and Gotch later had the accolade of it being bought by the Art Gallery of New South Wales, Sydney.

The *Portrait of Mrs John Crooke*, in a yellow dress and with a large fan, was well-regarded. This had been painted in Newlyn in early 1891 and Mrs Crooke, the wife of fellow Newlyn artist, John Crooke, had also featured in Stanhope Forbes' *The Health of the Bride*. When the painting had been first exhibited on Show Day in Newlyn in 1891, along with several other portraits, the local reviewer had remarked: 'The largest is a beautifully coloured life-size portrait of one of the artists' wives, Mrs Crooke, whose reputation for beauty is undisputed. The pose of the figure is superb and Mr Gotch has done ample justice to the symmetry of form, exquisite draperies, facial expression, dark curling hair and blue eyes of the fair model. The gold-tinted satin dress and bodice, with corsage spray of pink roses, and the white gloves over the well-moulded arms were boldly delineated against the light background.'[15] Whilst a colour image of the painting exists, the original appears to be lost.

Study of a Head was said to be of 'a dark haired girl, clad in one of the embroidered robes this artist loves so much, profiled against a rich background of red, gold and pale green, which contrasts well with the delicate flesh tints'. This work was purchased in 1979 by the Ferens Art Gallery, Hull and is now known as *Study of a Young Woman*. It has also been known as *A Study in Brocades*, as the frame is decorated to look like brocade as well.

The inclusion of watercolours in his group of works was unusual and these four works were, unsurprisingly, hung together. The *Portrait of a Lady* was said to be of an American woman in a white dress. This will be of Mrs Mabel Whitmore,

15. *The Cornishman*, 2 April 1891.

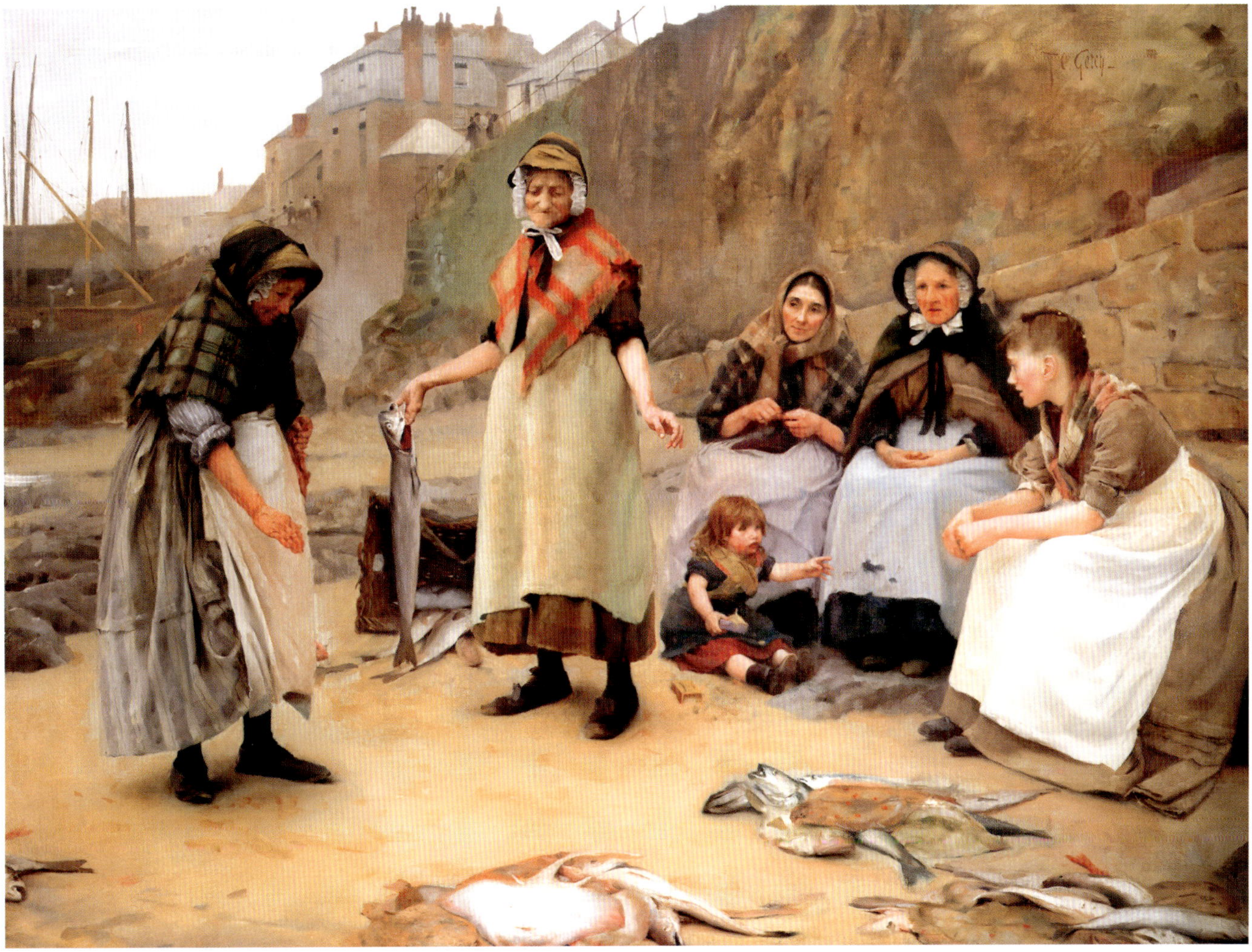

pl. 18 **Thomas Cooper Gotch**
Sharing Fish
oil on canvas • 120 x 160 cm
private collection, image courtesy Messum's

the wife of the American artist, William Russell Whitmore, for the Whitmores were an integral part of the Newlyn community in the years 1890–6 and were great friends with the Gotches. *Blue Hills Mines* had been painted at St Agnes in 1888, whilst *A Blossom*, later sold to Lady Laidlay, and *Study of a Child* were both small portraits of a round-faced baby.[16]

2015 EXHIBITS

Sharing Fish (pl. 18, private collection): When shown at the Royal West of England Academy in 1923, the catalogue entry read: 'This picture illustrates an old custom, now almost vanished, which obtained in Newlyn. A few fishwives would jointly buy a quantity of fish, and would then proceed to divide it into equal lots. When they were all satisfied that the lots were equal they would hail a passerby, and each giving him a token of identity, such as a key, a stone, a piece of seaweed, a scrap of wood, or what not, he would then, at hazard, throw them, one on each share, thus literally "casting the lot".' Gotch recorded in his diary that he began the painting in September 1890 and completed it over the winter of 1890/1. It is set in Newlyn under the slip leading to the old pier, with the Cliff behind, and the catch being shared out includes salmon trout, gurnett, ray, dory and plaice. The younger woman was Mary Rowe, who modelled for the bride in Stanhope Forbes' *The Health of the Bride* (Tate).

When the painting was exhibited on Show Day in Newlyn in 1891, it was well regarded. '[The fishwives'] crumpled and dilapidated bonnets, with white frills under the rims, brought out strongly the tanned and wrinkled faces beneath; and the old-fashioned red and green, red and black striped shawls and other portions of the fisher garb rendered the old women truly artistic subjects'.[17] However, when shown at the Royal Academy, it was 'skied' and, as Gotch had suffered a similar experience the previous year with *'Twixt Life and Death'*, he became quite disconsolate. However, these setbacks spurred him to move away from rustic naturalism and to develop his own individual vision.

Girl in a Cornish Garden (pl. 17, private collection): It is believed that this work, which is dated 1889, may have originally been entitled *Blossom*. It was painted in the garden of Gotch's home 'The Malthouse'.

GRIER, Louis Reginald James Monro

EMERALD HILL, MELBOURNE 1864–1920 ST IVES

At the time of the 1894 exhibition, Louis Grier was considered one of the leading St Ives landscape and marine painters. This early promise, however, did not result in commercial success, albeit he did become a valued art teacher in the colony.

Father Doctor from Ireland, mother Australian. Youngest of six children. Family moved to England when he was two. Educated in England and Canada (1879).
1880–4: Worked as a banker in Canada.
1884: First visited St Ives.
1884–6: Studied at Académie Julian, Paris, albeit Grier liked to claim that he was 'self-taught'.
1886–7: Visited St Ives again in 1886 before settling in the colony in 1887.
1888: Saturday evening socials held in his studio, The Foc'sle, that winter, leading to formation of St Ives Arts Club in 1890.
1890: 'Louis Grier's Company' put on 'Trial by Jury' in Penzance. Participated in Cornish Artists' Exhibition at Dowdeswells in December.
1891: Won gold medal at Paris Salon with *The Night Watch* (rejected by RA in 1890).
1892: Took 70 paintings out to Australia for an exhibition tour.
1895: Set up School of Landscape and Marine Painting in St Ives with Julius Olsson.

16. I am indebted to Gotch's biographer, Pamela Lomax, for details of Gotch's exhibits.
17. *The Cornishman*, 2 April 1891.

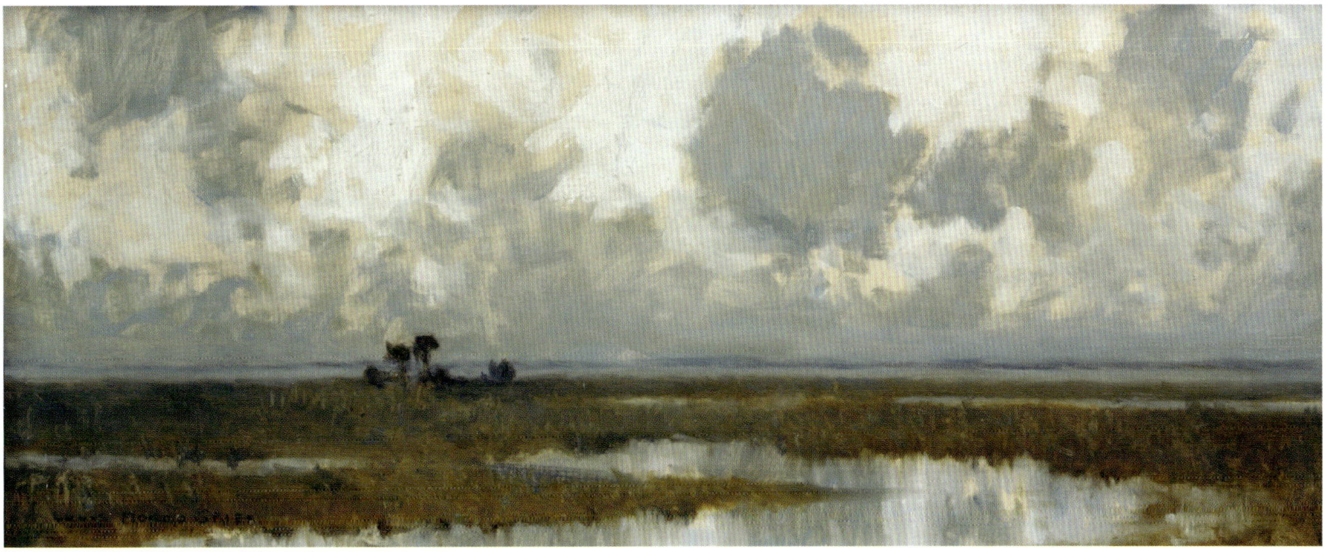

pl. 19 **Louis Grier**
Marshes – Winter
oil on canvas • 42 x 92 cm
St Ives Town Council

1898–1910: Split from Olsson in 1898 and ran rival school – students included Norman Wilkinson, Guy Kortright, William Parkyn and the New Zealander, Margaret Stoddart.
1898: Became Town Councillor.

WALLIS CORRESPONDENCE

Grier responded to Wallis from Wells-by-the-Sea in Norfolk, indicating that he was intending to stay there until 'nearly winter'. He tells Wallis that he is sending his very best work to Nottingham and adds, 'If you should hear of any students coming this way, you might be so very kind as to point out my advertisement in the current number of the *Studio*'.[18] He attended and spoke amusingly at the opening, albeit the content of his speech was not recorded.

1894 EXHIBITS

- ***The Moorland*** [194]
- ***Sea-Grass Meadows*** [195]
- ***A Fair Haven*** [196]
- ***The Night Watch*** (Gold medal at Paris Salon) [197]

***Nottingham Guardian*, 13 October 1894**: 'Mr Louis Grier's four canvasses show an artist who is doing strong work and prove that he is far from one-sided in what he is attempting with considerable success to produce. His *Night Watch* was judged worthy of a gold medal at the Paris Salon. It is a night effect most dexterously treated. The seine boats are riding at anchor at their nets on a calm sea, wrapped in the silence and semi-darkness of a summer night. It is a successful attempt to depict the contrast between moonlight and the glow from a brazier in the rear boat. The watchers have rigged up an awning with sail and oars and their faces are lit up by the burning coals, a glimmering lamp hanging above their heads. Beyond them a line of fishing boats fades away into the deep blue night, the lights in their mastheads and those in the more distant town faintly shining.

'*Sea-Grass Meadows* is a vast expanse of flat sea-marsh, the water channels winding through the coarse rank vegetation coloured by the red sun, while on the far horizon the sea is dimly seen. Another great sweep of country is *The Moorland*, in which rain is falling from the heavy clouds, blue sky and distant sea beyond. Both these pictures have breadth and good colour.

'His *A Fair Haven* is a view of Fowey Harbour, the grey houses hanging to the hillside, the rough pier circling round the anchored boats. It is getting late in the day and the high cliffs above have thrown a shadow over the water. In the centre of the foreground, a fishing boat has just glided in, the men taking down sail and preparing to land in the dinghy. There is some clever work in the picture, although it is not as good as those spoken of above.'

2015 EXHIBITS

Marshes – Winter (pl. 19, St Ives Town Council): Marshland scenes were very popular with the St Ives landscape artists. The flat landscape resulted in big skies, whose atmospheric effects were reflected in the patches of water dotted about the marsh. This painting is a good example of the mood pieces that Grier produced. Commenting on his work in 1898, *The Artist* said, 'His outlook is his own; his work is marked by a peculiarly individual sense of decorative qualities, seizing with remarkable felicity the salient lines of a composition, lines which have a pattern-making interdependence one upon the other ... To him landscape is not the imitation of forms merely, but the medium by which he carries an impression. His work is painter-like in quality, decorative in intention.'[19]

18. Letter dated 26 July 1894.
19. 'Some Landscape Painters in Cornwall', *The Artist*, 1898, pp. 142–3.

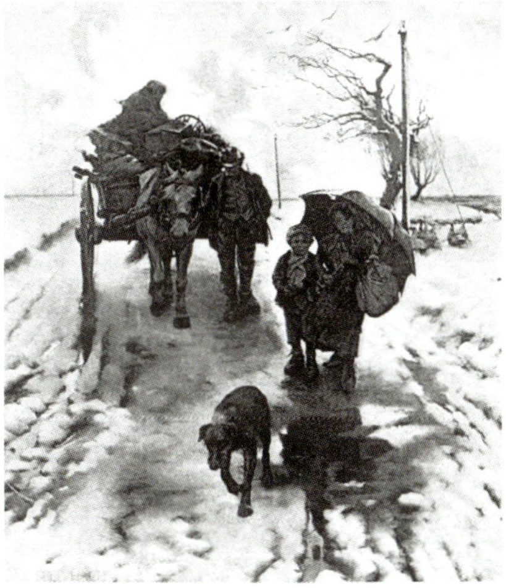

Fred Hall
Adversity
from the 1894 exhibition catalogue

HALL, Frederick NEAC

STILLINGTON, YORK 1860–1948 SPEEN, NEWBURY

Fred Hall, who was based in Newlyn, produced an eclectic mix of paintings, but was most successful as an impressionist landscape painter. However, he also was a highly competent animal and bird painter, and a portrait and figure painter. He often tackled typical Newlyn School subjects, but was inclined to lace some of these with the same sense of humour that saw him also gain recognition as a caricaturist.

Father physician. Family moved to Stoke Newington, London in 1875 and then to Lincoln in 1877.
1879–81: Studied at Lincoln School of Art, at same time as Frank Bramley.
1882: Studied at Verlat's Academy in Antwerp, also with Bramley.
1883: First exhibit at the RA.
1884: Visited Newlyn for first time, settling there soon after.
1885–97: Based in Newlyn, but frequented Porlock.
1890: Did series of caricatures of fellow artists. Participated in the Cornish Artists show at Dowdeswells.
1898: Married. After a year in Liverpool, and spells in Dorking and London, settled at Speen, near Newbury 1911, from where he concentrated on farm subjects.

WALLIS CORRESPONDENCE

Hall sent a list of owners of his paintings to Wallis from Newlyn on 17 June 1894, but commented, 'I trust that when writing to them it is not stated that it is any wish of mine that they should lend the pictures, as I have a great objection to borrowing works from purchasers.' In July, he agreed to the addition of his work *Adversity*. Despite being so well represented, with his contributions being praised in reviews, Hall seems to have taken little interest in the show, for he wrote to Wallis in December from R Wiggleworth's home in Harrogate, asking which works by him had actually been included.

1894 EXHIBITS

- ***Godfrey, son of R. Wigglesworth, of Beckwith Knowle*** (R. Wigglesworth) [1]
- ***April*** (A. Smith) [2]
- ***Ronald, son of R. Wigglesworth*** (R. Wigglesworth) [36]
- ***Mending Nets*** (W.H. Starkey) [111]
- ***Golden September*** (Messrs W&P Holroyd) [119]
- ***'The Goose'***, Tennyson (verse 4), (R. Wigglesworth) [145]
- ***'The Goose'***, Tennyson (verse 7), (R. Wigglesworth) [146]
- ***Twilight*** (Henry Tankard) [147]
- ***Adversity*** [148]
- ***Old Birds*** (RA 1887) (Mrs R.M. Hick) [149]
- ***'I know an old wife lean and poor, Her rags scarce hold together'***, Tennyson, 'The Goose', (Messrs W&P Holroyd) [150]
- ***'Cinderella'**: Grimm's Fairy Tale* (RA 1891) (A. Maschwitz) [198]

Only *'I know an old wife …'* and *Twilight* have come to light. *Adversity* was a Porlock scene, which depicted an evicted family battling through the snow, whilst *Old Birds* (a sketch for which is illustrated in *Pall Mall Gazette's Pictures of 1887*) showed an old woman plucking a goose, with a jackdaw pecking at the mass of white feathers on the floor. *Cinderella*, which was illustrated in *Pall Mall Gazette's Pictures of 1891*, showed a young woman surrounded by birds. R. Wigglesworth lived at Beckwith Knowle, near Harrogate, W.H. Starkey in Edgbaston, A. Maschwitz in Birmingham, A Smith in Bradford, Mrs R.M. Hick in Whalley, and Henry Tankard in London.

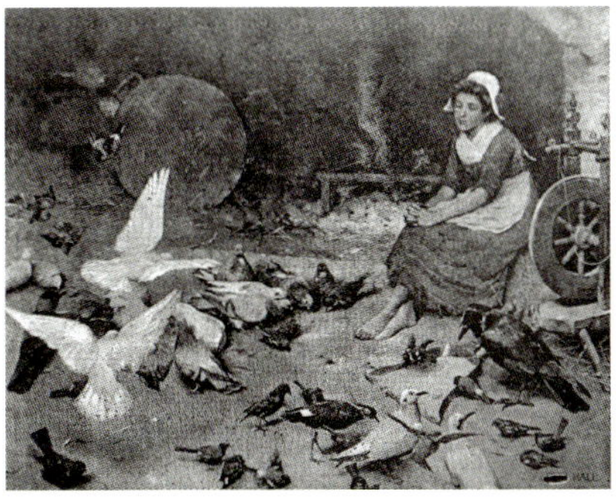

Fred Hall
Cinderella: Grimm's Fairy Tale
from *Pall Mall Gazette's 'Pictures of the Year'*

Nottingham Evening Post, 28 September 1894: 'Fred Hall was one of the artists singled out for especial comment by Henry Blackburn, in his speech at the Opening Luncheon. He said, "I remember when that artist's principal picture was painted, I thought the artist one of those impetuous men, who was to be one of the great painters of the time, who would go on from flight to flight until they lost him in the heavens".'

Nottingham Guardian, 6 October 1894: 'His picture *Twilight* is one of the chief features of this interesting exhibition, and delights us on seeing it a second time, as it did when it was exhibited in the New Gallery two years ago. A girl in a sun bonnet, with a hayrake on her shoulder, drives a cow and two calves across a field in the deepening twilight. A round yellow moon is rising, and thin, vague wisps of mist are beginning to cling about the grass, which is still reddened by the light of the departing sun. The glimmering atmosphere is full of delicate colour, and the word 'poetic' is the only fit one to apply to this unusually happy rendering of one of Nature's most poetic and beautiful effects. The picture is undoubtedly one of the best in the collection.

'[*Golden September*] is daring in colour and delightful in effect. It is a vivid impression of a flock of amusing geese in a field, everything bathed in a rich red glow from the sunset, a pale yellow moon just seen in a pale purple-gold sky. It is as fine a piece of colour as anything here.'

2015 EXHIBITS

Twilight (pl. 20, private collection): As noted above, this painting, which is dated 1891, was considered one of the outstanding works in the 1894 exhibition. It has recently been on the market under the title *Homeward Bound*.

'I know an old wife lean and poor, Her rags scarce hold together' (pl. 21, private collection): This was one of three of Hall's depictions of scenes from Tennyson's poem *The Goose* that were included in the 1894 exhibition. The poem was written in 1842, at the time of the Reform Bill agitation, as a political allegory showing how illusory were the supposed advantages held out by the Radicals to the poor and labouring classes. The old woman featured in these paintings typifies these classes, the stranger, who gave her the goose, the Radicals, the goose the Radical programme, which included Free Trade, the golden eggs such advantages as the proposed Radical measures might for a time seem to confer, the cluttering goose, the storm and whirlwind the heavy price which would have to be paid for them in the social anarchy resulting from triumphant Radicalism.[20]

No 145 illustrated the fourth verse, where the old lady has dropped the goose to clutch at the golden egg that it has laid, before running off to tell her neighbours, whilst No 146 depicts the seventh verse, by which time, the old woman has become tired of the goose cluttering here and chuckling there, and so starts hurling pots and kettles at the bird. Whilst *'I know an old wife ...'* were the first lines of the poem, the painting seems to depict the penultimate verse, where the old woman is surveying the wreckage caused by the departure of the goose and the stranger. *The glass blew in, the fire blew out, / The blast was hard and harder. / Her cap blew off, her gown blew up, / And a whirlwind clear'd the larder.*

The painting was first exhibited at the New English Art Club in 1888 and was illustrated in Alice Meynell's article on Newlyn in the *Art Journal* in 1889. This reveals that, at some juncture subsequently, the bottom of the canvas has been cut down by as much as a third, so that the glossy mouse on which the eyes of the old woman were fixed, has been removed. The original painting did have an unusual perspective, with a large area of flooring visible, but the narrative element in the work has been reduced by the alteration.

20. see www.online-literature.com/tennyson/4072/

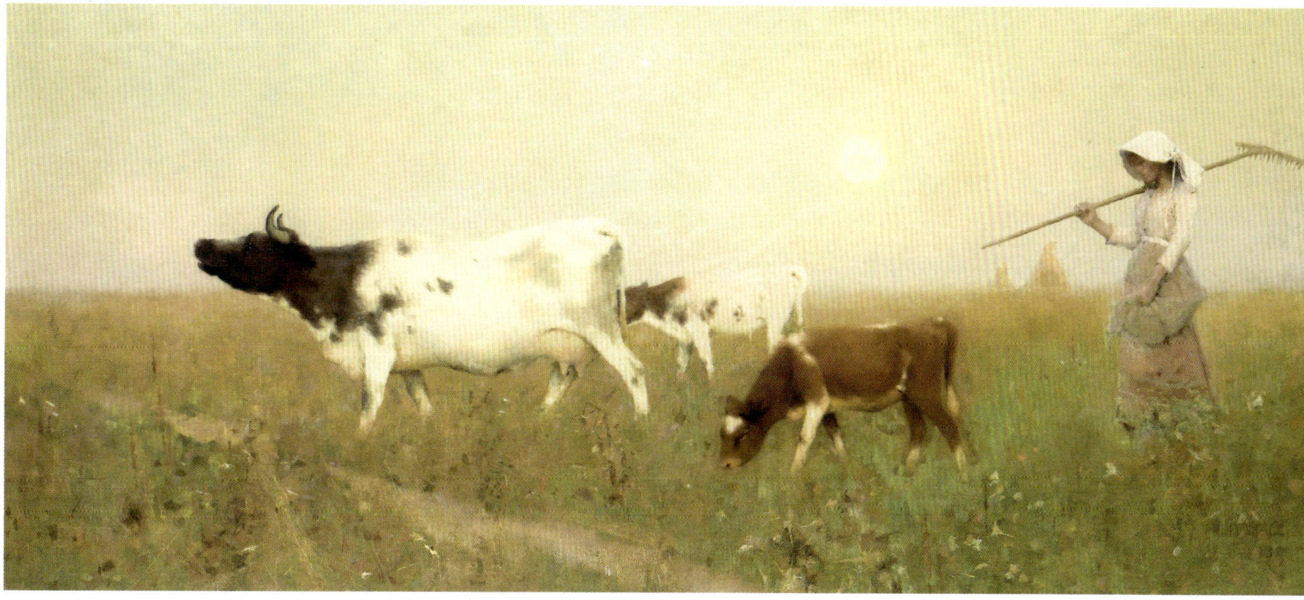

pl. 20 **Fred Hall**
Twilight
oil on canvas • 91 x 197.5 cm
private collection, image courtesy Bonhams; © Bridgeman Art Library

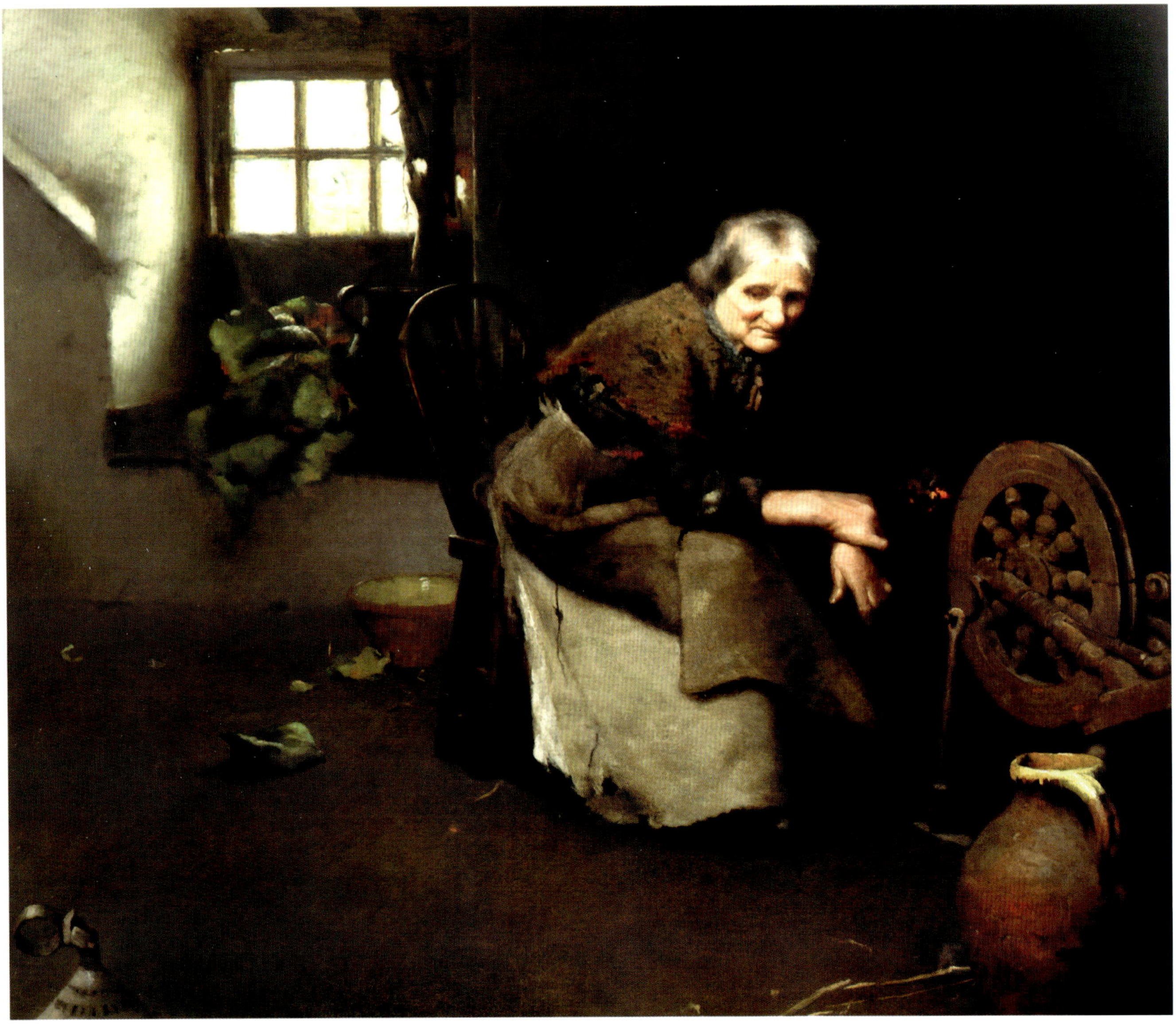

pl. 21 **Fred Hall**
'I know an old wife lean and poor, her rags scarce held together'
oil on canvas • 78 x 91 cm

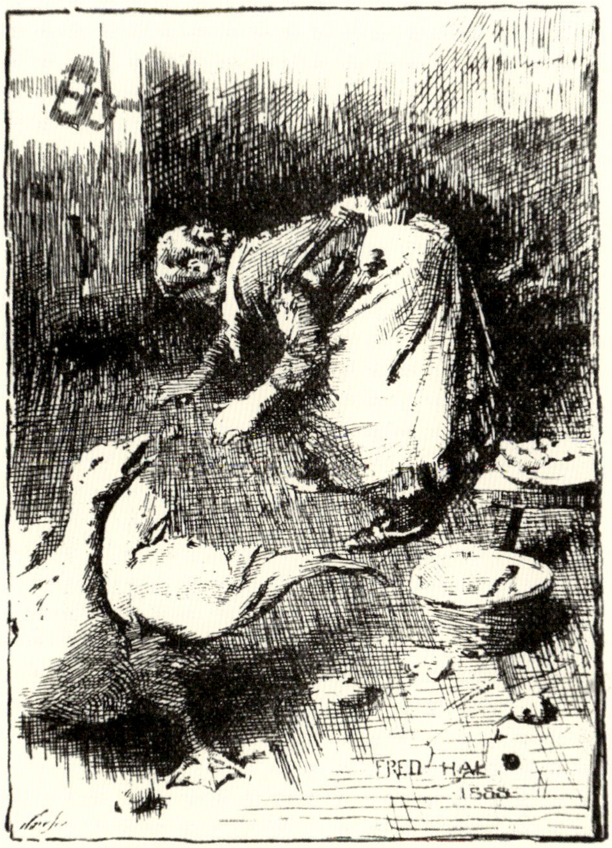

619.—The Goose.—FRED HALL. (Original Sketch.
" She dropt the goose, and caught the pelf,
And ran to tell her neighbours ;
And bless'd herself, and cursed herself,
And rested from her labours."—TENNYSON.

Fred Hall
'The Goose' (verse 4)
from *Academy Notes*

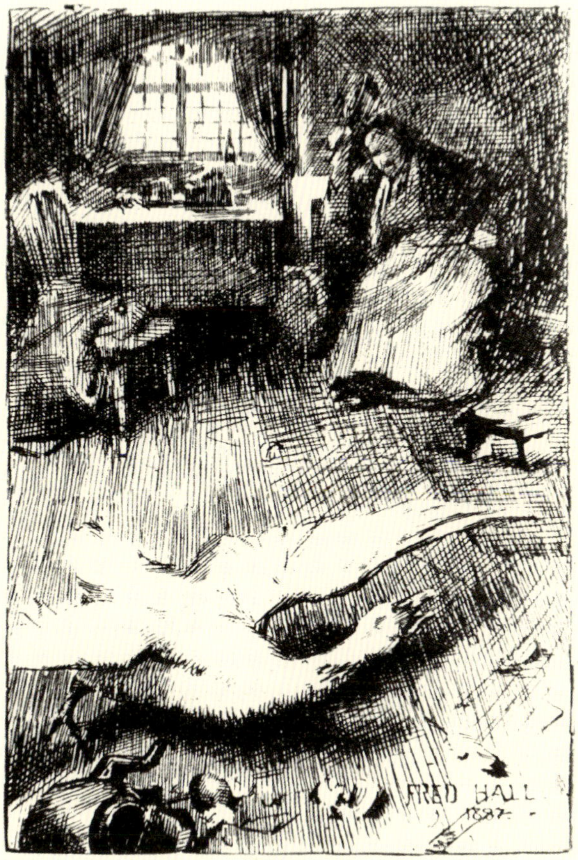

624.—The Goose.—FRED HALL. (Original Sketch.)
" It clutter'd here, it chuckl'd there ;
It stirred the old wife's mettle :
She shifted in her elbow-chair,
And hurl'd the pan and kettle."—TENNYSON.

Fred Hall
'The Goose' (verse 7)
from *Academy Notes*

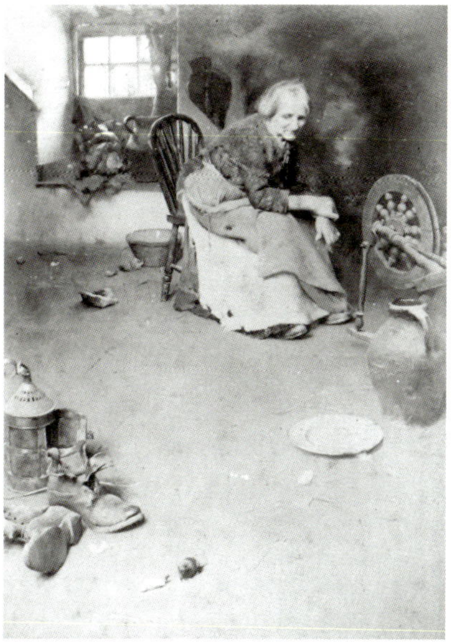

Fred Hall
'I know an old wife lean and poor, her rags scarce held together'
The painting has subsequently been cut down in size
from *Art Journal*, 1889

HARRIS, Edwin

LADYWOOD, BIRMINGHAM 1855–1906 CLEEVE PRIOR, EVESHAM

Harris was one of the early Newlyn colonists from Birmingham. As his first wife's uncle was an art dealer, he seems to have found a ready market for his depictions of pretty girls in simple cottage interiors, often sitting on or close to window seats. He introduces, on occasion, a narrative element to these scenes, but there is little in the way of social commentary. Their charm is enhanced by his carefully observed, and fluently realised, effects of light.

1869: Enrolled in Birmingham School of Art, later becoming an assistant master.
1880: Studied art in Antwerp under Verlat at same time as Frank Bramley (q.v.) and William Wainwright (q.v.).
1881: First visit to Newlyn.
1882: Worked in Pont-Aven, where met Elizabeth Armstrong (later Forbes) (q.v.).
1883: Settled in Newlyn.
1887: First wife died a painful death aged only 25.
1895: Left Newlyn, and concentrated on portraiture in Cardiff, Newport and Bristol.
1898: Returned to Birmingham.

1894 EXHIBITS

- ***One of the Lifeboat** Crew* [103]
- ***The Milk-maid*** (W.H. Starkey) [123]
- ***Uncle Dick*** (David Hedges) [124]
- ***The Captain of the Crew*** (W.H. Starkey) [125]
- ***Harbour Lights*** (David Hedges) [126]
- ***Flowers of Spring*** (Mrs A. Marshall) [157]

Only *Uncle Dick* has been located. As noted above, Starkey and Hedges were Birmingham collectors. Mrs A. Marshall lived in Huddersfield. None of the works were reviewed.

2015 EXHIBITS

Uncle Dick (pl. 22, private collection): Uncle Dick, who had been a marine pilot, was also painted by Walter Langley and William Wainwright.

A Pinch of Snuff (pl. 23, Penlee House Gallery & Museum): Harris draws on the motif of snuff-taking that characterises many images of the traditional fishwives of West Cornwall in this gently humorous portrait of old age.

HEMY, Charles Napier RA, ROI, RI, RWS

NEWCASTLE UPON TYNE 1841–1917 FALMOUTH

Napier Hemy, who lived in Falmouth, was one of the most highly regarded marine painters of his generation and he brought the activities and travails of the Cornish fishermen to the attention of an international audience. At the time of the 1894 exhibition, he had already been exhibiting at the Royal Academy for nearly thirty years, but his move to Falmouth in 1880 had proved a turning point in his career, and he shortly began to sell work regularly to public galleries.

1850: Emigrated with his parents to Australia, returning in 1852. The two sea journeys made a lasting impression on him.

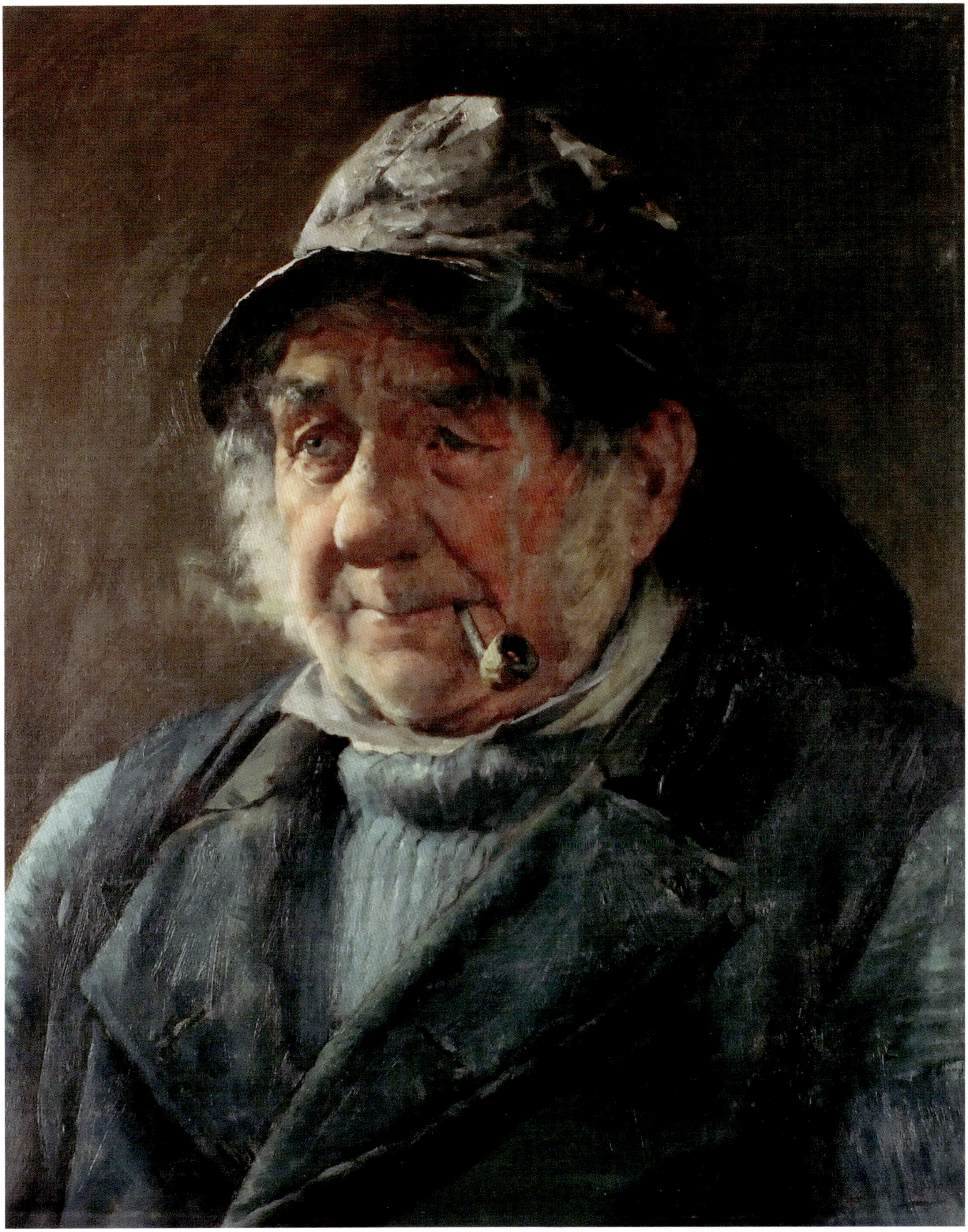

pl. 22 **Edwin Harris**
Uncle Dick
oil on canvas • 46 x 39.5 cm
private collection, image courtesy W.H. Lane & Son, Penzance

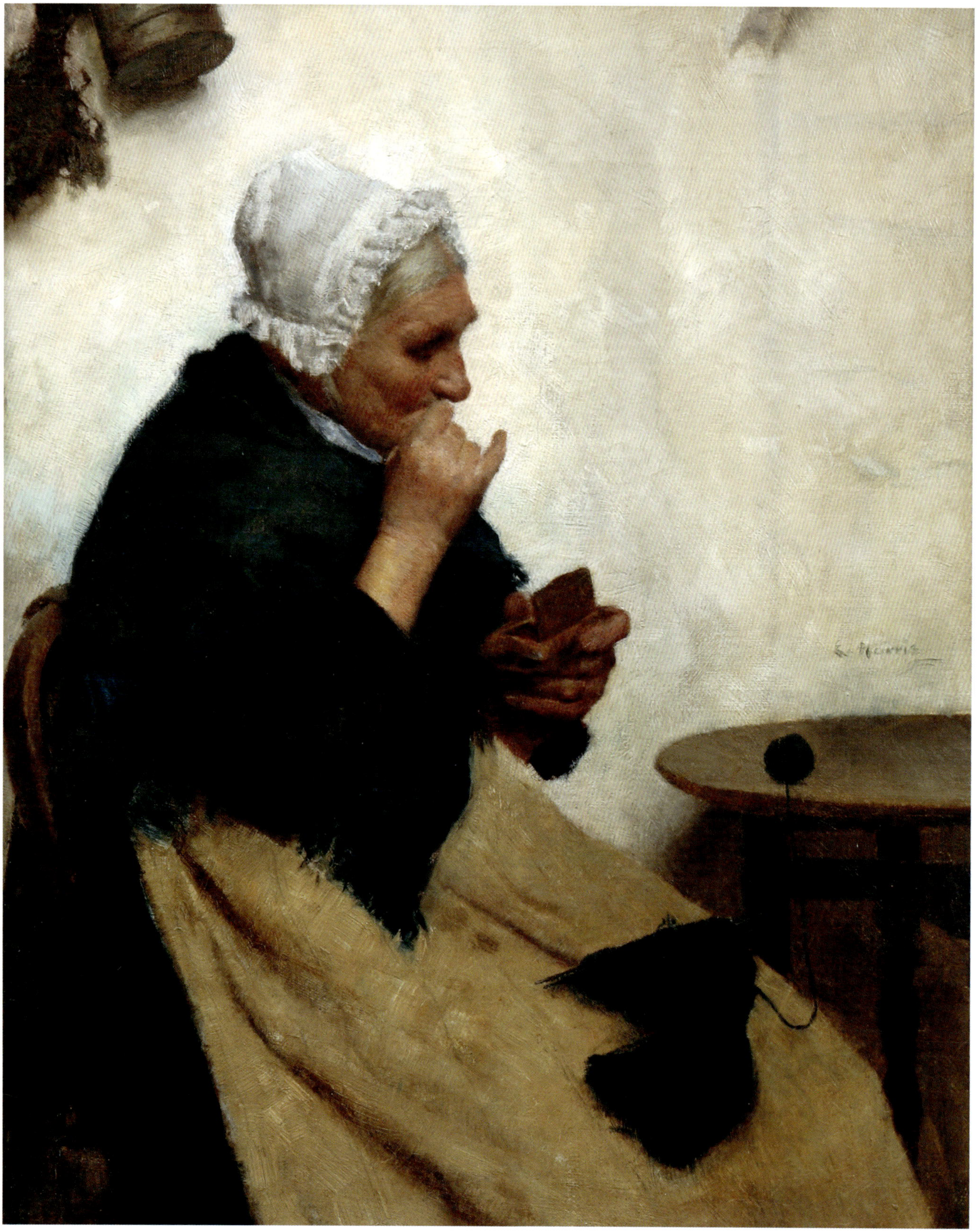

pl. 23 **Edwin Harris**
A Pinch of Snuff
oil on canvas • 37 x 29 cm
Penlee House Gallery & Museum

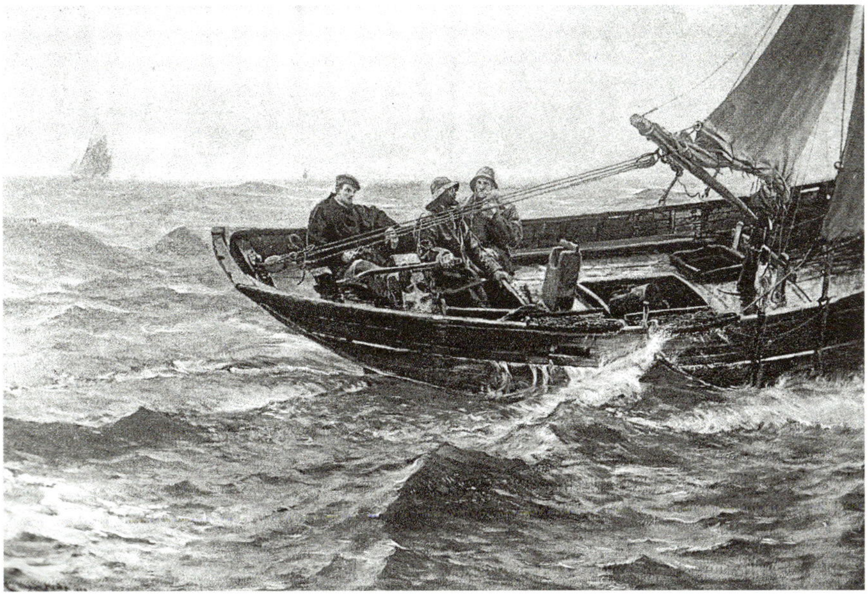

Charles Napier Hemy
Three Fishers
from the 1894 exhibition catalogue

1852: Enrolled in Newcastle's Government School of Design under the tutelage of William Bell Scott.
1860–2: Lived briefly as a Dominican priest in monasteries in Lyon and Carpentras, France.
1866: Married for first time.
1867–9: Studied with Belgian painter Baron Henri Leys, and at the Antwerp Academy.
1870: Exhibited paintings of St Ives, one of which now owned by Salford Art Gallery.
1869–80: Based in London, with a gallery studio in Fulham.
1880: Moved to Falmouth after the death of his first wife and married local girl, Amy Freeman, in 1881, with whom he was to have ten children. Built large property, Churchfield, as his home and constructed a floating studio, which he called the *Vanderveld*, from a seine boat.
1883: Sold *Old Putney Bridge* to Manchester Art Gallery.
1884: Elected member of RI.
1885: Elected member of ROI; sold *Grey Venice* to Manchester Art Gallery.
1887: Sold *Homeward* to Birmingham Art Gallery.
1890: Elected ARWS (RWS 1897).
1897: *Pilchards* bought by the Chantrey Trustees for £1200.
1898: Made ARA (RA 1910).
1904: *London River* bought by the Chantrey Trustees.
1917: By his death, had exhibited 156 works at RA.

1894 EXHIBITS

- ***Homeward*** (Birmingham) [133]
- ***Old Putney Bridge*** (Manchester) [134]
- ***Grey Venice*** (Manchester) [135]
- ***Three Fishers*** (RA 1889) (George Kenrick) [136]
- ***The Morning Light*** (Mrs Buxton Whalley) [137]

George Kenrick lived in Edgbaston, Birmingham, and Mrs Buxton Whalley in Newbury.

***Nottingham Guardian*, 6 October 1894**: 'The work of Mr C. Napier Hemy, who by now must be a true 'Falmouth native', is well known to all who care for good sea painting. Like Mr Tuke, he paints the sea upon the sea, taking his studio afloat with him. The various methods of catching fish by line and net, trammel, seine or trawl, have no mysteries for him, so often has he entered into their rites with

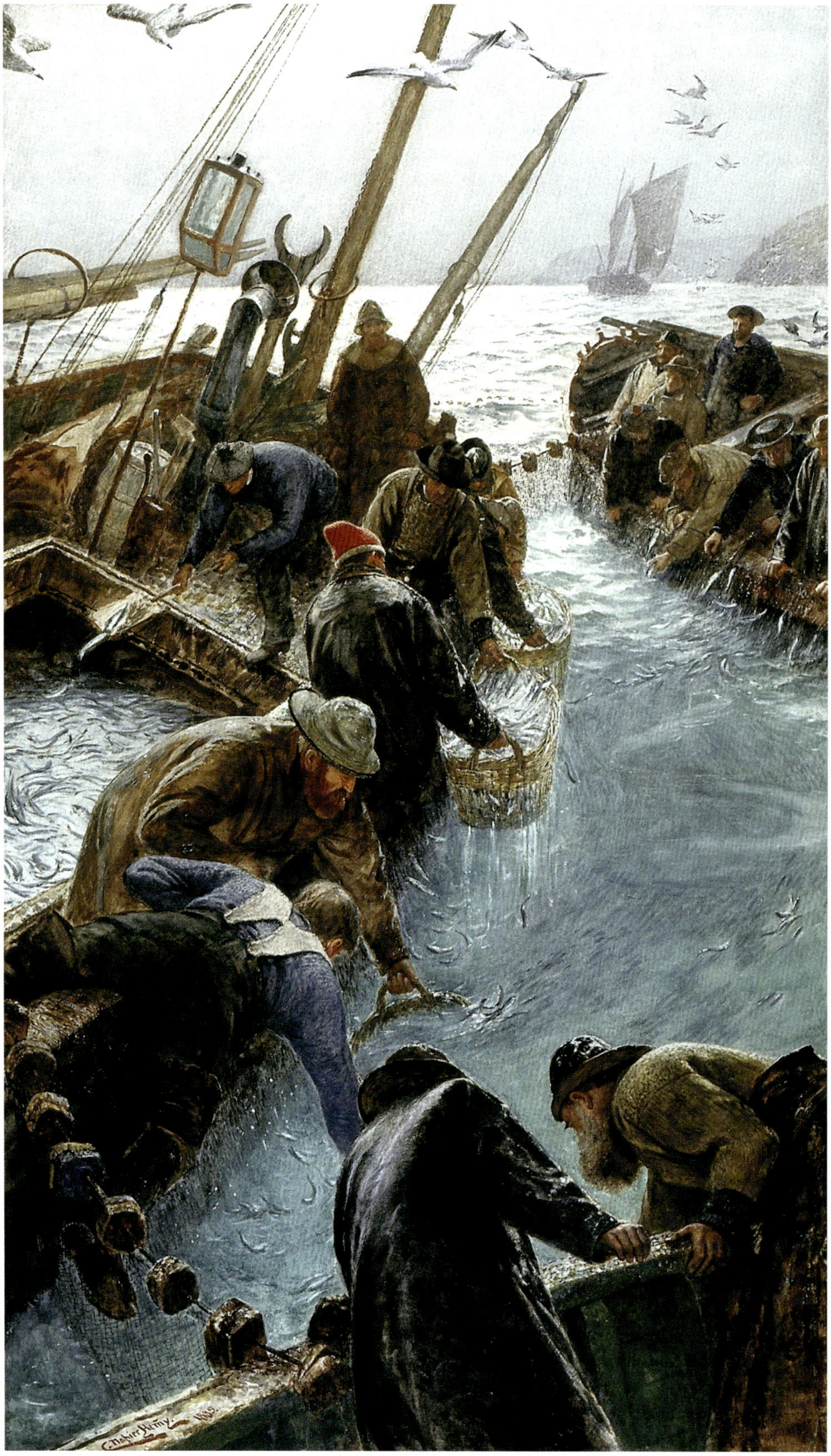

pl. 24 **Charles Napier Hemy**
How we Caught the Pilchards
1885 • watercolour • 136 x 79 cm
National Museums Liverpool, Walker Art Gallery

relish. In the painting of translucent water, grass green under the keel of a boat as she cuts through the water, there is probably no-one that can beat him. Three works here show his great power in this direction, while two others have a subject less usual with this artist. *Homeward* is filled with this fine skill in depicting the colour of the sea; two men in a boat, rowing, under the grey harbour wall, with the grey houses above. In the *Three Fishers*, we get only the stern of a fishing boat as she rushes through the green waves, under a fresh breeze, so that it refreshes one even to look at it, and makes one long to join the three sailors on their expedition. *The Morning Light* represents the landing of fish upon a rough stone pie from a boat, with a woman coming down the steps carrying a basket, the whole canvas filled with the bright, white light of the morning ...

2015 EXHIBIT

How we caught the pilchards (pl. 24, National Museums Liverpool, Walker Art Gallery): Seine fishing for pilchards was one of the most dramatic sights around the coast of Cornwall and, given that the seine boats tended to operate close to the shore, it was a spectacle enjoyed by locals, tourists and artists alike. Alerted to the presence of a shoal by the water colouring purple and by the presence of seabirds, it took considerable skill for the men in seine boats to manoeuvre a seine net, which could be a quarter of a mile in length, so as to secure the shoal. Sometimes a smaller tuck net was used within the confines of the seine net to bring the catch to the surface, but here the fishermen seem merely to be dipping wicker baskets into the seine net, which is fastened securely to the seine boats so that the shoal cannot escape. This watercolour dates from 1885, and Hemy reverted to the subject in the 1890s, doing numerous sketches before producing his huge canvas, *Pilchards*, which was bought by the Chantrey Trustees in 1897. Percy Craft, Alfred Warne-Browne and Frederick Sargent also produced impressive canvases of such a scene.

JEVONS, George Walter

BIRKENHEAD c.1855; *fl.* to 1904

Walter Jevons was a landscape artist of moderate ability, who was based in St Ives in the early 1890s and still retained connections with the colony after moving to The Lizard in 1894.

Father merchant. He was brought up and probably had early art training in Liverpool.
1886: Recorded as visitor at Tregenna Castle Hotel, St Ives.
Late 1880s: Studied in Paris at Académie Julian.
1889: Part of group of Paris students who visited Runswick.
1890: Came to St Ives in June with Dutch artist, Sigisbert Bosch Reitz. Joined later by others from the Runswick party, including Terrick Williams and Harry Bishop. August: Founder member of St Ives Arts Club.
1891: At time of Census, lodging with Eddy family at Zennor.
1892–5: Participated in Show Days and other activities in St Ives.
1894: Moved to Roswick Cottage, St Martin, on The Lizard, but retained connections with St Ives (for instance, being a coffin bearer at Harry Robinson's funeral in 1904).

WALLIS CORRESPONDENCE

Writing from Roswick Cottage, St Martin, Jevons initially indicated that he would send just one work to the exhibition, but clearly having picked up on the interest that other artists were demonstrating in the show, he wrote to offer, first, one more and then a total of four – two to be picked up from Liverpool and two from Cornwall. He also lent to the exhibition Arnesby Brown's *Study for A Northern Breeze*, which he had acquired.

1894 EXHIBITS

- ***Cornish Fir Trees*** [10]
- ***A Waterfall*** [54]
- ***A Summer Evening*** [55]
- ***Evening*** (Paris 1893, RA 1894) [56]

None of these paintings have been located.

***Nottingham Evening Post*, 6 October 1894**: 'Mr Walter Jevons is represented by several pictures, of which the best is *Evening*, one of those sweeps of marshland, river-riven, seen under the glow of evening, which this school so much effect.'

Evening was his most successful work, having been hung also at the Paris Salon in 1893 and the RA in 1894. When first shown in St Ives in 1892, it was described as 'essentially a beautiful picture, the poetic expression of a Suffolk landscape. The tender and sympathetic treatment of afterglow effects linger lovingly alike on distant hills, rush-strewn marsh and silvery stream, producing in its subtle way an effect of absolute tranquillity and rest'.[21]

LANGLEY, Walter RBSA, RI

BIRMINGHAM 1852–1922 PENZANCE

Walter Langley was generally recognised as the first of the Newlyn School artists to settle in Newlyn and was unusual in that the primary medium in which he worked was watercolour. Despite having rarely exhibited at the Royal Academy prior to the Nottingham exhibition, he had established a significant reputation for himself at the watercolour societies and sold his work for large sums. As a watercolourist, though, his style reflected more Dutch influences than the French ones which inspired his oil painting colleagues. Like Stanhope Forbes, Langley did not alter unduly his style or his subject matter as time passed, and his life-long output is now considered archetypal Newlyn School work.

Father was a tailor. Studied South Kensington Schools 1872–5.
1881: Brief visit to Brittany.
1882: First Newlyn School artist to settle in Newlyn, after visiting in 1880 and 1881.
1883: First exhibits of his watercolours in London resulted in considerable acclaim – immediately made member of RI.
1883–92: Repeated success for his watercolours depicting the lives of the fisherfolk, many dealing with bereavement, a subject that pulled at the heart-strings of the Victorian public.
1890: Participated in the Cornish Artists show at Dowdeswells.
1892: First exhibit at the Royal Academy and began to paint more in oils.
1893: One-man show at the Fine Art Society; medal at Chicago.
1895: Invitation to donate self-portrait to Uffizi Gallery, Florence.
1895–1922: Continued to paint similar subjects in oils and watercolours, with great success; regular at the Royal Academy; represented in a number of public collections.

WALLIS CORRESPONDENCE

On 22 May 1894, writing from 6 St Mary's Terrace, Penzance, Langley sent Wallis his first list of what he considered his best work, but he was aware that, as some

21. *St Ives Weekly Summary*, 26 March 1892.

of the owners had only just had work returned to them, they might be unwilling to lend again. This list included *Among the Missing* (1884 – then owned by Mr H.H. Bolton of Newchurch, near Manchester and now by Penlee House Gallery & Museum, Penzance), *'Disaster!'* (1889; then owned by Mr J.C. Holder of Pitmaston, Moor Green, Birmingham, now by Birmingham Art Gallery) and *The Departure of the Fleet*, (1886 – then owned by David Hedges of Yardley, near Birmingham, now by Penlee House Gallery & Museum, Penzance). He also mentioned a work, which he thought was called *Widowed* (possibly *The Widow*), which Wallis' brother, the Curator at Birmingham, had sold from an exhibition there. In July, he also mentioned *But men must work and women must weep*, an 1882 watercolour that had been acquired by Birmingham Art Gallery.

In August, Wallis wrote enquiring about his RA exhibit of the year *Ne'er morning wore to evening but some heart did break*, but Langley indicated that this had been promised to the contemporaneous Birmingham exhibition. He did, though, suggest his RI exhibit of the year *After the Storm*, which he called 'a very important work' and 'the largest work that I have ever done in watercolour'. This had been bought for £300 by William Lethbridge of Courtlands, Lympstone, Exeter, but he declined to lend. (The whereabouts of this work, having been donated to Birmingham Art Gallery in 1903, are now unknown.)

Another painting that Langley suggested in his correspondence with Harry Wallis was his large 1885 watercolour, *Waiting for the Boats*, which he had sold to W.A. Michael Q.C. of 4 Kings Bench Walk, Temple, from the 1885 RI exhibition for £315. Given that Michael was lending two other small works to the exhibition, Langley thought that he might lend this 'important work' as well. For some reason, he did not, and the painting in the exhibition entitled *Waiting for the Boats* was described as being lent by the artist. This work, completed in 1893, had been exhibited previously at the Country Fisheries Exhibition held in Truro in 1893. In a review of this show, it was described as follows: '*Waiting for the boats* is another of Mr Langley's serious studies that appeal to the reflective mind. The wrinkled old dame, whose hands are brown, knotted and large-veined through much toil, is waiting with fish cowal at her side, for the incoming boats; but weariness has apparently wafted her into dreamland.'[22]

It also apparently had been shown in a previous Nottingham exhibition, as there is correspondence between Langley and Wallis in April 1894 about an offer received for this and another work. Langley, writing from 1 Okement House, Okehampton on 12 April 1894, commented, 'My pictures were put in at a low price I would accept £25 for *A Lass that Loves A Sailor*. The other picture *Waiting for the Boats*, which I consider one of my best works, I could make no reduction on taking it by itself, but if the two works are taken, I would be prepared to accept £60 for both. This is the very lowest I can accept.' Clearly, these prices were not acceptable to the proposed purchaser, as both works were kept on by Wallis and included in the Cornish artists' exhibition. Accordingly, the group of work that was collected together was not as impressive as Langley had hoped.

1894 EXHIBITS

- ***An Old Pilot*** [86; watercolour]
- ***The Old, Old Story*** [87; watercolour]
- ***'Disaster!'*** (John Holder) [88; watercolour]
- ***A Lass that Loves A Sailor*** [89; watercolour]
- ***The Sunset of Life*** (W.A. Michael) [90; watercolour]
- ***'Jilted'*** (D. Hedges) [91; watercolour]
- ***Waiting for the Boats*** [92; watercolour]
- ***'Local News'*** (W.A. Michael) [93; watercolour]
- ***Village Gossip*** (D. Hedges) [94; watercolour]

'Disaster!' is now owned by Birmingham Art Gallery. As Langley tended to use the same titles on a number of occasions, it is difficult to pinpoint exactly which

22. *The Cornishman*, 27 July 1893.

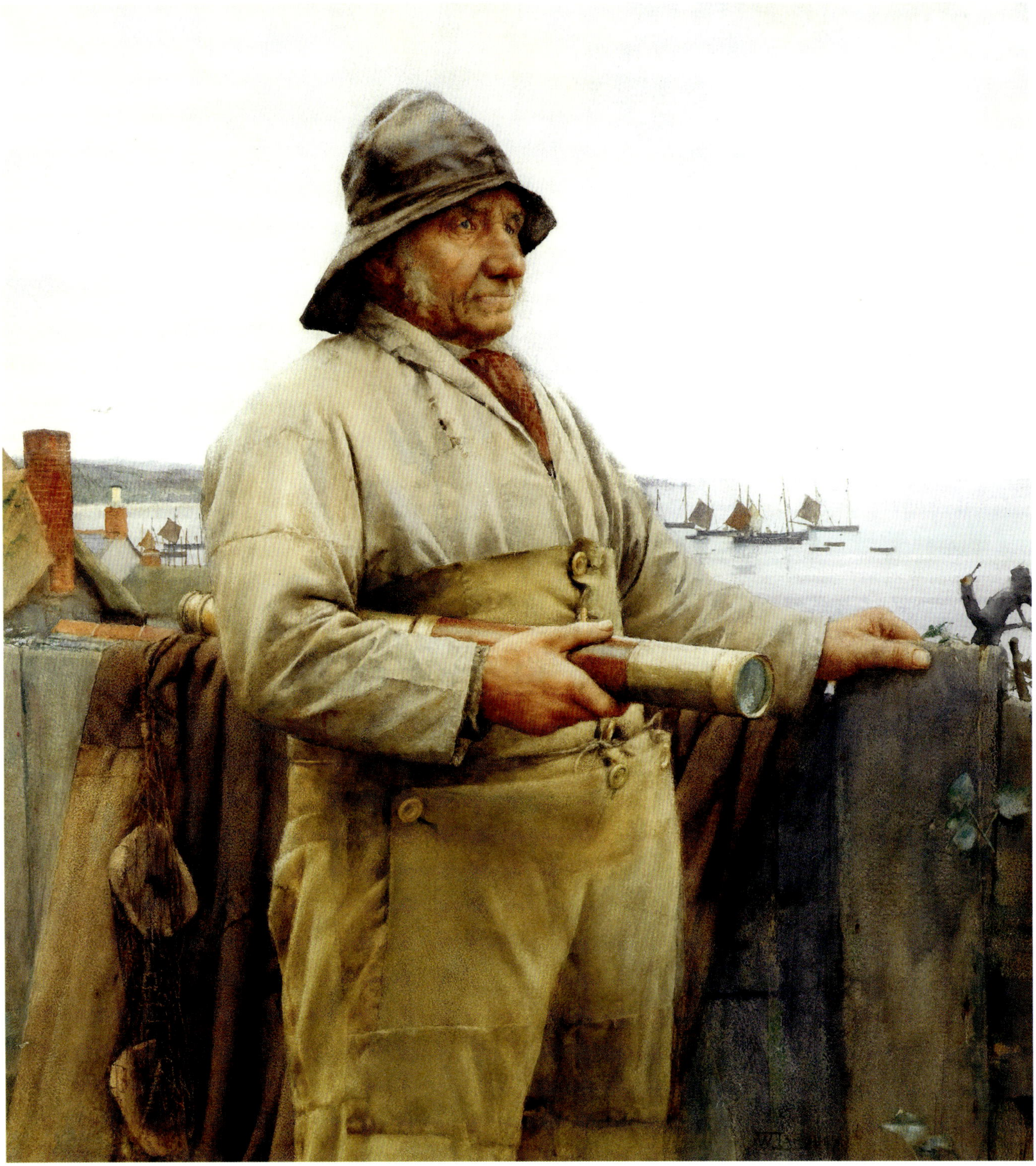

pl. 25 **Walter Langley**
An Old Pilot
watercolour • 81 x 71 cm
Bowerman Charitable Trust

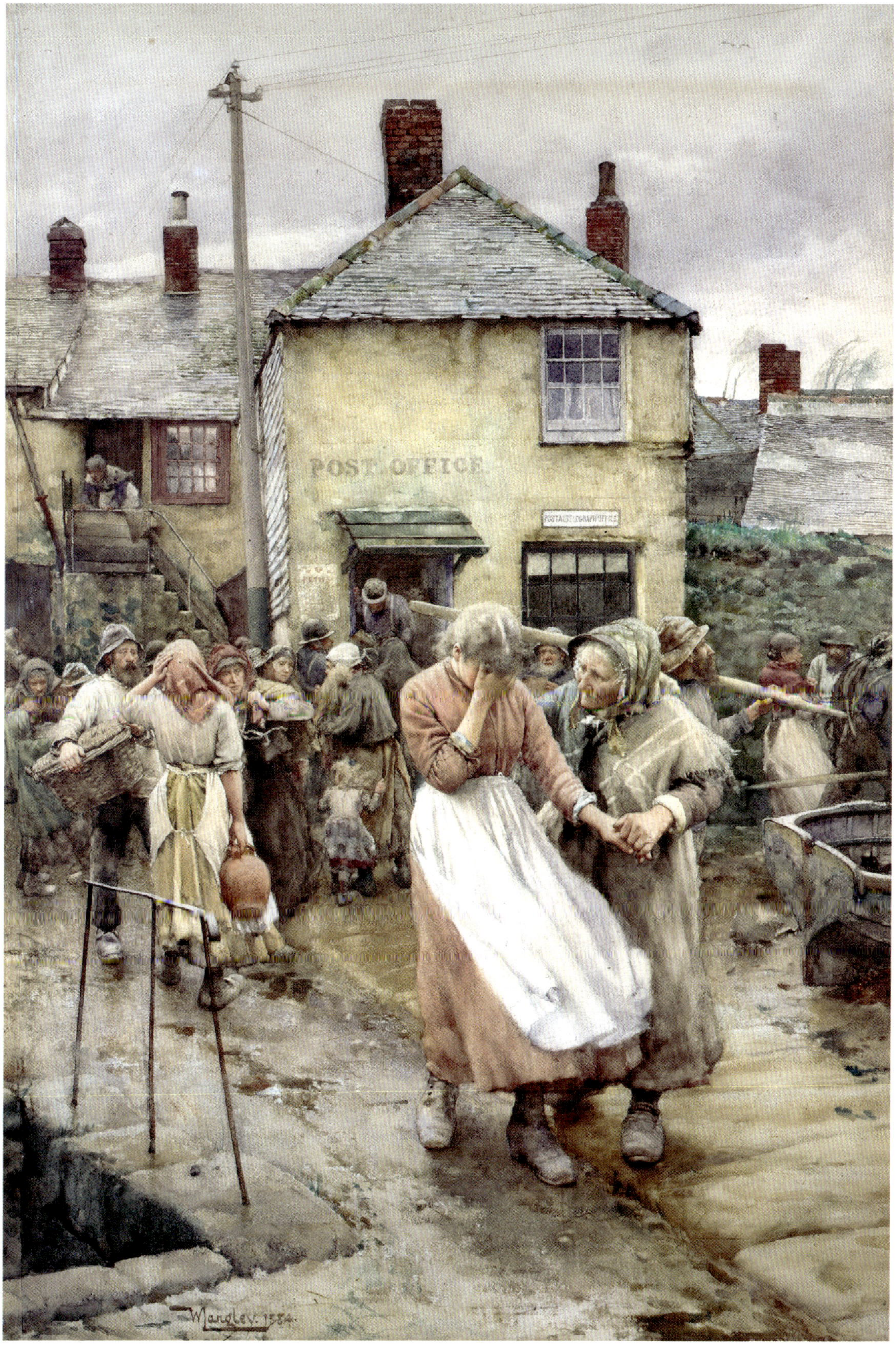

pl. 26 **Walter Langley**
Among the Missing – Scene in a Cornish Fishing Village
1884 • watercolour • 103 x 70 cm
Penlee House Gallery & Museum

works were in the original exhibition. For instance, he did at least three versions of *'Local News'*. However, as noted above, *Waiting for the Boats* was the 1893 version, not the large 1885 version, whilst *A Lass that Loves A Sailor* was the 1894 version, not the 1893 version, which had already been sold. This probably showed a girl leaning against a capstan, looking out to sea.

***Nottingham Evening Post*, 6 October 1894**: 'Mr Walter Langley should rightly be considered the father of the Newlyn branch, for when Mr Forbes arrived in that quaint village, he found that this artist, of whom the town of Birmingham is so justly proud, had been working there in solitude for some time. Mr Langley's work is so well known that we shall not attempt to describe it here. Luckily Mr Wallis has been able to procure the loan of some of his finest watercolour drawings, notably *Disaster* lent by Mr J.C. Holder, *Jilted* lent by Mr David Hedges, *Local News* and *The Sunset of Life* lent by Mr W.A. Michael, and six or seven others, all of them displaying work which in its direction is unrivalled. Not only does he enter into all the joys and sorrows, chiefly the latter, of those who go down to the sea in ships, depicting with high dramatic power the disasters that befall them, as in the picture belonging to Mr Holder, but his manipulative skill in the delicate handling of colour gives high pleasure to all those who care for this branch of painting. We will leave the wall on which his work is displayed to speak for itself.

2015 EXHIBITS

An Old Pilot (pl. 25, Bowerman Charitable Trust): This features a character known as Uncle Dick, who modelled for a number of the artists.

In a Cornish Fishing Village – Departure of the Fleet for the North (pl. 27, Penlee House Gallery & Museum): This is one of the paintings that Langley suggested should be included in the 1894 exhibition, but was not included because the owner refused to lend. This was probably because it had been sent to the Chicago World Columbian Exhibition 1893, where both it and *Disaster!* were awarded a gold medal. However, as Langley refused to pay the excise duty, he received a bronze medal instead! The occasion depicted was a major event in the calendar of the Cornish fishing ports. As there were few fish to be had around the Cornish coast in the summer months, many of the local fishing boats sailed around Britain to the north-east coast, where they fished for herring in the North Sea, often basing themselves at Whitby. Accordingly, fishing families had to get used to being separated for several months each summer. The fleet's departure would not have been an easy time for all concerned.

Among the Missing – Scene in a Cornish Fishing Village (pl. 26, Penlee House Gallery & Museum): This painting, again, recommended to Wallis by Langley, confirms that the worries held by families when their men-folk left to fish in the North Sea were not baseless. In Newlyn, when a storm had caused havoc off the East Coast, a notice would be put up outside the Post Office listing boats and men lost. Here, a young woman has just learnt that her husband is amongst those missing. The building depicted as the Post Office is thought to be one close to Langley's studio in Keel Alley in The Fradgen, but there is no record of its actually having been a Post Office. The painting was originally exhibited at the Spring Exhibition of the RI in 1884 and was highly rated, being reproduced in the *Illustrated London News* and *The Graphic*. It has a join down the left-hand side – either an addition, or to cover up a mistake, for, unlike with oils, an error in watercolour could not be overpainted.

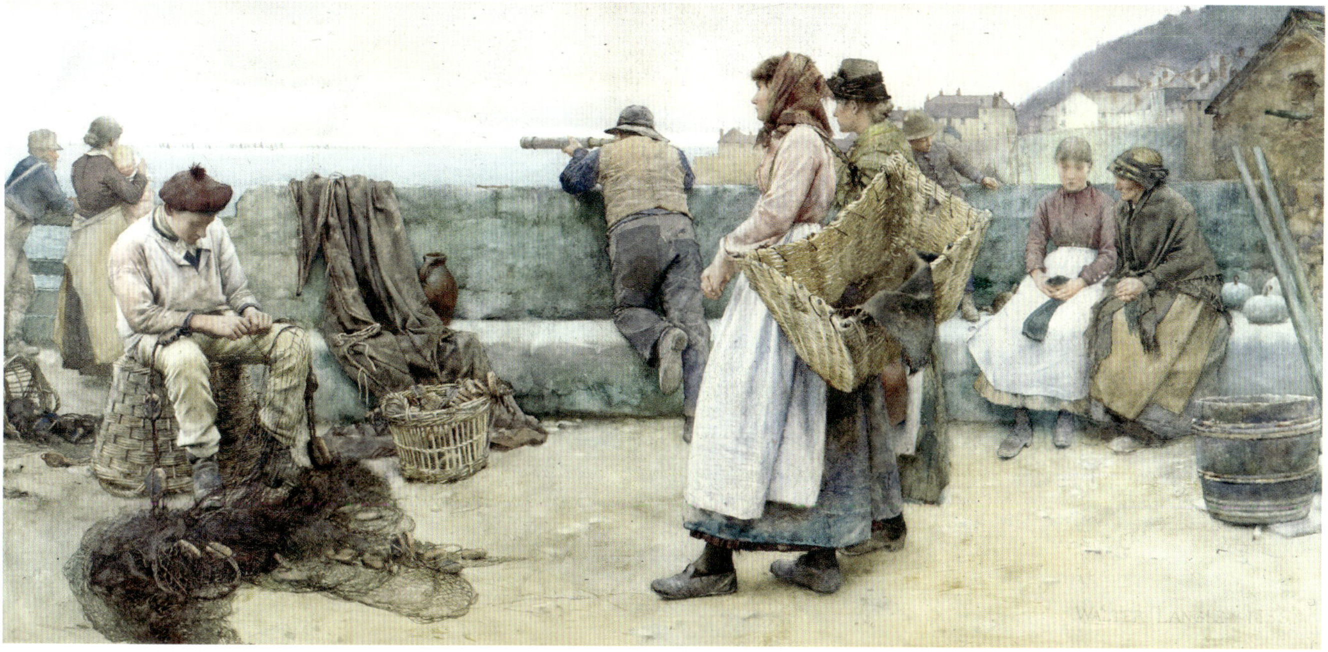

pl. 27 **Walter Langley**
In a Cornish Fishing Village – Departure of the Fleet for the North
1886 • watercolour • 91 x 137.5 cm
Penlee House Gallery & Museum

LAUENCE, Sydney Mortimer RBA

BROOKLYN, NEW YORK 1865–1940 ANCHORAGE, ALASKA

The American artist, Sydney Laurence, was a maverick. Having married in 1889, he came to St Ives on honeymoon with his wife, Alexandrina, and stayed for over a decade, before deciding to go gold prospecting in Alaska in 1904. Having lost everything, he never made contact with his wife and two children again, married bigamously, before becoming revered as Alaska's leading artist and the subject of the film *Laurence of Alaska*.

Father Australian, mother English. Educated at Peekskill Military Academy.
1888-9: Studied at the Art Students League, New York. Also had lessons from Edward Moran. Exhibited at the National Academy of Design in 1888 and 1889.
1889: Married in New York, honeymooned in St Ives and decided to settle in the colony.
1890: First success at Paris Salon. Included in Dowdeswell exhibition.
1890–8: Mixed life in St Ives with continental travel and some study in Paris.
1895: Elected to RBA.
1898: Whilst his wife remained in St Ives, Sydney returned to New York and then became a war artist for the *New York Herald* to cover the Spanish-American war.
1900: After a period back in St Ives, left for South Africa to cover the Boer War for *Black and White*, but soon caught enteric fever and returned home.
1901: Moved with family to Tonbridge.
1901–4: Continued reporting for *Black and White* on international events.
1904: Deserted family in England to go gold prospecting in Alaska.

WALLIS CORRESPONDENCE

Laurence initially wrote to Wallis from Hotel Suisse in Paris on 24 May 1894, indicating that Wallis had asked to include his Salon work of that year, *The Setting Sun – Coast of Cornwall*, and he agreed to this, as long as Nottingham paid for both packing and carriage. Laurence indicated that he was leaving Paris that week, and, when he next wrote to Wallis on 22 July 1894, he was based at Maison Petit, Vétheuil, Seine et Oise. In this letter, he urged Wallis to leave the Salon number and Mention Honorable card on the picture! He also indicated that he would not put a price on the work but would be glad to receive offers. However, in the end, he seems to have put a figure of £500 on it, which he reduced to £200, in an unsuccessful attempt to get Nottingham Castle to acquire it.

1894 EXHIBITS

- ***Sunlit Waves*** (C.H. Palethorpe) [183]
- ***The Setting Sun – Coast of Cornwall*** [190]
- ***The 'Cornishman'*** [191]
- ***Passing Shadows*** [192]

Other than *The Setting Sun – Coast of Cornwall*, now at Southampton Art Gallery, none of the other works have been located. C.H. Palethorpe lived in Dudley.

***Nottingham Guardian*, 13 October 1894**: 'Mr S M Laurence's large canvas *The Setting Sun – Coast of Cornwall* is a really powerful piece of wave painting, and has received honourable mention at the Paris Salon. The crimson sun, about to sink out of sight, lights up the sky and touches, as with blood, the crests of the long line of great waves which are roaring with anger as they break upon the sandy shore, which gleams with red and green reflections. This is one of the finest and freshest studies of waves in an exhibition where the colour and form of waves is so constantly sought after.

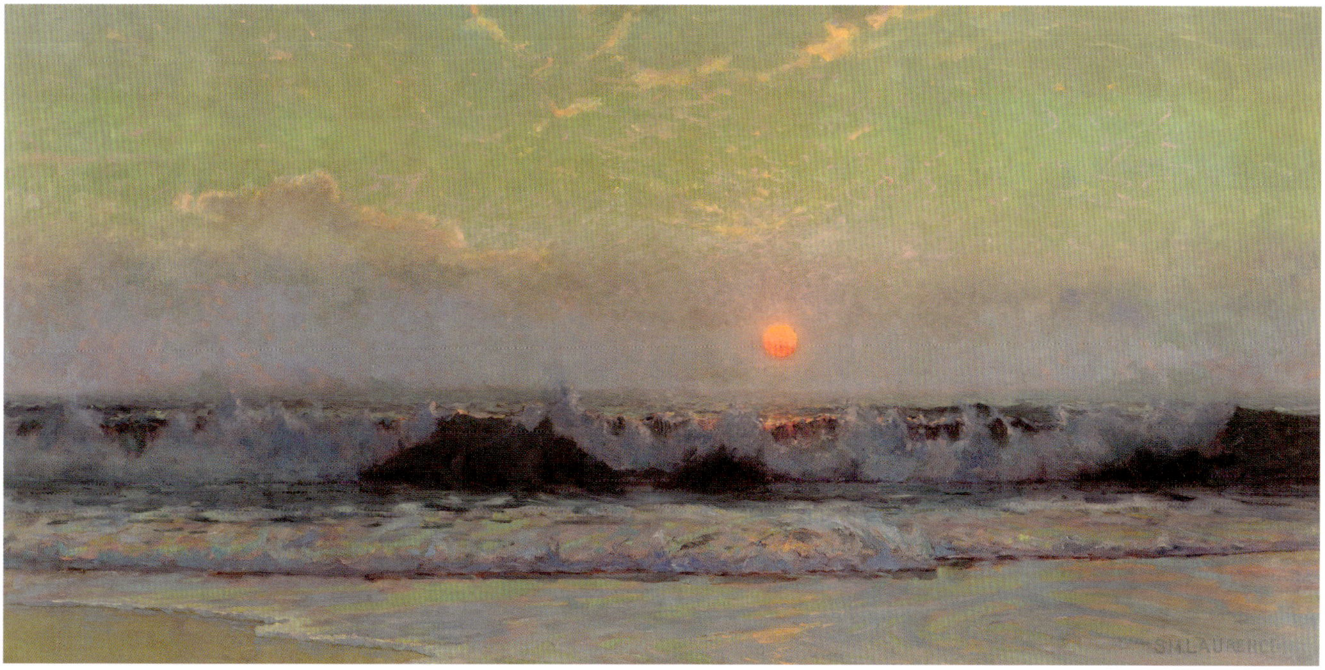

pl. 28 **Sydney Mortimer Laurence**
The Setting Sun – Coast of Cornwall
1894 • oil on canvas • 137 x 274 cm
Southampton City Art Gallery

'*The "Cornishman"* shows the railway embankment over the Marazion Marshes with the London express rushing across. The marsh water and brown reeds are covered with the clinging smoke from the engine, which floats over and gradually sinks into them. This vanishing smoke and the effect of speed in the train are cleverly caught. *Sunlit Waves*, lent by Mr Palethorpe, is another good rendering of translucent green waves curving over and breaking in a white foam, while distant sea and sky are filled with a yellow glow.'

2015 EXHIBIT

The Setting Sun – Coast of Cornwall (pl. 28, Southampton City Art Gallery): This is the finest painting produced by Laurence during the 15-year period that he was based in England, most of which was spent in St Ives. The scene depicted is Porthmeor Beach, St Ives, overlooking which Laurence had a studio in the early 1890s. The subject and the elongated format show the influence of *The Wave* (Pennsylvania Academy of the Fine Arts), a painting by fellow American, Alexander Harrison, which had caused a sensation at the Paris Salon in 1885. Given its success in Paris, it is notable that Laurence did not succeed in getting it hung at the Royal Academy. Victorians still considered pure seascapes boring – they wanted marine paintings full of dramatic incident.

Given his true story, Laurence was inclined to embellish accounts of his career and indicated later in life to American admirers that this picture was bought by the French Government, leading numerous art historians to make enquiries in vain. David Tovey located it sitting unrecognised in the stores of Southampton Art Gallery, to whom it had been donated in the 1930s by the heirs of Frederick Griffin, a Southampton doctor, who was the brother of the Reverend Edward Griffin, the vicar of St Johns-in-the-Fields, Halsetown, near St Ives, a good friend of the artist. Frederick Griffin, in fact, acquired fifteen oils and eighteen watercolours from Laurence, but these were mostly modest works. Griffin family folklore indicates that, in 1904, Laurence was desperate to raise funds for his Alaskan gold prospecting adventure and that Frederick, whom he clearly knew well, for he had given him a painting as a wedding present in February 1896, obliged by buying his 1894 Paris Salon success for just £100. Accordingly, Laurence's lie about its ultimate purchaser is perhaps understandable, as a sale to the French Government sounded rather better than having to admit that, after failing to find a buyer for a decade, he had ended up flogging it, for a song, to his Vicar's brother, to finance a madcap venture, which resulted in his not only deserting his wife and children, but also losing everything.

MEADE, Arthur RBA, ROI

BOROUGHBRIDGE, SOMERSET 1864–1942 ST IVES

Meade, another former Bushey student, was to become one of the stalwarts of the St Ives art colony, living in the town for over fifty years, and also one of its leading landscape painters, exhibiting at the Royal Academy over sixty times.

Father poulterer and fishmonger.
1881: At time of census, lodging in Bath with the artist, Eliza Gibbs.
Mid-1880s: Studied in Paris under Gerome.
1888: First RA exhibit a Tangier scene.
1890–1: Studied at Herkomer Art School, Bushey.
1891: At time of Census, lodging with his wife, Mabel, in St Ives and settled in town the following year.
1895: Elected member of RBA.
1909: Elected member of ROI.

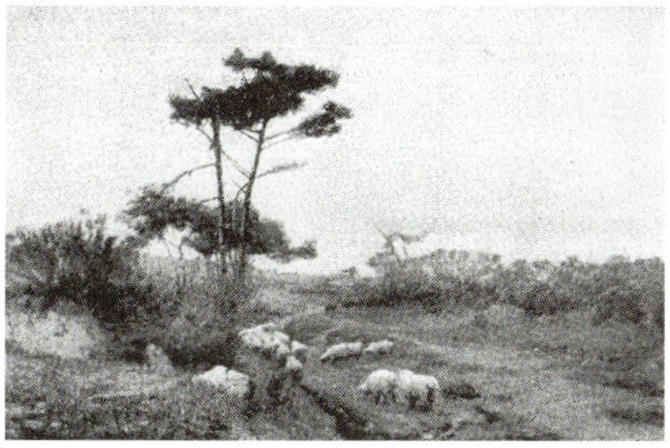

Arthur Meade
When Day is Waning
from the 1894 exhibition catalogue

WALLIS CORRESPONDENCE

In response to Wallis' initial suggestions as to potential exhibits, Meade responded in a letter dated 10 July 1894 'I am sorry to say that those pictures you mention are still on my hands, but I feel they would not be very representative of me, the work I am doing now being so much better. If you would care, I should like to send a marine that I have at St Ives [*A Breezy Day*] ... If you really wanted a fifth, both *Lengthening Shadows* and *A Cornish Road* are at a friend's studio in London – Mr Sargent's 17 Holland Park Road, Kensington.'[23] This suggests that a mistake was made in the catalogue and that instead of there being two works called *Passing Shadows*, one was his 1892 RA exhibit *Lengthening Shadows*. His letter, which was from 8 Alexandra Terrace, Dorchester, wished Wallis an enjoyable summer and commented, 'We are lazily living in Dorset doing nothing'. However, Dorset scenes were to feature a lot in his output over the next few years. In a subsequent letter dated 13 July 1894, Meade also suggested his 1893 RA exhibit *In Hardy's Country*, which he said was lying idle at his London agent, Stewart of 51 Rathbone Place, but he needed to hire another 60" x 40" frame, as he had used the frame of this work for his other 1894 RA exhibit *Gorse by the Sea*, which he had promised to Manchester. Clearly, this proved impossible. The work *A Breezy Day* may have become one of his five RA exhibits of 1895 – *Breezy Afternoon*.

1894 EXHIBITS

- ***Passing Shadows*** (should be ***Lengthening Shadows***) [159]
- ***The Wrestlers*** (RA 1894) [171]
- ***A Breezy Day*** [177]
- ***Passing Shadows*** (RA 1894) [179]
- ***When Day is Waning*** (RA 1894) [181]
- ***A Cornish Road*** (RA 1891) [223]

When Day is Waning was one of the works shortlisted for possible acquisition by Nottingham Castle for its permanent collection. None of the works have been located.

Nottingham Guardian, 13 October 1894: 'Mr Arthur Meade is represented by seven or eight canvases of unusual interest and fine feeling for effects of colour and atmosphere. *When Day is Waning*, is filled with the quiet charm of the evening. The foreground is in shadow, all green and purple, with a rough road down which go a flock of sheep past a clump of fir trees and bushes, touched with autumn colours. Beyond, running across the centre of the picture, are trees and the golden fields, all bright and ruddy in the dying sunlight; and then the blue-green sea, backed by distant headlands, capped with a straight bank of purple cloud and a green sky, pale and delicate. It is all quiet and most harmoniously in colour and displays an artist who has the gift of a true and sympathetic insight into Nature's moods.

'Another good picture of Mr Meade's is No 179, *Passing Shadows*, a sandy cart track running across a moor, with blue hills and water far away on the horizon and dark patches thrown on the beach by the clouds overhead. *A Breezy Day* shows this artist at home with the sea, deep blue waves streaked with lighter green, and tipped here and there with white crests, and over all a finely coloured sky. His *Wrestlers*, from this year's Academy, is a clever effect of bare flesh under intense sunlight – a party of lads seen under a very bright light on the sands against a sandcliff, almost white in the sunshine.

'A second *Passing Shadows* of his (No 159) [this is probably *Lengthening Shadows*] shows the distant meadows and woods glowing in sunlight and dotted with cattle, and the foreground darkened with the shadow of one of the few clouds in a bright sky – all quiet and reposeful in tone.'

23. This will be Frederick Sargent, who surprisingly was not included in the show himself.

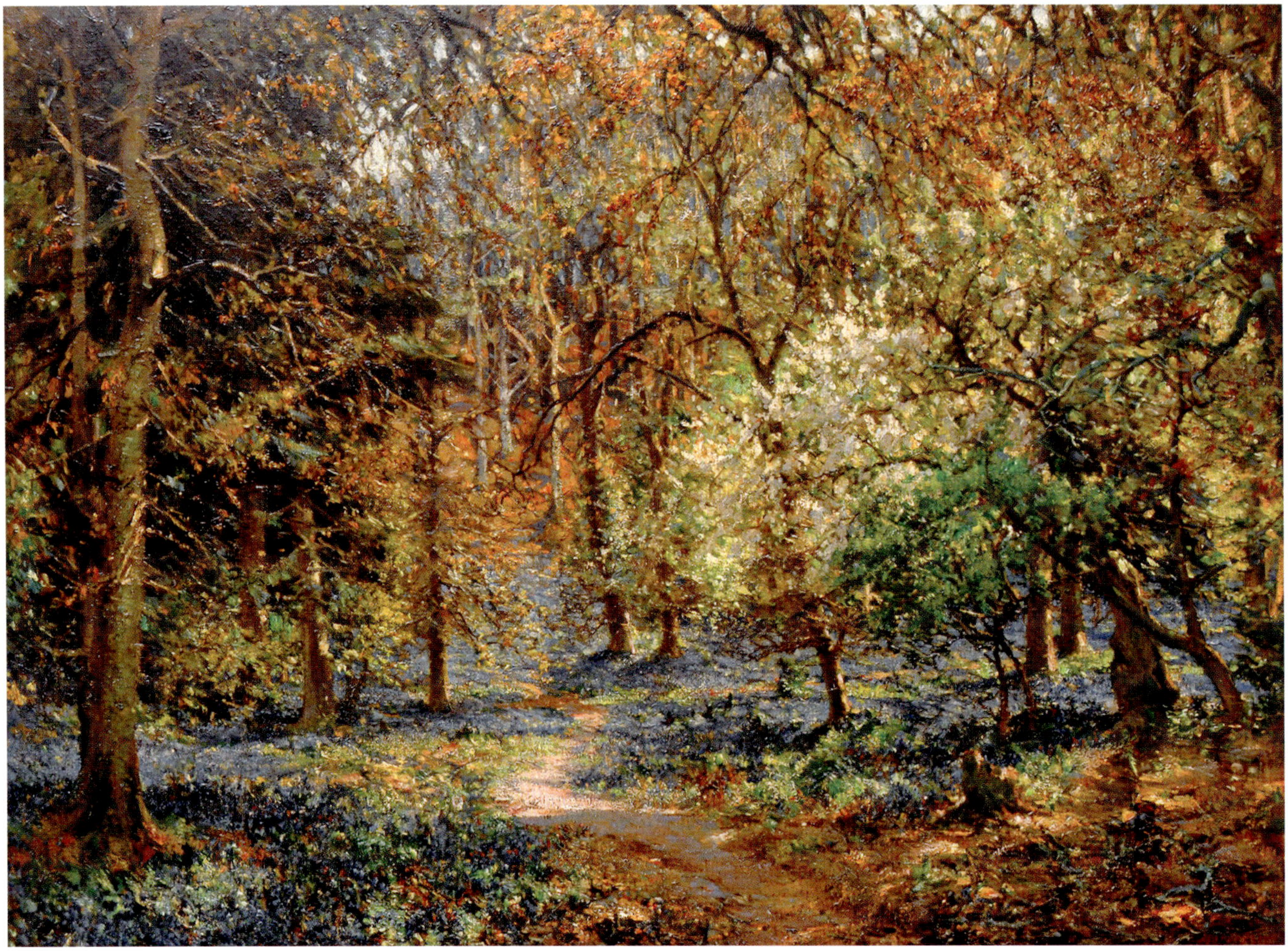

pl. 29 **Arthur Meade**
The Merry Springtime
1905 • oil on canvas • 114 x 151.5 cm
private collection

2015 EXHIBIT

The Merry Springtime (pl. 29, private collection): This painting, which was hung at the Royal Academy in 1905 and described as 'a dream of colour', was one of Meade's major successes, winning a medal at the Carnegie International Exhibition in Pittsburgh in 1907 and also being hung at the Franco-British Exhibition of 1908. On Meade's death, Borlase Smart still recalled the impact of this 'bewitching subject' when he had seen it at the Academy – 'how beautiful it looked in contrast to the browns and greys of the majority of the surrounding pictures'. As, following this success, he concentrated on such subjects for a few years, the artist became known as 'Bluebell Meade'.

MILNER, Frederick RBC, RWA

unknown c.1855–1939 ST IVES

Fred Milner went on to become a long-term resident of the St Ives art colony and an important figure in the landscape section. However, in the early 1890s, he was based in Cheltenham and was more a regular visitor than a permanent member of the community. His speciality was tranquil landscapes.

Studied at Wakefield and Doncaster Schools of Art.
1880: Earliest known painting, but initially worked as a bank clerk.
1889: By now, married and living in Cheltenham.
1890: Visited Carbis Bay with fellow Cheltenham artist, Laurence Scott, and met Alfred East, who became life-long friend.
1892: First RA exhibit *Low Tide on the Bar*.
1898: Settled permanently in St Ives.
1901: Moved to 'Zareba', Trelyon Hill, St Ives, where based until his death.
1905–1939: Long-term occupant of the enormous 2 Piazza Studios.

1894 EXHIBITS

- ***Noonday in Summer*** [142]
- ***Low Tide on the Bar*** (RA 1892) [143]
- ***In September*** [144]

None of these works have been located.

***Nottingham Guardian*, 13 October 1894**: 'Mr Fred Milner sends three works. *Noonday in Summer* is a river almost white under the noonday heat, which runs between two meadows, with one great cloud reflected in its waters. *Low Tide on the Bar*, he gives as a good colour effect, with the waves of the deep blue sea breaking upon the bar in the distance, with a set of posts marking the course of the stream, which runs over the red sands to join it, which will be lost to sight when the incoming tide rushes over the flats. *In September* is a stretch of marshland and river, pale green in tones, with a peculiar winged cloud in the sky.

MORRIS, Charles Greville RBA

SALFORD, LANCASHIRE 1861–c.1923 PARKSTONE, DORSET

Morris was a good friend of Adrian Stokes and was one of the first Bushey students to settle in the town. He was an integral part of the landscape section in the colony during the early 1890s, and returned to visit on a regular basis, as his mother had settled in the town.

Father cotton spinner.
Early 1880s: Studied in Paris under Bollinger, Collin and Courtois.
1886: Worked in Pont-Aven with Adrian Stokes and exhibited Breton scenes at RA and Paris Salon in the years 1886–8.
1888–90: Studied at Herkomer Art School, Bushey.
1888: Attended Stokes' Chantrey Supper in St Ives in August.
1890: Founder member of St Ives Arts Clu, and contributed to Dowdeswell's exhibition.
1891–2: Based at Mount Trafford, Eccles, Manchester.
1892: His widowed mother, Fanny Louisa Morris, settled in St Ives.
1893: Back in St Ives for most of the year and contributed to Cornwall Fisheries Exhibition in Truro.
1894–1900: Irregular visitor, occasionally using St Ives exhibiting address and participating in Show Days, but subjects tend to be of Berkshire.
1901–2: Based in Bath, but revisited St Ives.
1905: Now based in Dorset, where remained for rest of his life, revisiting St Ives on occasion to see his mother, who lived in Albany House until her death in 1918.

WALLIS CORRESPONDENCE

Charles G. Morris was back in Bushey when he responded to Wallis' letter. The five works included in the exhibition were the ones that he recommended, mentioning that *Marshland* was the painting that Wallis had seen in his studio. This, being hung at that year's RA exhibition, was to be picked up from his London agent, whereas the others, with the exception of *The Haunt of the Coot and Heron* (91 x 61 cm), which was being lent by its purchaser, Mr Knowles, were to be collected from his Manchester agent. Morris clearly liked to work on a vast scale for *The Last Warm Blush of Fading Day* was 127 x 102 cm, *Marshland* was 168 x 122 cm and *Evening* was a massive 198 x 152 cm.

1894 EXHIBITS

- ***Marshland*** (RA 1894) [53]
- ***A Cornish Marsh*** [106]
- ***The Haunt of the Coot and Heron*** (RA 1890) (R.M. Knowles) [112]
- ***The Last Warm Blush of Fading Day*** (RA 1891) [175]
- ***Evening*** (RA 1893) [176]

Marshland was donated to Manchester Art Gallery in 1909 by William Hill, but is currently unexhibitable. None of the other paintings have been located, albeit *Evening* was owned by St Ives Town Council until sold off in 1968. R.M. Knowles was a J.P. in Bingham, Nottinghamshire. Morris was one of the artists whose work was shortlisted for acquisition by Nottingham Castle for its permanent collection.

***Nottingham Guardian*, 13 October 1894**: 'In *Evening*, Mr C Greville Morris has produced a picture which places him among the best of the Cornish landscapists. As the title of the picture suggests, the subject is a quiet English scene in that last lingering light that clothes with pathetic beauty even the ugliness of a modern town and doubles the mysterious loveliness of the countryside. We have here simply a rough and rut-covered road with pools of water after heavy rain, leading to some farm buildings, surrounded by tall bare trees. On one side the cultivated ground rises sharply, all ploughed and purple earth, with the distant hedgerow showing black against the pale sky strewn with sunset coloured cloudlets. Along the road, the cows wander towards their distant sheds, after being milked. The shadows of evening are creeping over the face of the earth and the landscape has that touch of sadness that suggests the coming of winter.

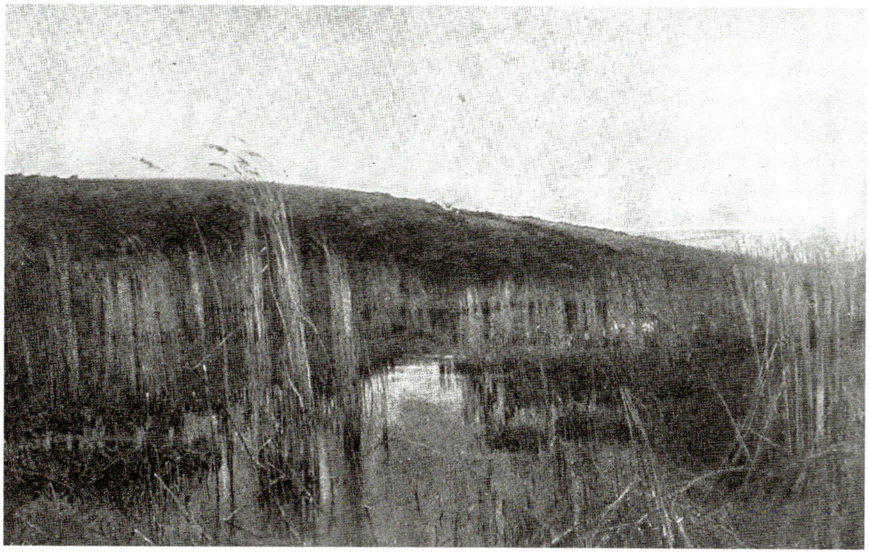

Greville Morris
Marshland
from the 1894 exhibition catalogue

'Another good work by Mr Morris is *The Haunt of the Coot and Heron*, a tract of marshy land with trees in the centre, with pale grey and purple clouds above the brown rushes; and a similar subject *A Cornish Marsh*. Again in *The Last Warm Blush of Fading Day*, we get that poetic insight into the last fair moments of the spent day.'

The Last Warm Blush of Fading Day had been highly rated when it had been exhibited on Show Day in St Ives in 1891: 'In this sunset picture, Mr Morris has simply surpassed himself. Still, calm and restful, it is full of gorgeous light, so subtly dealt with that the harmony of the composition is never disturbed. In the foreground stands a grand old tree – partly in the after-glow, partly in soft twilight – whilst around the trunk a grey tangle of wild undergrowth climbs and twines for a little way and then snakelike glides weirdly away into the night, until it is lost among the reeds, pools and weeds of the marshes.[24] The work was paired with Sir John Millais' *Glen Birnam* at the RA to good effect, as both paintings had similar colouring

NORTH, Arthur William (the late)

HUDDERSFIELD 1857–87 HUDDERSFIELD)

Given that little-known artist, Arthur North had died, aged only 29, in 1887, and had only been involved briefly with the Newlyn colony in 1885–6, his inclusion in the 1894 exhibition is a surprise. However, the two works were lent by Messrs Holroyd of his home town of Huddersfield, who also contributed works by Fred Hall, Chevallier Tayler and Julius Olsson, and so it was probably at their suggestion that he was represented.

1882: Studied at Antwerp
1885: Visited Newlyn.
1886: RA exhibiting address given as Cliff House, Newlyn.

1894 EXHIBITS

- ***A Studio*** (Messrs W&P Holroyd) [37]
- ***Net Making*** (Messrs W&P Holroyd) [38]

24. SIWS, 11 April 1891.

OLSSON, Albert Julius RA, RBA, PROI, RWA, RBC, NEAC

ISLINGTON, LONDON 1864–1942 DALKEY, COUNTY DUBLIN

At the time of the 1894 Exhibition, Julius Olsson, who was of Swedish extraction and who was largely self-taught, was only just beginning to make a name as a marine artist. The following year, he established a School of Painting in St Ives, devoted, uniquely, almost exclusively to landscape and marine art, which was to gain an international reputation, whilst he himself became hailed as the leading British seascape painter of his generation.

Father Swedish timber merchant. Brought up in London but educated for some years in Sweden. Worked four years in a bank, and spent some time in the Channel Islands, with a 'pot-boiling' marine painter.
1887: Visited Cornwall and exhibited a Newlyn scene.
1888: Exhibited a St Ives scene at the RBA. Married.
1890: Settled in St Ives. First successes at RA and Paris Salon. Participated in Cornish Artists' Exhibition at Dowdeswells in December.
1895: Opened Cornish School of Landscape and Marine Painting, working initially with Louis Grier (q.v.) and then, from 1898, with Algernon Talmage (q.v.).
1903: Won medal at Paris Salon with *The Storm*.
1911: *Moonlit Shore* purchased by the Chantrey Trustees.
1914: Elected ARA.

WALLIS CORRESPONDENCE

Olsson was in Walberswick, another coastal area that was frequently visited by artists, when he responded to Wallis on 6 May 1894. He commented, 'I hope to be able to send one (or two) large ones and perhaps half a dozen smaller sea pictures, which I trust you will be able to hang together.'[25] One of the paintings had been on show at Leeds.

1894 EXHIBITS

- ***Moonrise*** [68]
- ***Bleak North Wind*** [170]
- ***Rippling Breeze*** (Messrs W&P Holroyd) [184]
- ***Eastern Glow*** [185]
- ***Afternoon Sun*** [186]
- ***Evening*** [187]

None of these works have been located. *Bleak North Wind* was illustrated in *Black and White's Handbook to the Royal Academy and New Gallery* in 1894.

***Nottingham Guardian*, 29 September 1894**: 'Mr Julius Olsson is another artist who revels in the sea. His *Rippling Breeze, Eastern Glow and Afternoon Sun* are three excellent studies of breaking wave or tumbled sea, under different aspects of light. A more important picture of his is *Evening*, a bold and dexterous painting of a great bay of sand and distant headlands, as seen from the high cliffs above, which are crowned with grey wind-torn thorn trees. Great clouds touched with the reflected lines of the banished sun, fill the sky, which occupies a large part of the canvas, forming a harmonious whole with the somewhat sad tones of the landscape.

'His *Bleak North Wind* is a clever rendering of a blue-green sea, with white sailed boats under a cold sky, massed with battalions of white and purple clouds. He is also represented by a Moonlight sketch.'

25. Letter dated 5 June 1894.

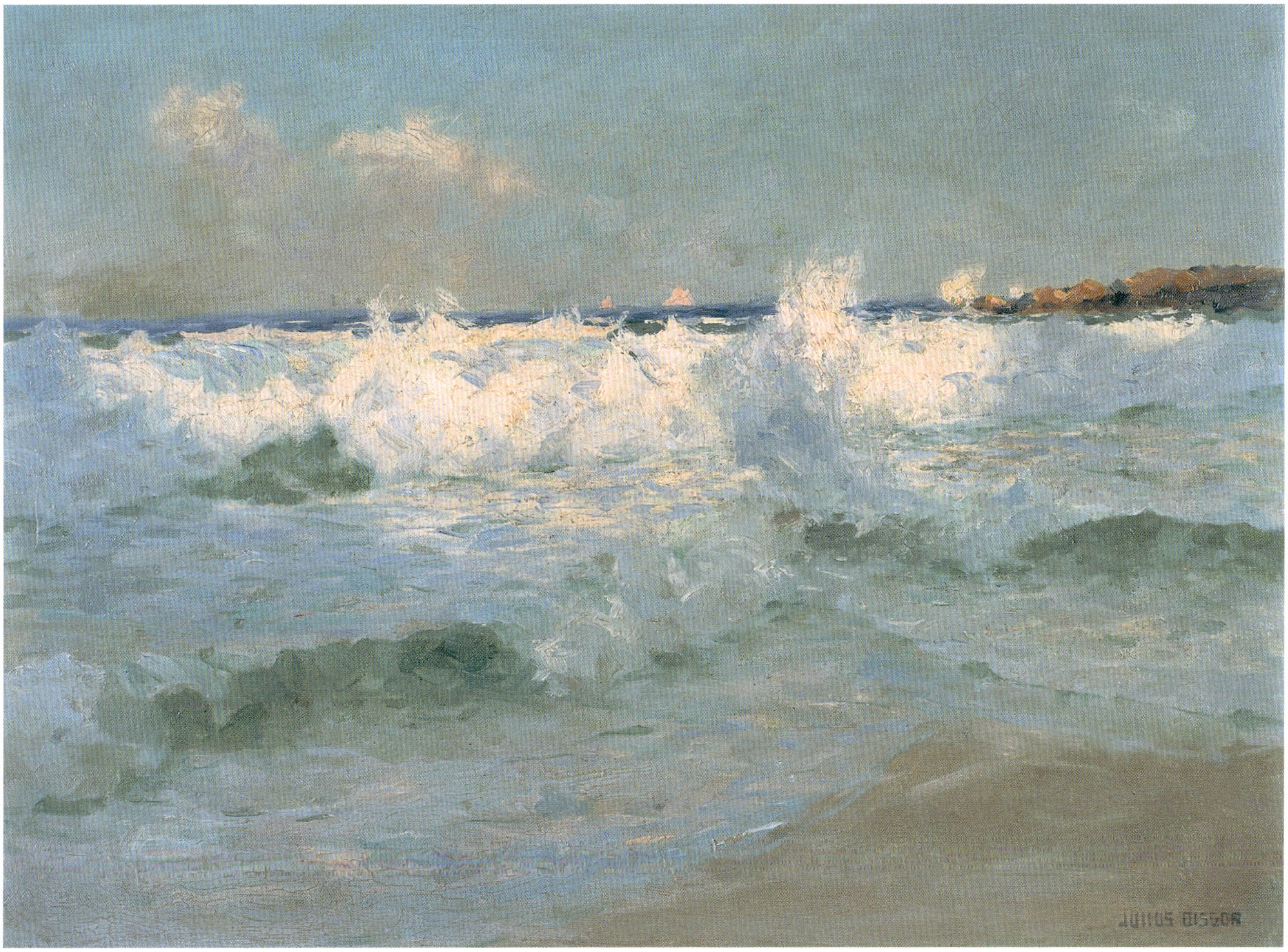

pl. 30 **Julius Olsson**
Porthmeor Beach Seascape
oil on canvas • 61 x 76 cm
St Ives Arts Club

2015 EXHIBIT

Porthmeor Beach Seascape (pl. 30, St Ives Arts Club): Pure seascapes were not in favour with Victorian viewers, who liked their marine paintings filled with drama and incident. St Ives artists, like Olsson, were at the forefront of making the genre more acceptable. This work was given by Olsson as a wedding present to fellow artist, William Titcomb (q.v.), in April 1892, and was donated by Titcomb's daughter, Loveday Cogan, to the St Ives Arts Club in the 1980s.

OSBORN, William Evelyn

CHELSEA 1868–1906 CHELSEA

Will Osborn was a landscape painter, fond of depicting evening effects, who was briefly involved with the St Ives art colony during the early 1890s, during which time he met his wife, fellow artist, Dorothy Worden. His premature death has resulted in his work being little known and, for some time, he was mistakenly referred to as an Australian.

Father Inspector of Factories. Nephew of the celebrated artist, Emily Mary Osborn (1828–1925).
1886: Living in Rochdale with his family when first exhibited.
1891: First recorded as a visitor to St Ives in June and spent winter in the town.
1892: Took part in Carnival Masquerade and Show Day.
1893–6: Regular visitor to St Ives.
1896: Married in Exeter fellow artist, Dorothy Worden, whom he is likely to have met in St Ives, and they settled in Exmouth.
1906: Now living in Chelsea, with his wife running the Blue Kailin Restaurant, frequented, inter alia, by Augustus John and Henry Lamb, who befriended the normally 'dejected' and 'melancholy' Osborn. Accordingly, his death, from an overdose of chloroform, which he used to get to sleep as he had been suffering from neuralgic pains, may not have been accidental.

1894 EXHIBITS

- ***April Twilight*** [3]
- ***Fading After-glow, St Ives Bay*** [4]

***Nottingham Guardian*, 13 October 1894**: 'Mr Will E. Osborn is another St Ives landscape painter, who attempts to extract as much poetry as he can from the subjects he depicts. Both his pictures in this exhibition are filled with the last lingering light of day. *April Twilight* is a great bay of blue sea, sand-fringed, with the foreground already darkened by the coming night, whilst above the distant coastline, with its sandhills, the daylight still lingers, and above it the clouds are yet faintly tinged with red. In his *Fading After-glow*, we have the sweep of St Ives, with its grey sand curving round to the little town, where the lights are beginning to twinkle faintly. All this is seen through the branches of some almost leafless trees, with bunches of blossom, which rise among the roofs of houses on the immediate foreground, which adds a quaint effect to his study in pale grey and purple.

2015 EXHIBITS

St Ives Pier (pl. 31, Falmouth Art Gallery): In 1888, Smeaton's Pier was extended and a second lighthouse erected on the end of the new breakwater. However, the original 'pepperpot' lighthouse was not removed. Here, Osborn only shows the original pier and lighthouse, but there is no indication that he visited St Ives

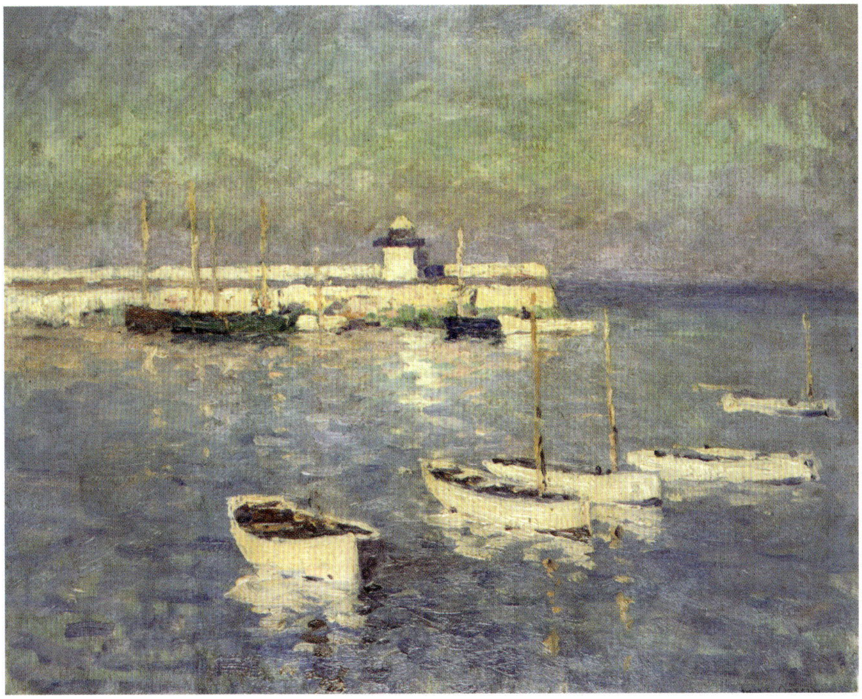

pl. 31 **Will Osborn**
St Ives Pier (Smeaton's Pier)
oil on canvas • 51 x 61 cm
Falmouth Art Gallery Collection

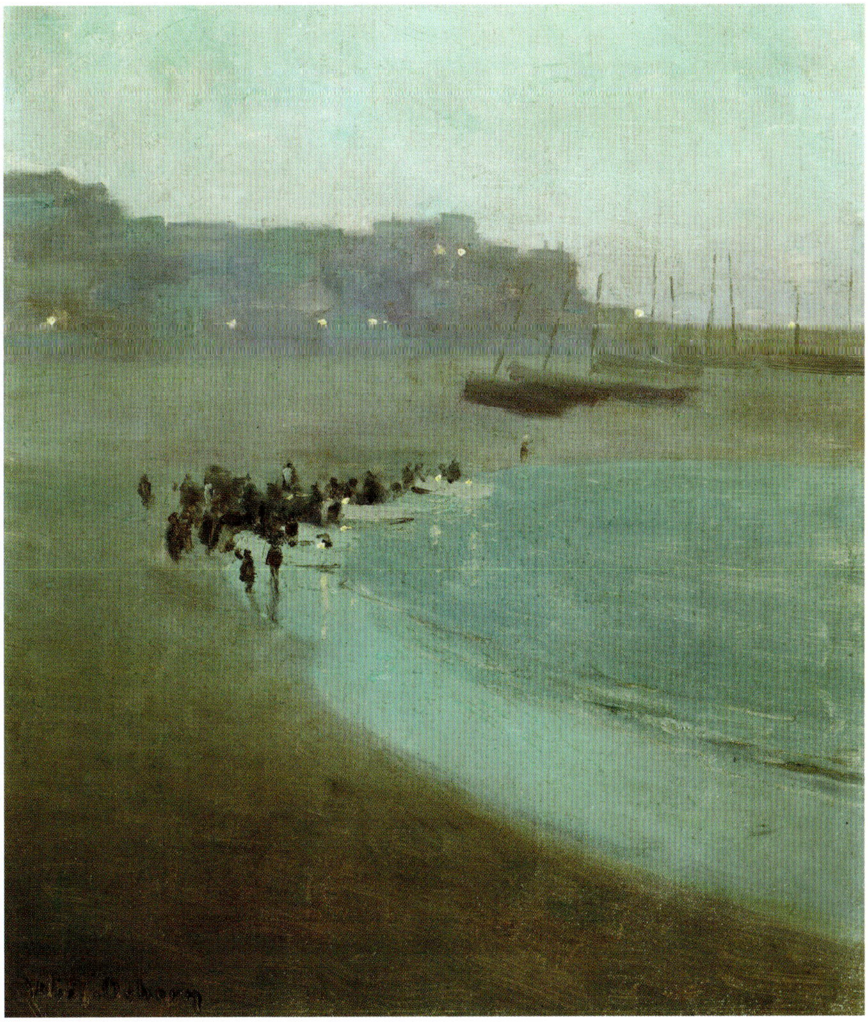

pl. 32 **Will Osborn**
Beach at Dusk, St Ives Harbour
c.1895 • oil on canvas • 51 x 61 cm

prior to 1888, and a number of artists, preferring the unique shape of the old lighthouse, chose to ignore the extension and the new lighthouse in their paintings of the harbour.In depicting this sunset scene, Osborn appears to have worked at great speed, using thick brush strokes and a loose, impressionistic painting style to capture the fleeting effect of the evening light on the quiet waters of the harbour.

The painting was part of a group gifted to Falmouth Art Gallery in 1923 by Alfred Aaron de Pass (1861–1952), a South African businessman and art benefactor, in memory of his sons, Sub-Lieutenant Crispin De Pass, who died in 1918 at Cambrai serving with the tank corps, and John De Pass who was killed in a skiing accident on the Chamossaire mountain, Switzerland, in January 1923.

Beach at Dusk, St Ives Harbour (pl. 32, Tate; appearing at Penlee only): This is a typical example of the tranquil, dusk, mood pieces that the St Ives artists were renowned for at the time, with flashes of golden light emanating from lanterns on the boats and around the harbour. The painting was presented to the Tate anonymously in memory of Sir Terence Rattigan in 1983.

RHEAM, Henry Meynell

BIRKENHEAD 1859–1920 PENZANCE

Henry Rheam, who was a first cousin of Henry Tuke, was a Newlyn-based figure painter, who worked primarily in watercolour. His early work conformed closely with the rural realist ethos of the Newlyn School, but he went on to develop a romantic, late Pre-Raphaelite style.

Family Quakers.
Early 1880s: Studied in Germany, in London at Heatherley's (1884) and in Paris at Academie Julian (1886).
Late 1880s: Worked in Polperro, but played cricket for artist teams in West Penwith from 1887.
1890: Settled in Newlyn. Participated in the Cornish Artists show at Dowdeswells.
Mid-1890s: Concentrated on more romantic subjects hereafter.
1897: Became the Hon Secretary/Curator of the Newlyn Society of Artists, a post he retained until his death.
1900: Married Alice Elliott and lived at Boase Castle Lodge, Belle Vue, Newlyn.

WALLIS CORRESPONDENCE

Whilst initially responding to Wallis from Newlyn in April, Rheam sent in list of four works that he wished to include in July, whilst staying at Hilston, Burstwick, near Hull. However, he subsequently managed to sell two of these works and so he was only represented by two paintings in the exhibition. He may also have sold *Wrecked* as he asked for it to be sent to George Hidderley of Stockport, when the show finished. He commented to Wallis, in a letter dated 12 December 1894, 'It is rather disappointing that so few pictures have been sold from such a good exhibition.'

1894 EXHIBITS

- ***A Study*** [98]
- ***Wrecked*** [99]

Neither of these works have been located.

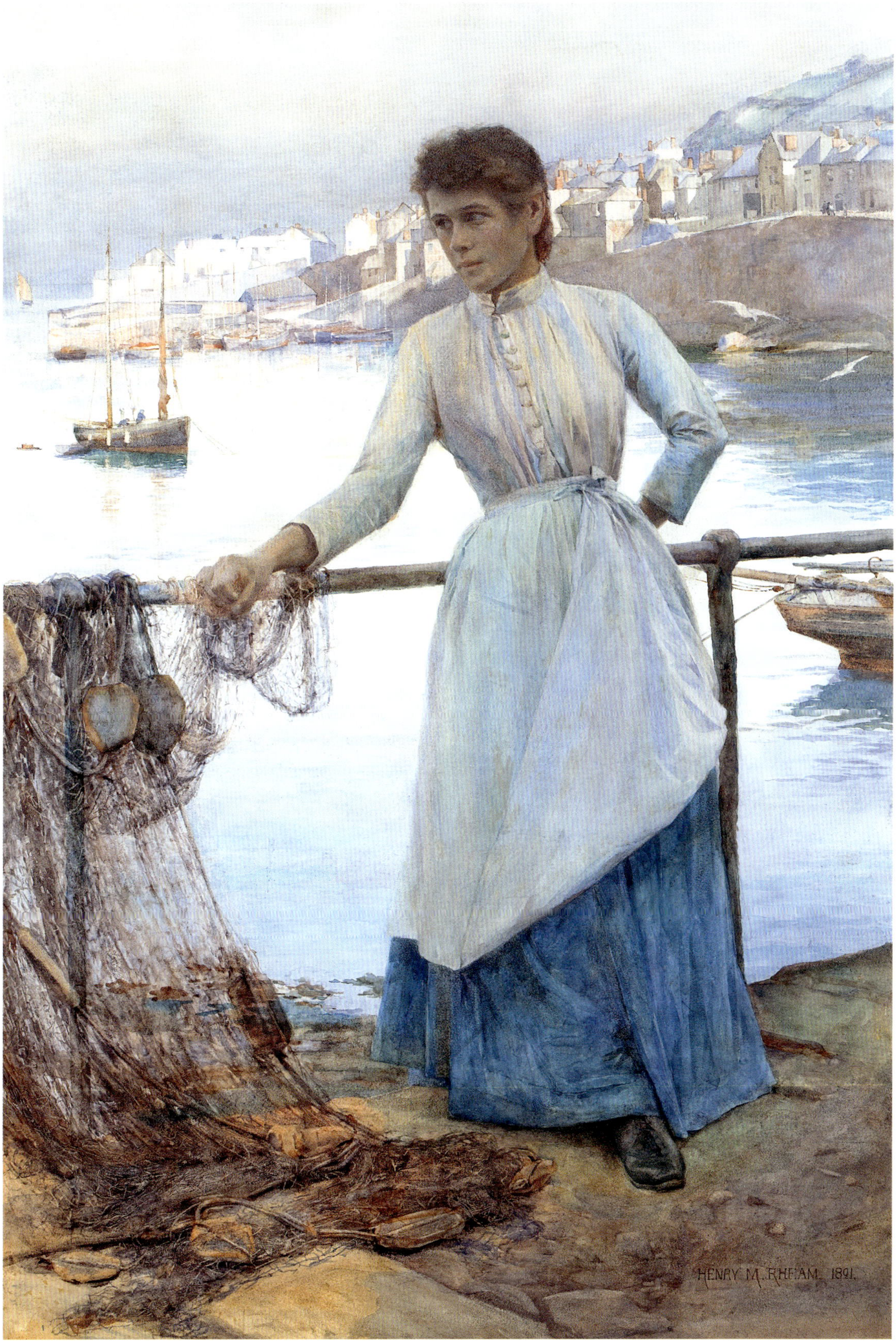

pl. 33 **Henry Meynell Rheam**
Girl in Blue
1891 • watercolour • 89 x 58 cm
Penlee House Gallery & Museum

***Nottingham Evening Post*, 6 October 1894**: 'We must also pass over the very excellent watercolour work of fine quality which is to be found in Mr Henry Meynell Rheam's pictures, notably an interesting study of a pretty girl, whose dark brown hair falls on her shoulders, clad in dark blue bodice and white apron, and a book on her lap; and a dramatic figure of a woman called *Wrecked*. She has just sprung up from her chair, the newspaper dropped upon the ground, and one hand flung up to her head, as she realizes her loss with sudden acuteness.'

Wrecked had been exhibited at the RI in 1892, where it had been very well received, and when it was included amongst the artist's Show Day exhibits in Newlyn in 1893, the reviewer for *The Cornishman* had commented that 'the expression and pose of the figure defy adverse criticism'.[26]

2015 EXHIBITS

Girl in Blue (pl. 33, Penlee House Gallery & Museum): This attractive work, dating from 1891, may well feature the same model, as in *A Study* included in the 1894 exhibition. It was clearly painted *en plein air*, as the girl's blouse and apron have taken on colour from the reflections upon the water in the harbour. The painting, which was included in the seminal 'Artists of the Newlyn School' exhibition in 1979.

RICHARDS, Frank RBA

BIRMINGHAM 1863–1935 BOURNEMOUTH

Frank Richards was a landscape and figure painter from Birmingham, who was involved with the Newlyn colony from 1890-95, before settling in Dorset, and concentrating on portraiture and watercolours of local scenes. In addition to doing a portrait of Queen Victoria for a Shanghai Club, he was also patronised by Sir Merton Russell-Cotes and has a number of works held by the Russell-Cotes Art Gallery & Museum, Bournemouth, where he spent the last years of his life.

1884: Believed to have moved to Bournemouth area and, in 1885, recorded as working from Lulworth, Dorset.
Late 1880s: Having an interest in sculpture, toured Italy and did illustrations for periodical magazines.
1890: Dated paintings place him in Newlyn and he took part in the Dowdeswell exhibition.
1895: In an article for *The Studio*, entitled *Newlyn as a Sketching Ground*, he wrote that he had been in and around Newlyn for five years and knew it under 'all its various changes and aspects, according to time of year and weather ...'
1896: Moved to London before settling in Wareham, Dorset by 1902.

WALLIS CORRESPONDENCE

Richards' correspondence with Wallis was written from Addison Studios, Blythe Road, West Kensington. His initial letter was not dated until 26 July 1894, perhaps suggesting that he was not initially considered eligible. Wallis had clearly requested *Christchurch Minster, Hampshire* and Richards gave him the address of the current owner. He also said that *The Last Match*, a smaller picture then at York, would be available, and suggested that Wallis made contact with his father to request the three works that he did lend to the show, which he indicated were all Newlyn scenes. He added, 'They are the only ones worth having – don't accept others'.

26. *The Cornishman*, 30 March 1893.

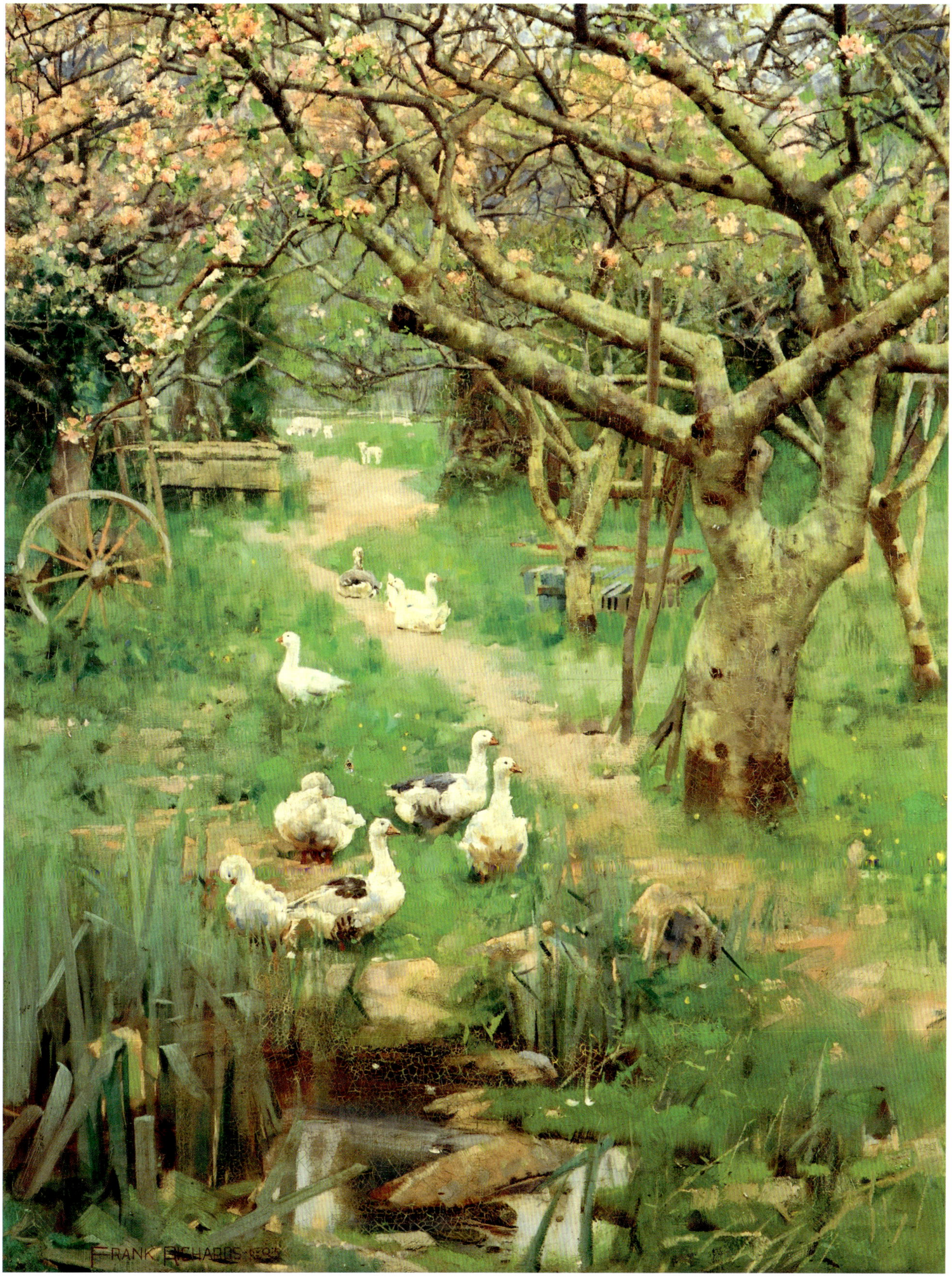

pl. 34 **Frank Richards**
In a Cornish Orchard
1893 • oil on canvas • 101 x 75 cm
The Russell-Cotes Art Gallery & Museum, Bournemouth

1894 EXHIBITS

- ***The Last Match*** [9]
- ***Gone Down with all hands!*** (S. Wall Richards) [22; watercolour]
- ***A Cornish Courtyard*** (S. Wall Richards) [79; watercolour]
- ***A Street Scene*** (S. Wall Richards) [100; watercolour]
- ***Christchurch Minster, Hampshire*** (RA 1892) (Joseph Cooke) [169]

Samuel Wall Richards, the artist's father, and Joseph Cooke lived in Bournemouth. Other than *Christchurch Minster, Hampshire*, none of the works have been located and his contributions to the 1894 exhibition were not reviewed.

Christchurch Minster, which combines a long-distance view of Christchurch Priory (incorrectly termed by the artist a Minster), with a foreground of geese and boats drawn up out of the water, was exhibited in an unfinished state in Newlyn on Show Day in 1892.[27] Both its size and its unusually bright colouring were remarked upon, and the church was deemed a very picturesque structure. Richards did manage to finish it in time for the RA exhibition, as it was, apparently, 'a much discussed exhibit' there. Since it was shown at Nottingham, a figure standing by the boats has been added. The painting is now owned by Shepton Mallet Town Council, and is on loan to Highcliffe Castle.[28]

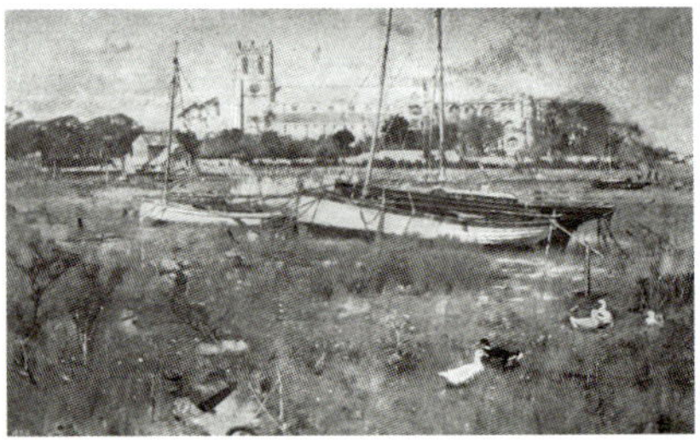

Frank Richards
Christchurch Minster, Hampshire
from the 1894 exhibition catalogue

2015 EXHIBIT

In a Cornish Orchard (pl. 34, Russell-Cotes Art Gallery & Museum, Bournemouth): This painting, which is dated 1893, was painted for the famous actor, Sir Henry Irving, to remind him of scenes from his Cornish childhood. It is said to have been done by Richards whilst working in a studio in St Ives.[29] It was later acquired by Sir Merton Russell-Cotes (1835–1921), who, at the turn of the twentieth century, designed and built for himself a sumptuous private residence on Bournemouth's East Cliff, with the intention that it should continue as a permanent art museum after his death. Reviewing the work in the *Bulletin of the Art Gallery* in March 1935, the year of Richards' death, it was said that it 'must have been at that period a daring flight into a high-keyed melody in complementary pink and green. Though he allowed himself considerable liberty in the use of colour, the artist has carefully restrained the whole by a faultless display of a knowledge of tree forms and a judicious use of cool greys in moulding their limbs.'[30]

ROBINSON, Henry Harewood

ALMONDBURY, YORKSHIRE 1850–1904 ST IVES

Harry Robinson was one of the initial settlers of the St Ives art colony in 1885 and, although not a major artist, was an integral figure in the local community, becoming a J.P., and a key officer of the St Ives Arts Club.

Father wool merchant. Trained as a barrister before studying art.
1882–3: Studied at Académie Julian, Paris. First exhibit at Paris Salon in 1883.
1884–5: Worked in Concarneau. First exhibit at RA in 1884.
1885: Settled in St Ives with Dorothy Webb, whom he married in April 1886.
1890: Very involved in establishment of St Ives Arts Club, where served as Secretary for nine years and President for two. Participated in Cornish Artists' Exhibition at Dowdeswells in December.
1897: Elected J.P.
1904: Died prematurely.

27. *The Cornishman*, 24 March 1892.
28. *Bulletin of the Russell-Cotes Art Gallery & Museum*, March 1935, p. 6.
29. Ibid., p. 5.
30. Ibid., pp. 5–6.

WALLIS CORRESPONDENCE

As Wallis' initial letter to Harry Robinson of 2 April 1894 had not been answered, he wrote again on 9 July and received a reply on 13 July from Hotel Mallet, Marlotte, Seine-et-Marne, France, where Robinson and his wife were based that summer whilst working in the Forest of Fontainebleau. Initially, Robinson did not put forward *Evening*, which had been hung at the Paris Salon that year, as 'it was a variant of the same motive' as *Between the Wood and the Sea* and he feared that 'they might injure each other'.

In a subsequent letter dated 2 August 1894, he also suggested his 1889 RA exhibit *The last hour of daylight*, which had been bought by a D.J. Tonkin of Highbury New Park, but the purchaser had died recently and he did not have details of his personal representatives. In that letter, he indicated that he and his wife were likely to be leaving their hotel in a week or so and intended to pass through Nottingham on their way back home. He also mentioned that he had done that summer some twenty pastels of the Forest of Fontainebleau, some of which might be of interest. As seven were included in the exhibition, it seems likely that the Robinsons did meet Wallis in Nottingham and agreed the inclusion not only of these pastels and *Evening* but also further works that came up from St Ives. However, the Robinsons did not visit the exhibition whilst it was on.

1894 EXHIBITS

- ***On the Cornish Coast*** [19]
- ***Seascape*** [23]
- ***At A Devon Farm*** (George H. Ball) [61]
- ***St Ives Bay*** [65]
- ***The Edge of the Forest, Forest of Fontainebleau*** [72; pastel]
- ***Pines, 'Long Rocher', Forest of Fontainebleau*** [73; pastel]
- ***'In the Gorge aux Loups', Forest of Fontainebleau*** [74; pastel]
- ***Near the 'Mare aux Fees', Forest of Fontainebleau*** [81; pastel]
- ***Thunder Cloud, 'Long Rocher', Forest of Fontainebleau*** [82; pastel]
- ***Near the 'Mare aux Fees', Forest of Fontainebleau*** [83; pastel]
- ***'Near the Mare aux Fees', Forest of Fontainebleau*** [97; pastel]
- ***Between the Wood and the Sea*** (RA 1894) [163]
- ***Evening*** (RA 1891) [164]

Robinson's work appears on the market very rarely and none of these works have been located. George Ball lived in Liverpool.

***Nottingham Evening Post*, 6 October 1894**: 'Mr Harewood Robinson is represented by a number of canvases, of which *Between the Wood and the Sea*, exhibited in this year's Academy, and *Evening* are the best. In the former, three girls are burning sticks at a small fire at the edge of a cliff wood, which overlooks the sea and the distant coast-line. The foreground grass and the stooping girls are already in shadow, but another of the maids and the trunks of the trees are gilded with the last rays of the sun, while the full, round, yellow moon is every moment growing more golden. This picture, tender in tone, is the artist's best. *Evening* is a similar effect – great, bare, sunlit tree trunks, with glimpses of sea and red roofs between them, and a man burning sticks at a small fire. Mr Robinson also exhibits some studies of the sea of lesser interest and a series of small pastels done among the woods of Fontainebleau.'

Robinson clearly considered *Between the Wood and the Sea* to be his best work, as he invariably lent it to subsequent exhibitions.

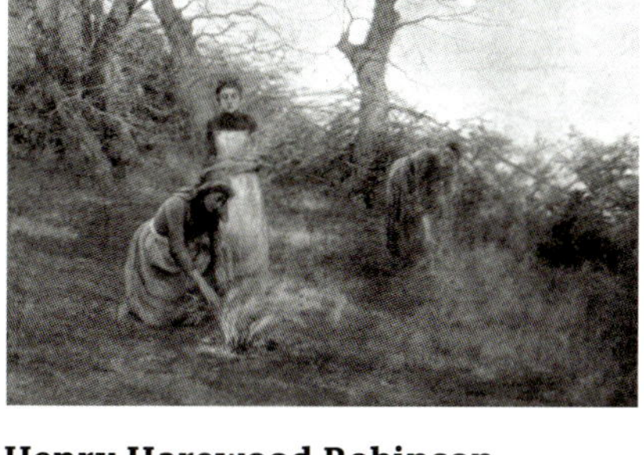

Henry Harewood Robinson
Between the Wood and the Sea
from the 1894 exhibition catalogue

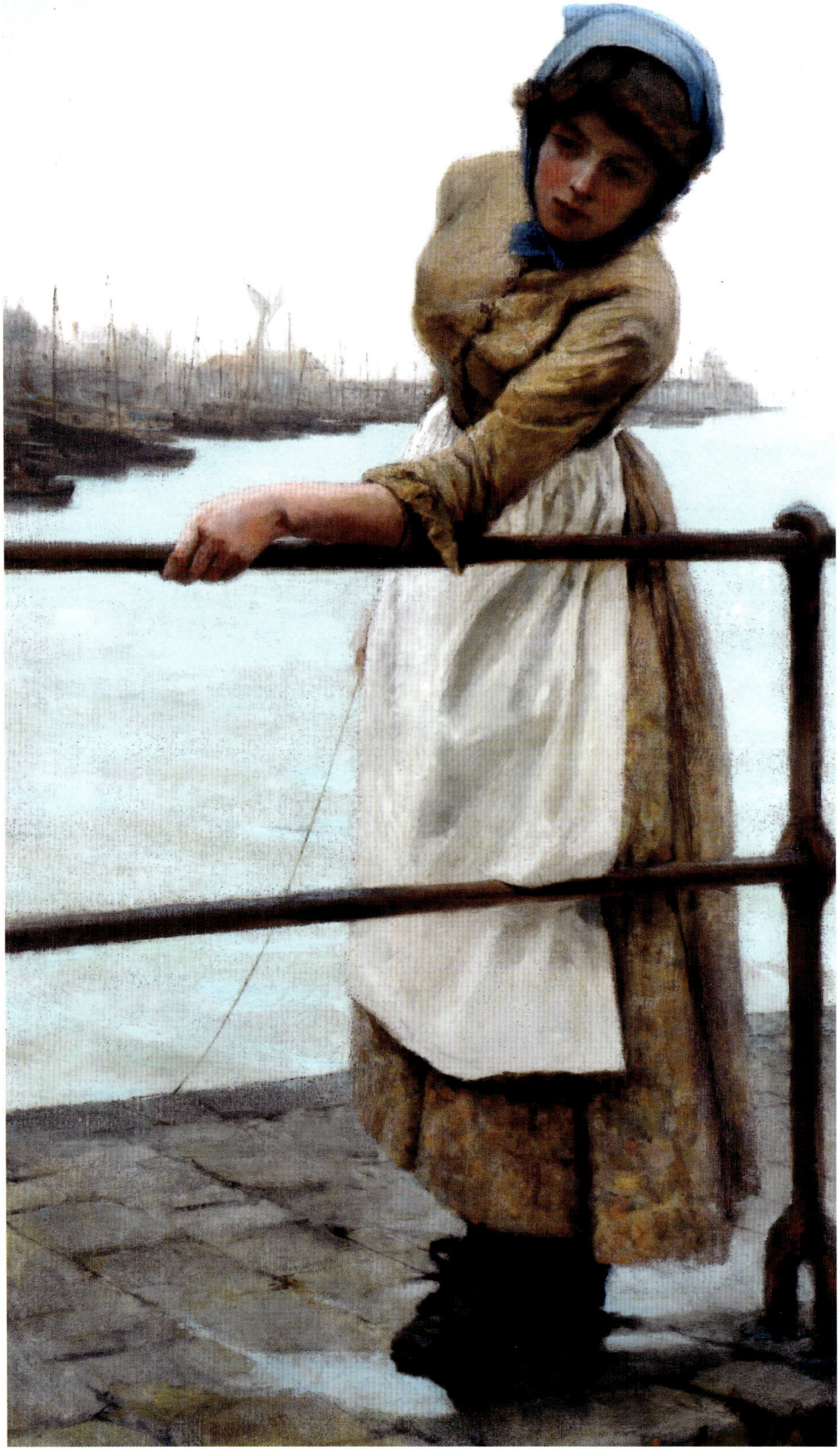

pl. 35 **Henry Harewood Robinson**
Two Nibbles
oil on canvas • 80 x 45 cm
Bowerman Charitable Trust

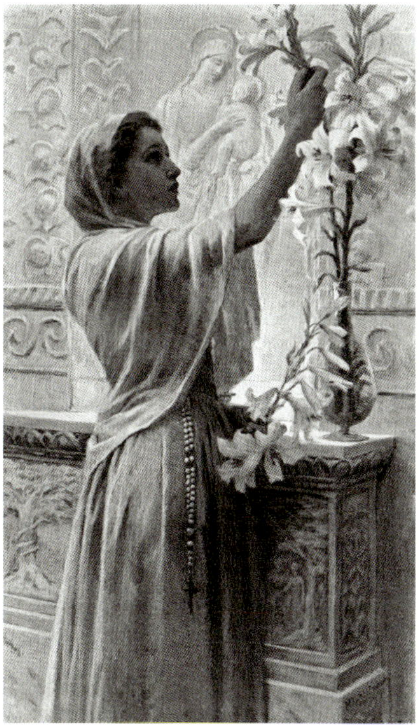

Dorothy Webb Robinson
The Shrine
from the 1894 exhibition catalogue

2015 EXHIBIT

Two Nibbles (pl. 35, Bowerman Charitable Trust): This painting depicts a local St Ives girl, wearing a blue scarf around her head, standing with a fishing line on a breakwater. In the background can be seen Smeaton's Pier, terminating with the pepperpot lighthouse. This would suggest that the painting dates from before 1888, when the extension to the pier was built, but it is difficult to place the breakwater on which the girl is standing, if this is not the West Pier, which was not built until 1894. So far, no record has been found of the painting being exhibited, unless it was shown as *A Fisherman's Wife* (RHA 1889: £50).

ROBINSON, Maria Dorothea Webb

BELFAST 1840–1920 YORK

Irish-born Dorothy Robinson was one of the initial settlers of the St Ives art colony in 1885 and developed a considerable reputation as a figure painter in the 1880s and 1890s.

Father muslin and shawl manufacturer. Family strict Quakers.
1848: Family moved to Dublin.
1857–79: Occasional study at Dublin School of Art.
1880–3: Studied at Académie Julian, Paris.
1883–5: Based in Concarneau with future husband, Harry Robinson.
1885: Settled in St Ives with Harry Robinson, whom she married in April 1886 in Randalstown, Northern Ireland.
1890: Founder member of St Ives Arts Club in August. Participated in Cornish Artists' Exhibition at Dowdeswells in December.
1890s: Her work was regularly illustrated in Royal Academy Pictures, and she enjoyed good sales to public collections and American private collectors.
1904: After death of her husband, rarely painted again.

WALLIS CORRESPONDENCE

The initial response made to Wallis, when he finally made contact with the Robinsons in Marlotte, Seine-et-Marne, France, was made by Harry Robinson on behalf of his wife and, in this letter dated 13 July 1894, he indicated that she would like to be represented by *The Shrine*, *Too Late* and *At a Breton Farm*, which had been exhibited at the Paris Salon in 1884. However, she herself wrote to him on 23 July 1894, enclosing the authority to the RA to release to Nottingham her exhibit of that year, *The Three Fisher Wives*, and urging him also to make application to Mr Armitage, who had been the purchaser of *A Volunteer for the Lifeboat*, 'as it represents quite another type of subject from the others that I can send'. She also lamented that two of the pictures which she also would have liked to have contributed were 'the property of gentlemen in New York and are therefore unavailable'.

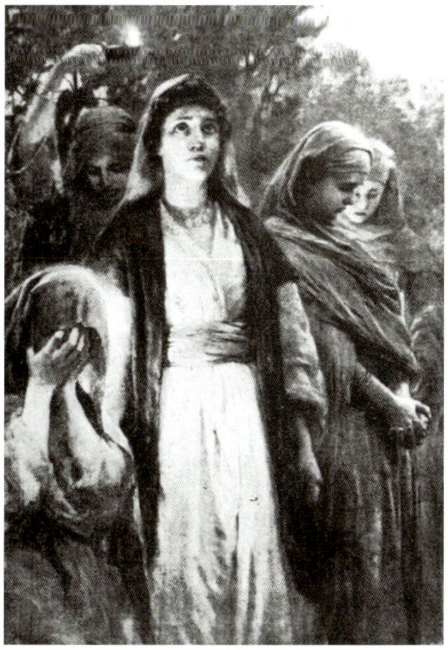

Dorothy Webb Robinson
Too Late
from *Royal Academy Pictures 1892*

1894 EXHIBITS

- ***Too Late*** (RA 1892) [32]
- ***The Shrine*** (RA 1893) [128]
- ***'Three wives sat up in a tower, And they trimmed their lamps as the sun went down'*** (RA 1894) [129]
- ***A Volunteer for the Lifeboat*** (RA 1892) (B. Armitage) [130]

The first two works have not been located and, surprisingly, her contributions were not mentioned in reviews. *Too Late!* featured the five foolish virgins and

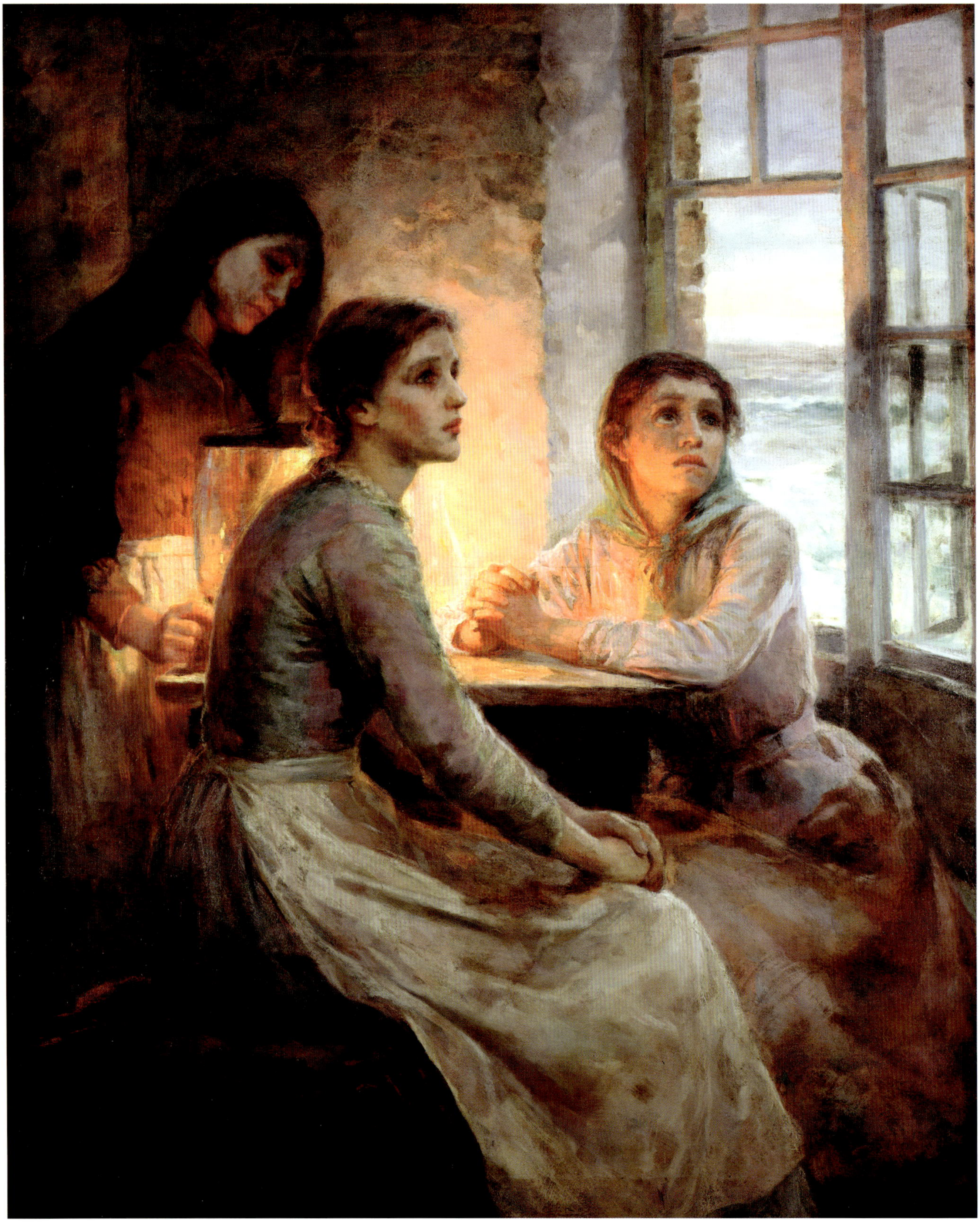

pl. 36 **Dorothy Webb Robinson**
'Three wives sat up in a lighthouse tower, And they trimmed their lamps as the sun went down'
oil on canvas • 117 x 94 cm
Leeds Museum and Galleries (Leeds Art Gallery)

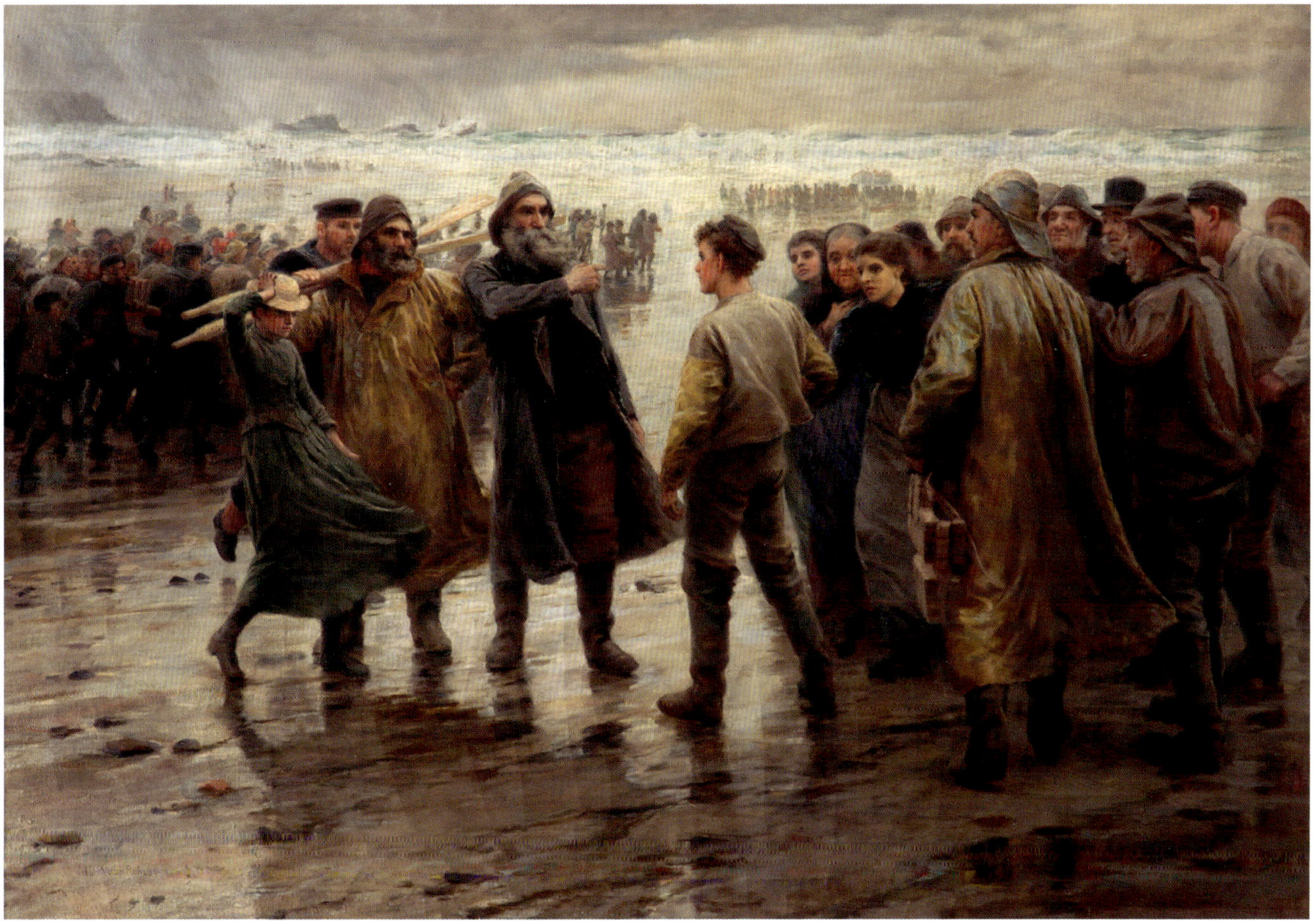

pl. 37 **Dorothy Webb Robinson**
A Volunteer for the Lifeboat
oil on canvas • 115 x 160 cm
Salford Museum & Art Gallery

was expected to be one of the Pictures of the Year, when it was first exhibited on Show Day in St Ives in 1892, whilst *The Shrine* depicted a young woman adjusting a display of lilies on a memorial in a chapel. The ornateness of the carving, and the girl's clothing, indicate that it may have been painted whilst the Robinsons were in France.

2015 EXHIBITS

'Three wives sat up in a lighthouse tower, And they trimmed their lamps as the sun went down' (pl. 36, Leeds Museum & Galleries – Leeds Art Gallery): This title was drawn from Charles Kingsley's popular poem, *The Three Fishers*, written in 1851, which also contained the well-known refrain *But men must work and women must weep*, which had been used as a title by many artists, including fellow Cornish colonists Walter Langley (1882), Frank Emanuel and even her husband, Harry (RA 1889).

The first verse of the poem commences *'Three fishers went sailing away to the west, Away to the west as the sun went down'* and, at the time of the Nottingham exhibition, Dorothy was working on a depiction of this scene, showing three fishermen in a boat, weighing anchor at sunset, with Smeaton's Pier, St Ives, in the background. Her Nottingham exhibit, though, dealt with the second verse, in which three worried wives sit cramped in the lighthouse tower, trying to see how their husbands' boat is coping with a storm. One fiddles with the lamp, as the other two look with concern at the deteriorating weather. A glimpse of the raging sea can be seen through the window. All Victorian viewers would have known that the third and final verse commenced *'Three corpses lay out on the shining sands, In the morning gleam as the tide went down'*. The painting was acquired by Leeds Art Gallery in 1895.

A Volunteer for the Lifeboat (pl. 37, Salford Museum & Art Gallery): Whilst normally known as *A Volunteer for the Lifeboat*, the full title of this painting is *Second Crew for the Lifeboat: A Volunteer!*, with the sub-title *'Those dread sands where doomed ships come, To cast their wrecks upon the steps of home.'* It caused a sensation when it was exhibited on Show Day in St Ives in 1891. The reviewer for the local paper sets the scene, 'Through the driving storm mist – beyond the white crested breakers, is the dim form of the fated ship, drifting helplessly on shore. Already the lifeboat has attempted once to reach her, but after bravely battling with the fury of the gale for hours, has been compelled to return – her men exhausted – for a fresh crew. The hurricane is at its height – the sea is a madness of foam, and the air is full of the noises of the wind and thick with the flying spray and drifting rain. Yet there is no hanging back amongst the men – all are pressing forward eager to volunteer, and the choice of the last man has fallen upon a young lad whose mother is tearfully entreating him not to risk his life in such weather. This great work of Mrs Robinson is full of movement – grand in scenic effect, faithful in detail, and will doubtless be one of the pictures of the year.' An enormous work, it depicted a large number of the local fishermen, including, of course, the lifeboat crew and the coastguard. In this respect, the work of Robinson was unlike that of any other female artist working in Cornwall, for she alone seems to have overcome the local prejudices that considered it unseemly for a woman to be seen painting out of doors and for an adult male to be a model for a female artist.

It is not known whether *A Volunteer for the Lifeboat* was inspired by an actual scene witnessed by Robinson, but she will have observed the considerable team effort required to get the boat launched and have admired the bravery of the lifeboat crew, as, in the age of steam, they battled tempestuous seas in an oar-propelled craft. The addition of a sub-title drawn from literature seems quite superfluous in this instance, but her major works rarely lacked a literary reference, and so the local fisherfolk and local landmarks were adapted to fit an imagined literary scenario.

ROWE, Tom Trythall NEAC

BRIDGWATER, 1858–1937[31]

Trythall Rowe, both of whose parents were Cornish, had fraternised with Stanhope Forbes in Brittany and, in the 1880s and early 1890s, he paid a number of brief visits to Cornwall. His inclusion in the 1894 exhibition was the result of a recent stay in St Ives.

1881: Recorded in Census as an art student in Chelsea.
1882–3: Working in Brittany; in autumn of 1883, shared rooms with the American, Arthur Hoeber, at Quimperlé and accompanied Stanhope Forbes on his visit to Pont-Aven.
1884: Paid brief visit to Newlyn in October.
1886: Founder member of NEAC. Also became member of Nottingham Society of Artists, with whom exhibited regularly, leading to his work being in the permanent collection of Nottingham Castle Museum.
1889: Visited St Ives and exhibited at Falmouth in 1890.
1894: Worked in St Ives in June-July and so asked to be included in the Nottingham show.
1901–1911: Recorded as living at the Wickersley Institute, South Yorkshire, owned by William Titcomb (q.v.).

1894 EXHIBITS

- ***Street Scene, St Ives*** [80]
- ***Old Houses, Digey, St Ives*** [95]
- ***Back Street, St Ives*** [96]
- ***A Hay-field*** [121]

None of these paintings, probably watercolours, and no other Cornish works by Rowe have been located. They were not reviewed.

STOKES, Charles Adrian Scott RA ROI, VPRWS, NEAC, RWA

SOUTHPORT, LANCASHIRE 1854–1935 LONDON

Adrian Stokes was the leading St Ives artist at the time of the 1894 exhibition. Having spent the best part of a decade working alongside French and American landscape masters on the Continent, he introduced into St Ives a new style of landscape painting, which emphasized the effect rather than the subject, and drew on the Barbizon School artists' concentration on tones and values. The purchase by the Chantrey Trustees of his work *Upland and Sky* in 1888 had led to an influx of landscape students down to St Ives.

Father was an Inspector of Schools. Studied at Royal Academy Schools 1872–5.
1876: First success at Royal Academy; visited Pont-Aven for first time.
1881–6: Regular visitor to both Concarneau and Pont-Aven.
1884: Married Austrian artist, Marianne Preindlsberger (q.v.) in Pont-Aven.
1886: Visited Skagen, Denmark to see Pedr Kroyer.
1887: Settled in St Ives.
1888: *Upland and Sky* bought by the Chantrey Trustees for the nation.
1889: Won medal at Paris World Exposition with *On the Dunes, Cornwall*.
1890: Founder member of St Ives Arts Club in August. Participated in Cornish Artists' Exhibition at Dowdeswells in December.
1891: Left St Ives briefly to live in Italy.
1893: Won medal at Chicago for *The Setting Sun* (Harris Museum, Preston).

31. His date of birth is normally given as in 1856, but the 1861 Census records him as aged two.

1898: Left St Ives and visited Holland.
1905: First of five trips to Hungary, which resulted in a book.
1919: Made Royal Academician (ARA 1910).
1925: Published book *Landscape Painting*.

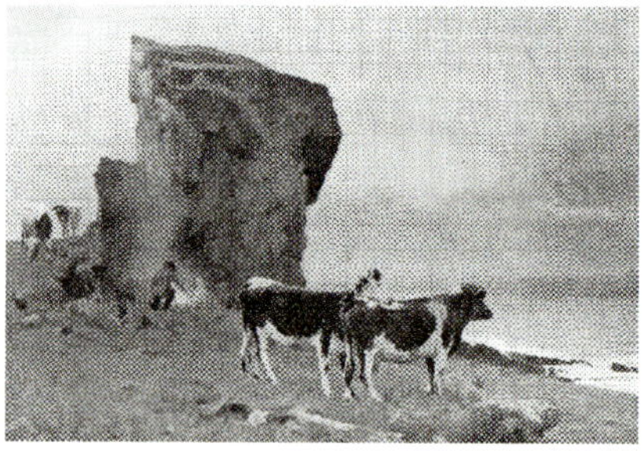

Adrian Stokes
On a Cornish Cliff
from the 1894 exhibition catalogue

WALLIS CORRESPONDENCE

Stokes wrote to Wallis initially on 20 April 1894 from 27 Avonmore Road, West Kensington. Wallis had clearly requested the loan of *The Setting Sun*, a work hailed as *the* landscape of the year when it was first exhibited, in the place of honour, at the New Gallery in 1891. However, this had been bought by leading Australian collector, George McCulloch and Stokes responded, 'With regard to *The Setting Sun*, Mr McCulloch has been so kind as to lend it to the Chicago exhibition and, since its return to The Guildhall, so that though I would much like to be represented at Nottingham by that picture, I fear that I cannot ask for it. His expressed wish to hang it immediately on his own walls seems to forbid me to do so.' In its place, Stokes suggested *On A Cornish Cliff*, which needed to be collected from Leeds, where it was in a show, and *Breezy Pastures*, then at the Atkinson Art Gallery, Southport.

On 28 July 1894, Stokes wrote to Wallis from Longpre les corps saint, Somme, France, indicating that, as he had not seen the paintings to be exhibited at Nottingham for some time, he anticipated that they might need washing and varnishing, and requesting Wallis to arrange for someone suitable to do that.

At the end of the exhibition, Stokes asked for *Breezy Pastures* to be sent on to an exhibition in Dublin.

1894 EXHIBITS

- ***On a Cornish Cliff*** (RA 1893) [213]
- ***Breezy Pastures*** [214]
- ***Off St Ives*** (RA 1890) (Edwin Walker) [215]

Edwin Walker lived in Huddersfield. None of these paintings have been located.

***Nottingham Evening Post*, 6 October 1894**: 'Mr Stokes is a landscape artist of high poetic power, and he is an animal painter as well. *Breezy Pastures* is a fine rendering of green wind-swept downs, with the sand showing in places, and the blue sea with distant coastline on the horizon. White clouds, pale purple in the shadows, are hurried along through a blue sky in the wind, which also blows about the wool of the sheep that graze along the upland. It is a delightfully breezy canvas, with fine colour. A large rock of extraordinary shape, partly covered with a green growth, fills the centre of *On a Cornish Cliff*, against which a man is lighting a fire. Both sea and sky are grey with the evening light. Two large cows stand in the foreground. The whole tone of the work is a quiet grey-green. *Off St Ives* ... is his best work here. It is a beautiful breezy day, and the green waves break in small rollers, running up over the flat sandy shore, with golden and purple reflections from the blue sky above, while the small fishing boats with brown sails go scudding along. This is a beautiful picture, filled with the freshness of the salt air.'

2015 EXHIBIT

The Harbour Bar (pl. 38, Leeds Museum and Galleries – Leeds Art Gallery): This painting was originally exhibited on Show Day in St Ives in 1889 under the title *Over the Bar*. It was painted from below the ferry on the Lelant side of the Hayle river, at eventide and, like his Chantrey work, *Upland and Sky*, the majority of the picture is devoted to the sky. Such works were intended to evoke a mood and to inspire poetic associations, and clearly the local reviewer was so moved,

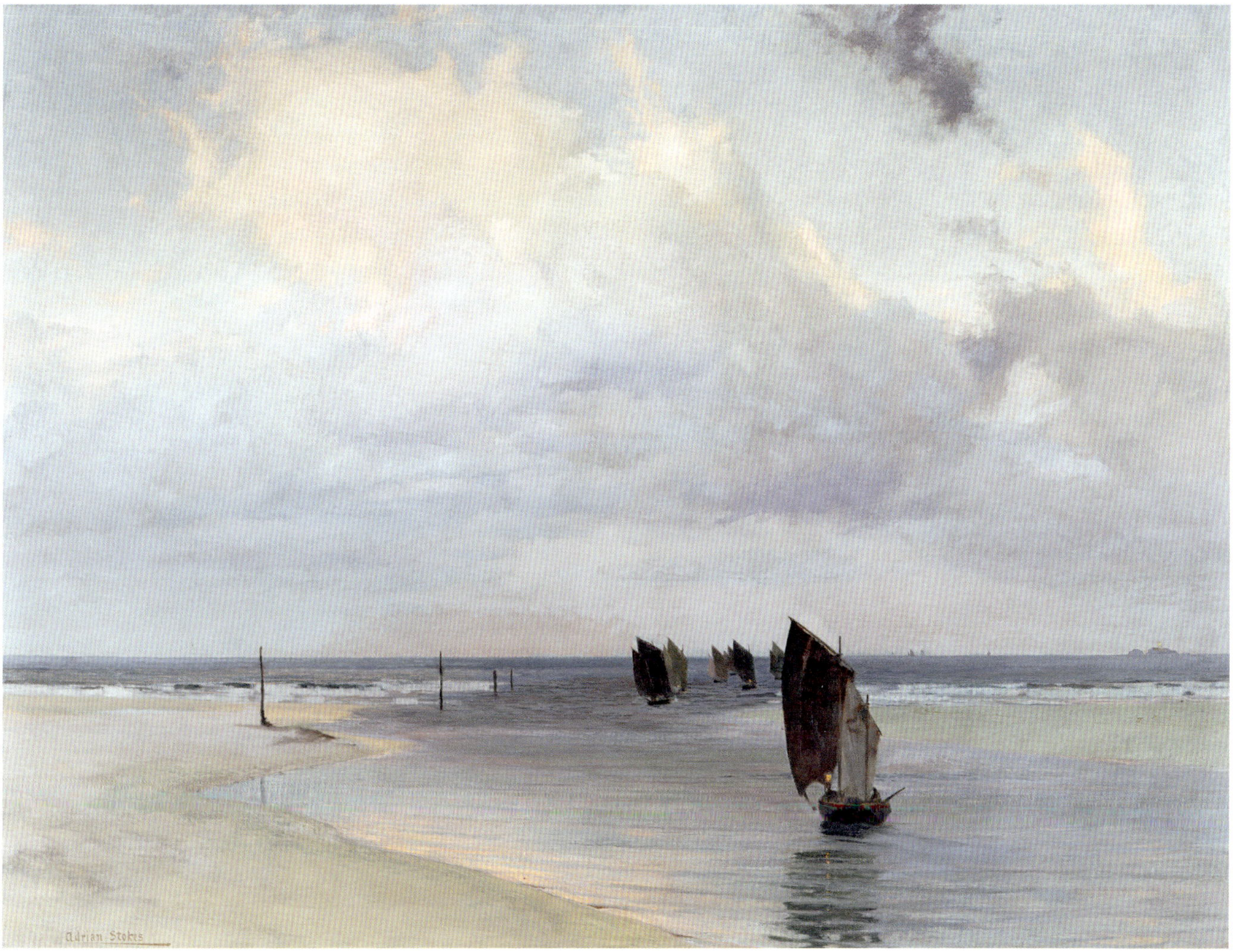

pl. 38 **Adrian Stokes**
The Harbour Bar
oil on canvas • 140 x 183 cm
Leeds Museum and Galleries (Leeds Art Gallery)

'He shows us the mouth of the winding river, the tumbling waters on the bar, the wet sands from which the tide has just withdrawn, the curve of the eastern shore, the darkly-lit waters of St Ives bay, deeply shadowed in the distance by clouds which hang low in the northern sky. Overhead is a mass of cumulus cloud, which an hour ago was dazzlingly white in the afternoon sun: now the flush of evening has enriched and mellowed it, and on its background of blue ether, it glows delicately warm in tone, like the flesh of a salmon-trout. Godrevy, the mariner's ministering angel, is holding out her newly-lit beacon light, and the lug-sailed fishing boats, slipping out on the ebb, also bear their lights, gleaming yellow while the twilight lasts; soon, however, in the darkness to deepen to a spark of crimson fire. The quiet peacefulness of the evening light, the softly sliding boats, the superb sky, whose warmth is reflected in the waters on the edge of the bay, combine to produce in the spectator a feeling of infinite restfulness.'[32] When Stokes left St Ives temporarily in 1891 it was his peculiar gift 'of feeling and transmitting the spell that comes with the contemplation of lovely and tranquil scenes' that was most remembered.[33]

STOKES, Marianne Leopoldine (née Preindlsberger) ARWS

GRAZ, AUSTRIA 1855–1927 LONDON

Marianne Stokes, the Austrian wife of Adrian Stokes, was a highly regarded artist in her own right. By the time of the 1894 exhibition, she was beginning to move away from the rustic naturalist depictions of children, which characterised her early Cornish work, to more decorative compositions with subjects drawn from folk-lore, myth and religion.

Father was commercial book-keeper. Studied at Graz under Schwach (1870–4), Munich (1874-80) and Colarossi's, Paris (1880-2 – silver medal 1882).
1881–5: Visited Concarneau and Pont-Aven; married Adrian Stokes in Pont-Aven in 1884.
1884: Awarded Mention Honorable at Paris Salon for her Pont-Aven scene *Condemnée à Mort* (later re-named *A Parting*).
1885: Exhibited for first time at the Royal Academy. *A Parting* sold to Walker Art Gallery, Liverpool.
1887: Settled in St Ives.
1890: Won gold medal in Munich with *Go thou must play alone, my boy, Thy sister is in heaven*. Founder member of St Ives Arts Club in August. Participated in Cornish Artists' Exhibition at Dowdeswells in December.
1891: Sold *Edelweiis* to the Prince Regent of Bavaria.
1893: Won medal at Chicago for *'Hail Mary!'*.
1895: After a trip to Italy, started to work in tempera on *gesso grosso* inspired by the Renaissancc masters.
1898: Left St Ives; later productive visits to Holland and Hungary.

1894 EXHIBITS

- ***'Hail Mary!'*** (RA 1891) [63]
- ***Little Things Amuse Little Minds*** (W.A. Michael) [69]
- ***A Parting*** (RA 1885) (Liverpool) [166]
- ***The Magic Flute*** (RA 1887) (H. Fernie) [167]
- ***Childhood's Treasures*** (W.A. Michael) [168]

Childhood's Treasures is now owned by Nottingham Castle Museum and *'Hail Mary!'* is in New Zealand. Neither *Little Things Amuse Little Minds*, which showed a boy dancing a paper figure on a straw taken from an overturned basket of onions, nor this version of *The Magic Flute* have been located, albeit it was illustrated in *The Graphic* in 1887.

32. *The Cornishman*, 11 April 1889. *The Times* (1 June 1889) felt that it was his best work yet: 'the sea is painted with a rare sense of beauty, and the sky is admirable'.
33. SIWS, 23 May 1891.

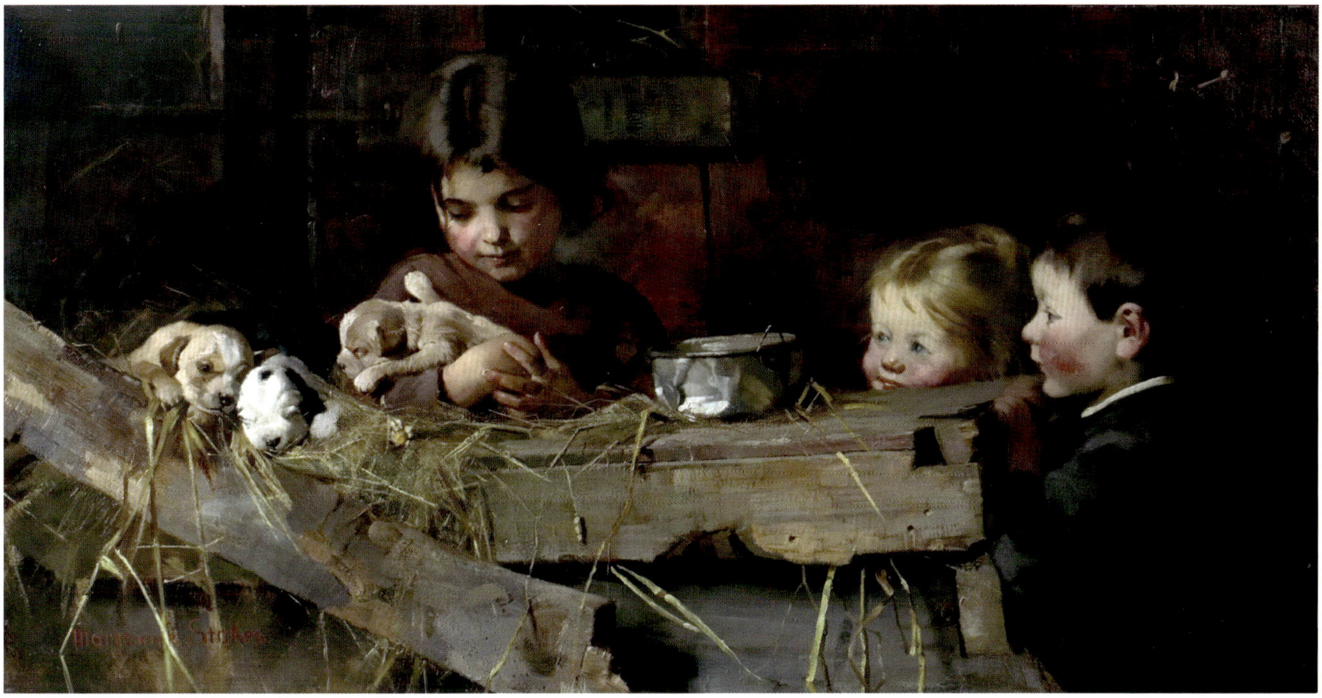

pl. 39 **Marianne Stokes**
Childhood's Treasures
1886 • oil on canvas • 68 x 127 cm
Nottingham City Museums and Galleries/
© The Artist's Estate

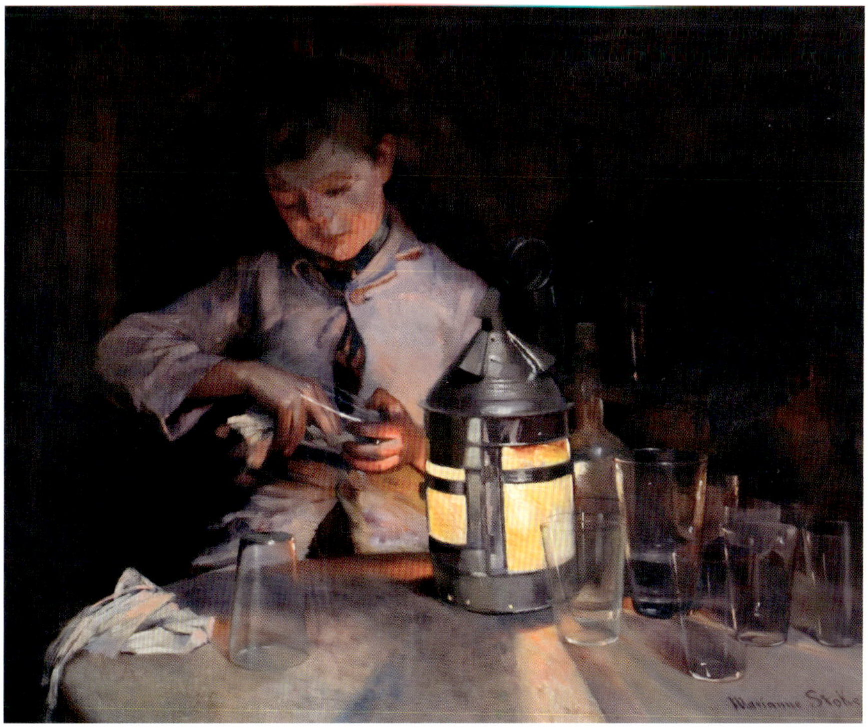

pl. 40 **Marianne Stokes**
Lantern Light
1888 • oil on canvas • 83 x 102 cm
Penlee House Gallery & Museum/
© The Artist's Estate

Nottingham Evening Post, 6 October 1894: 'Four of Mrs Marianne Stokes' pictures will delight all lovers of young children and young animals, whilst artists will admire the fine quality of the vigorous painting. *A Parting* represents a small boy seated on straw against a white wall in some stable. A young calf with its four legs tied together, has its head resting on the boy's lap, and the two young creatures gaze into one another's eyes with all the despair of a first parting. *The Magic Flute* is a charmingly humorous portrait of a small boy seated in the corner of a shed against a heap of mangold wurzels. His legs are stretched in front of him and an old blanket is over his shoulders. He has turned some of the roots around him into magic pigs, by the aid of four wooden sticks for legs, and holes for eyes, and, with fat cheeks blown out, he solemnly blows his penny whistle, and, in his imagination, they are dancing round him, as Ulysses' comrades did around Circe. This picture will appeal vividly to all those who love to watch children at their games... Very different is her *'Hail Mary!'*, in which the Angel of the Annunciation, red-haired, with a branch of a lily in his hand, is partly hidden behind the figure of the Virgin, who stands facing the spectator with a rapt look on her face. The two haloes cut one another, Mary's falling partly across the Angel's face, giving a peculiar effect, cleverly managed.'

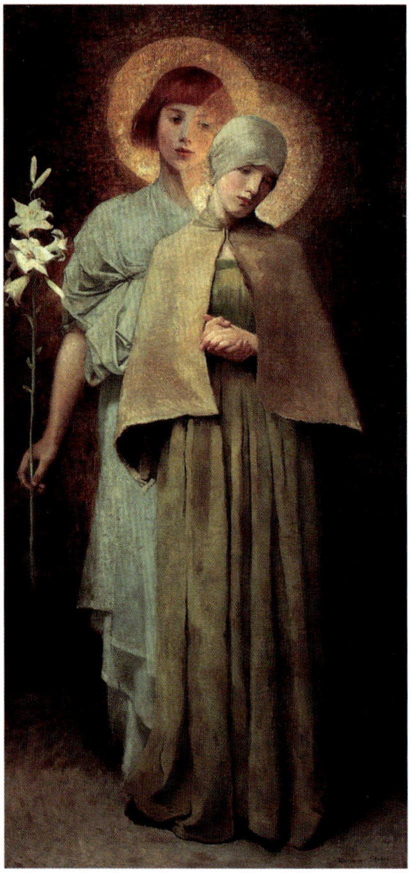

Marianne Stokes
'Hail Mary!'
1891 • oil on canvas • 190.5 x 89 cm
image courtesy the Artist's Estate

2015 EXHIBITS

Childhood's Treasures (pl. 39, Nottingham City Museums & Galleries): This painting was completed during a visit by the Stokeses to Ireland in 1885–6 to link up with Edith Somerville (1858–1949), whom Marianne had met at Colarossi's atelier in Paris. Edith commented that the pair were 'awfully clever and they are better than any master to me in fact'.[34] They stayed at Castletownshend for some time and also at Lismore, but the precise location for this delightful scene is unknown. The children are clearly from rustic stock, but are rosy-cheeked, healthy and well-fed, thus providing a comforting image for the middle classes of happy poverty. The painting was initially exhibited at the Royal Academy under the title *Childhood's Wonders* (see illustration in *Academy Notes*, 1886). It was not included in the short list of works for potential acquisition at the time of the 1894 exhibition, but when it was lent once more by W.A. Michael to Nottingham for an exhibition in 1896, it was acquired for the permanent collection.

Lantern Light (pl. 40, Penlee House Gallery & Museum): The subject matter of this painting bears similarities to that of *Polishing Pans*, now owned by the Walker Art Gallery, Liverpool. Whilst that work showed a young girl diligently cleaning brass and copperware, this shows a boy wiping glasses, the interior scene being illuminated solely by a lantern. In both paintings, the reflections on and off the vessels are an integral feature, and demonstrate Marianne's great skill as an artist.

TALMAGE, Algernon Mayow RA, ROI, RBA

OXFORD 1871–1939 SHERFIELD ENGLISH, ROMSEY

Algernon Talmage was one of the students of the Herkomer Art School, Bushey, who had recently come down to St Ives to learn *plein air* landscape painting alongside Adrian Stokes. Consequently, he never studied in France. He later became a highly regarded teacher of landscape and marine painting in St Ives, before being elected a Royal Academician in 1929 (ARA 1922).

Father clergyman.
1890–1: Studied West London School of Art.
1892–3: Studied at Herkomer Art School, Bushey.

34. Quoted in Magdalen Evans, *Utmost Fidelity: The painting lives of Marianne and Adrian Stokes*, Sansom & Co, Bristol, 2009, p. 32.

1893: Settled in St Ives. First exhibit at RBA.
1895: First exhibit at RA.
1898: Assistant at Julius Olsson's School of Landscape and Marine Painting, before becoming Principal in 1903.
1903: Elected member of RBA.
1907: Left his wife and moved to London.
1908: Elected member of ROI.

1894 EXHIBITS

- ***Moonrise After Rain*** [114]
- ***'Through the Twilight Mists, Rises the Autumn Moon'*** [115]

Neither of these works has been located.

***Nottingham Evening Post*, 6 October 1894**: 'Mr Algernon Talmage has two very good pictures of moonrise here. No. 114 shows a deep blue sky after rain, over a group of scotch firs, with the *Queen of the Night* reflected in marshy waters, while in No. 115, we look down a path to some houses in the midst of trees, below which the blue river makes a great circular twist under the hills, with one boat gliding upon its waters, while the round orange moon struggling through mists, is reflected upon its surface, making one of the best 'evening' effects in the exhibition.

TAYLER, Albert Chevallier NEAC, ROI, RBA

LONDON 1862–1925 LONDON

Chevallier Tayler was never a long-term resident of Newlyn, but regularly visited the colony and was well-liked. In addition to typical Newlyn School scenes, he painted religious and Society subjects and found a ready market for his work, for the list of lenders demonstrates that he had made a number of successful sales. He was very well represented in the exhibition, and his group of works was highly rated.

Father was solicitor. Studied at the Slade School (1879) and then in Paris under J.P. Lauren (1881–2).
1883: Visited Normandy with Henry Tuke.
1884: Won gold medal at the Paris Salon.
1884–95: First visited Newlyn in 1884, but never really settled and came and went with some regularity; however, he produced a few typical Newlyn School scenes.
1887: Converted to Roman Catholicism, which was to influence a number of his subjects.
1890: Visit to Boulogne. Participated in the Cornish Artists show at Dowdeswells.
1895: Left Newlyn finally and settled in Kensington, where painted drawing room scenes, dinner parties and other socialite gatherings with some success.

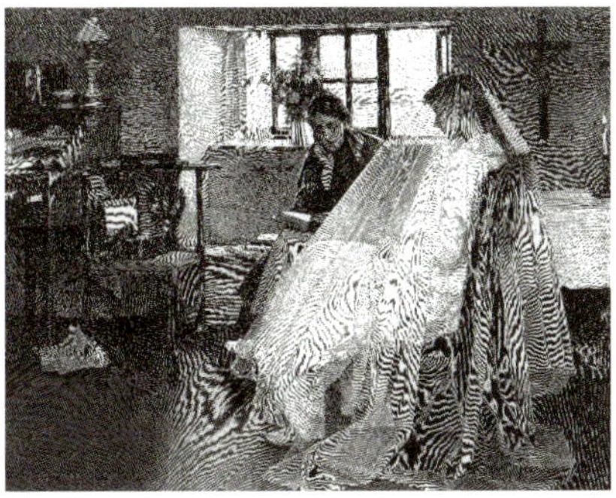

Albert Chevallier Tayler
Confirmation Day
from the 1894 exhibition catalogue

WALLIS CORRESPONDENCE

Not all letters from Tayler have survived, but it appears that a number of works included in the Nottingham exhibition had previously been shown in Plymouth, whose exhibition closed at the end of August. Tayler also communicated with Wallis in his capacity as business manager, on artistic matters, for Frank Bourdillon (q.v.), who had emigrated to India.

1894 EXHIBITS

- ***A Quiet Afternoon*** (Messrs W&P Holroyd) [5]
- ***Confidence*** (RA 1889) (Mr P. Phillips) [6]
- ***As Good as New – A Dress Rehearsal*** (Lever Bros, Port Sunlight) [11]
- ***The Pedlar*** (Gold Medal, Paris Salon, 1884) [21]
- ***Trying them on*** [25]
- ***On the Look-Out*** (W.H. Starkey) [60]
- ***The Legend of St Imelda*** [71]
- ***Sunday Morning*** (W.H. Starkey) [108]
- ***Street Scene, Venice*** (David Hedges) [110]
- ***Departure of the Fishing Fleet, Boulogne ('La Vie Boulonnaise')*** (RA 1891) (Birmingham) [210]
- ***Confirmation Day*** [211]
- ***A Summer Dinner Party*** (RA 1893) (Basil C. Fothergill) [212]

Messrs Phillips, Hedges and Starkey all lived in or near Birmingham. The Holroyds were based in Huddersfield, and Basil Fothergill in Liverpool. One of his works was shortlisted for possible acquisition by Nottingham Castle for its permanent collection.

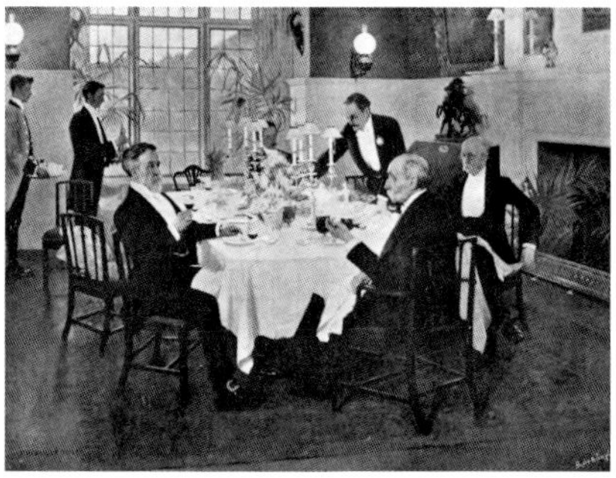

Albert Chevallier Tayler
A Summer Dinner Party
from the 1894 exhibition catalogue

Nottingham Evening Post, 6 October 1894: 'Mr A Chevallier Tayler's work is second to none in its interest and its high artistic quality. He is well represented by about a dozen pictures, though we would have liked to see his *Last Confession* among them, probably his finest effort so far, which has unfortunately gone to that land of revolutions and republics, South America.[35] But two of his pictures here, *La Vie Boulonnaise* and *A Summer Dinner Party*, are most admirable specimens of his skill. The former, now called *The Departure of the Fishing Fleet*, is lent by the Corporation of Birmingham. It is a large subject, crowded with figures happily and dramatically grouped. The boats are slowly moving out of the harbour in long lines, while the fisherwomen are watching and waving from the quay. The whole is backed by the houses of Boulogne. In the centre, a kneeling fisherman is tempting two girls with his fish – a striking group cleverly arranged. Notice also the masterly painting of the pinks and whites of the skate and other fish on the wet pavement, and the lovely browns in the sails of the departing boats. It is full of colour and of the life of a busy crowd of humble French people.

'Very different is *A Summer Dinner Party* ... which gives a brilliant effect of candlelight on a table sparkling with white cloth, silver and glass, and the amber and ruby glow of wine and fruit. The huge window at the end of the room is uncurtained, and in the twilight can be seen outside the dark hills, wood-covered. The candles are covered with green shades, and their faint gleams on the white panelled walls of the room is most dexterously given. Four men are seated round the table, their black garb contrasting with the glow of light in front of them. This is another of those effects of mingled twilight and candlelight which has so often been sought after by the 'Newlyners', and seldom with so much success as in this picture of Mr Tayler's.

'This artist is particularly clever in his cottage interiors with girls gossiping, making dresses, trying on finery and kindred subjects. Two or three of his best efforts in this direction are to be seen here. He has a happy power of dealing with white, white upon white, and against white. He seems to love a white wall, as the whitewashed interiors of the Newlyn cottages give him. His *Dress Rehearsal*, lent by Messrs Lever, has not been vulgarised, although it has been used for advertising purposes.[36] In the centre of a room, a girl in white, with white satin shoes, is holding out her dress for the inspection of an old lady in a high-backed chair, and three girls behind, one of whom sits upon the table, and all of whom examine the new garment with critical eyes. The colour, as in all Mr Tayler's pictures, is unforced and is delightful, and the painting of the numerous details, the open bonnet-boxes, the blue and white china on the shelves, the boots hastily thrown aside to make place for the satin shoes, is excellent.

35. This will be a reference to his RA exhibit of 1890, *The Last Blessing*.
36. The advertising slogan used was 'As Good as New'.

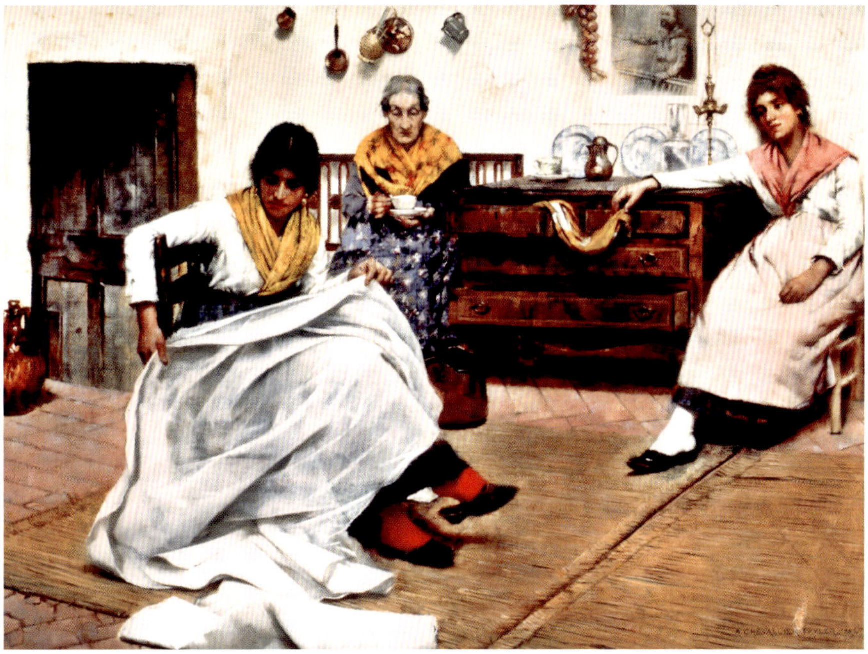

pl. 41 **Albert Chevallier Tayler**
A Bolt of Cloth
1887 • oil on canvas • 51 x 66 cm
Bowerman Charitable Trust

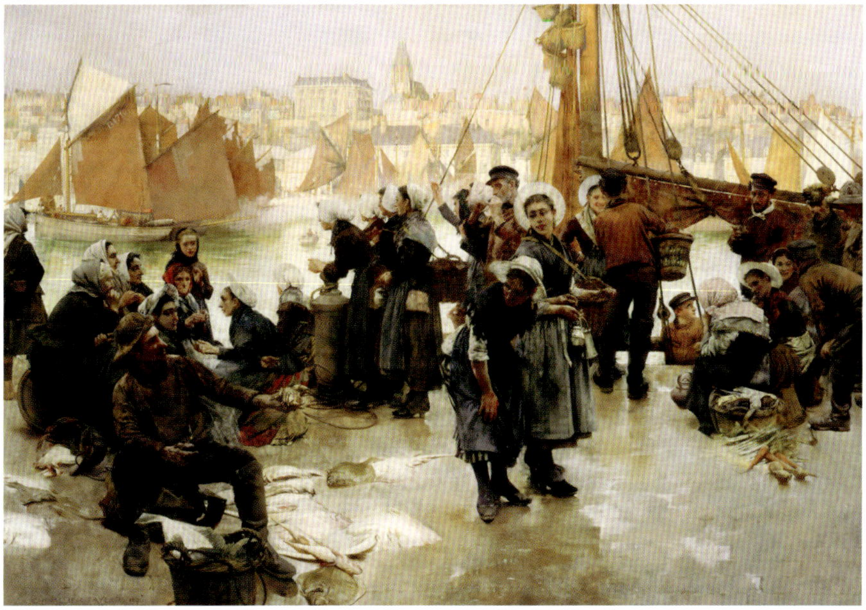

Albert Chevallier Tayler
Departure of the Fishing Fleet, Boulogne
1891 • oil on canvas • 137.5 x 194 cm
© Birmingham Museums Trust

'An equally good picture is *Confidences*, two girls on a chintz covered sofa, whispering over a love-letter, while an old lady in a pink curtained window seat, sits behind a round table covered in tea-things. *A Quiet Afternoon* is another cottage interior with a woman sewing in a window-seat and a young girl reading an illustrated paper, the whole tone of which is charming ...

'In all of these pictures the artist shows what high quality he can put into anything he attempts and how he can add distinction and beauty to scenes of human life.'

2015 EXHIBIT

A Bolt of Cloth (pl. 41, Bowerman Charitable Trust): This painting, dated 1887, is another fine example of Tayler's depictions of local Cornish women in a white-washed cottage interior. A young woman has rolled out a bolt of white cloth and is judging the length that she will need for her next dressmaking project, watched by her sister, who is sitting with their mother at the back of the room, on either side of a chest of drawers, from which tumbles out a piece of exotically coloured silk, which the sister fingers longingly. Once again, the painting demonstrates Tayler's interest in different whites – in the bolt of cloth, the walls and the background sister's socks, whilst that girl's pink scarf contrasts with her sister's pink socks. The foreground sister's yellow scarf also contrasts with the darker yellow of that of her mother, and the sheen on various pieces of clothing caught in the light is well observed. The painting of the incidentals in the picture, such as the china and the brass candle-stick on the chest of drawers, and the copper and brass, and the onions hanging on the wall, is also excellent. There is no doubt that it is a modest home – the door is rough, the furniture is scant and the only picture is a print stuck on the wall. However, notwithstanding their challenging circumstances, these women still loved a piece of finery and were keen to present themselves as well as they could. This was an idyllic vision of cottage life, which the middle classes liked to hold, and the artists were happy to perpetuate.

TITCOMB, William Holt Yates RBA, RBC, RI, RWA

CAMBRIDGE 1858–1930 BRISTOL

Titcomb, habitually referred to in the London press as a 'Newlyner', was, in fact, the leading figure painter in St Ives, but his time in Antwerp and Paris meant that he shared the same outlook and approach as the figure painters in Newlyn.

Father, Jonathan Holt Titcomb, was a clergyman, who became the first Bishop of Rangoon (1877–81) and the first Bishop of Northern and Central Europe (1884–6).
Late 1870s: Studied at South Kensington schools, and at Antwerp under Verlat.
1880–1: Joined his father in Burma, where painted the local inhabitants.
1881–9: Studied in Paris at various ateliers and at Bushey under Hubert Herkomer (1883–5).
1886: First exhibited at Royal Academy.
1887: First visited St Ives.
1890: Won medal at Paris Salon for *Primitive Methodists at Prayer, St Ives*. Founder member of St Ives Arts Club in August. Participated in Cornish Artists' Exhibition at Dowdeswells in December.
1890–1905: Based in St Ives; had a particular interest in depicting the faith of the fisherfolk; regular exhibitor at Royal Academy; in many public collections.
1893: Won medal at Chicago for *Old Sea Dogs*.
1905: Moved from St Ives to Dusseldorf.

WALLIS CORRESPONDENCE

Titcomb communicated with Wallis from his recently inherited property, the

Wickersley Institute, in South Yorkshire, where he was spending the summer. The three works included in the exhibition were his initial choices, in a letter dated 4 June 1894, but Wallis also asked if his 1890 Salon success, *Primitive Methodists at Prayer, St Ives*, might be added. However, Titcomb responded on 11 July 1894 that he had not thought it appropriate to include it, as it had been shown at Nottingham before, and he was now unable to do so, as he had promised it to Birmingham.

Titcomb was a perfectionist and, despite the fact that both *Piloting Her Home* and *Market Day, Etaples* had been hung at the Royal Academy, he asked Wallis if it would be possible to spend a day or two working on them in one of the Castles' galleries before they were hung. Some small detail had clearly irked him when he had seen them hung before.

1894 EXHIBITS

- ***Market Day, Etaples*** (RA 1893) [160]
- ***Piloting Her Home*** (RA 1894) [161]
- ***Old Sea Dogs*** (RA 1891) [162]

Old Sea Dogs was brought from the exhibition for the permanent collection of Nottingham Castle Museum and *Piloting Her Home* was subsequently acquired for the Art Gallery of Ontario, Toronto.

***Nottingham Evening Post*, 6 October 1894**: 'Of Mr W.H.Y. Titcomb's three pictures, *Piloting Her Home*, from the last Academy, is the best. It is a dramatic conception, with a rather unusual colour scheme of delicate purples running through it, ably carried out. The old lady, in white on her white bed, her arms stretched up in a dying ecstasy, her face lit up by a glad smile, is surrounded by kneeling relations, who, in varying attitudes, are offering up fervent prayer. One man, erect, with closed eyes, clasps a bible to his side, and with his right hand points above. The light comes through a small window with muslin curtains at the back. His *Old Sea Dogs*, three old men seated on a bench on a sandy beach, is a good work of characterisation and is filled with light and life, while *Market Day, Etaples*, is a successful attempt to deal with the effect of vivid light upon a well-arranged group of peasants, with baskets of flowers and vegetables, admiring a baby. The shadows fall blue and purple and the sun is dazzling.'

2015 EXHIBITS

Old Sea Dogs (pl. 43, Nottingham City Museums & Galleries): This painting, which had recently been medalled at the Chicago World Columbian Exhibition of 1893, was one of two bought for Nottingham Castle Museum's permanent collection from the 1894 Exhibition. Titcomb reduced his price from £250 to £100 in recognition of the help that the Exhibition had been 'to us as a Colony of painters' and in the hope that this would enable the Nottingham Committee 'to effect the purchase of another work by one of my brother artists'. However, this self-less gesture did not have the desired effect.

The painting features three of Titcomb's favourite models, 'One-Eyed' Barber, on the right, 'Prussian Bill', in the middle, and Ephraim Perkin, on the right. 'One-Eyed' Barber, whose proper name was William, was one of the true characters amongst the fisherfolk. A.G. Folliott Stokes described him as 'a man of fine physique, with the face and brow of an old prophet', who possessed 'a remarkable store of interesting facts, and not less interesting fancies'.[37] He was loved by the children of St Ives, not only because of the wooden dolls, called Joannies, that he would carve out of broken oars, but also because of his rhymes, which he could make up in his head at a moment's notice. Stokes commented, 'I have heard him addressing his wife in sonnet after sonnet of amusing conceits'.[38]

37. A.G. Folliott Stokes, *From St Ives to Land's End*, London, 1908, p. 37.
38. Ibid.

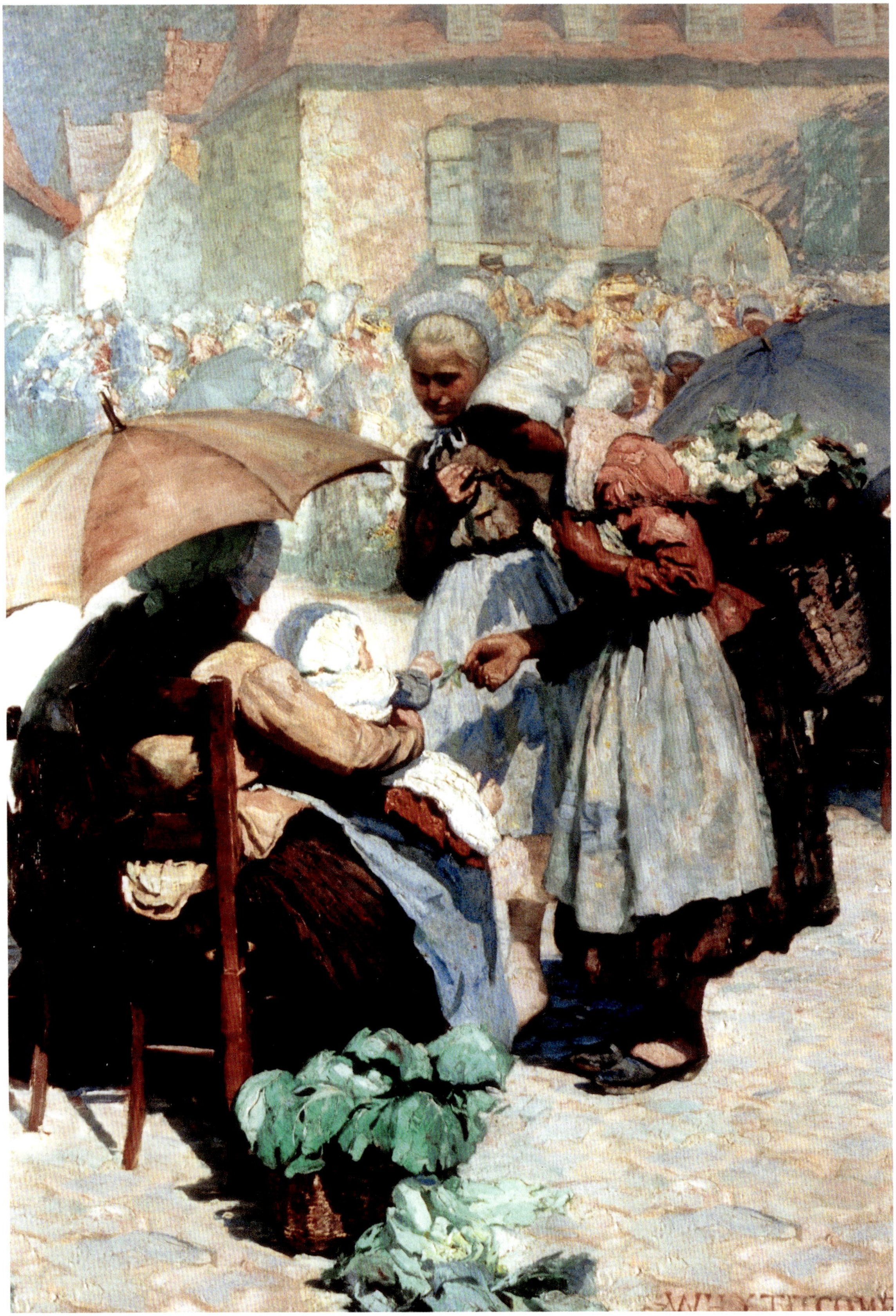

pl. 42 **William Titcomb**
Market Day, Etaples aka ***Baby's First Market Day***
oil on canvas • 135 x 91 cm
private collection

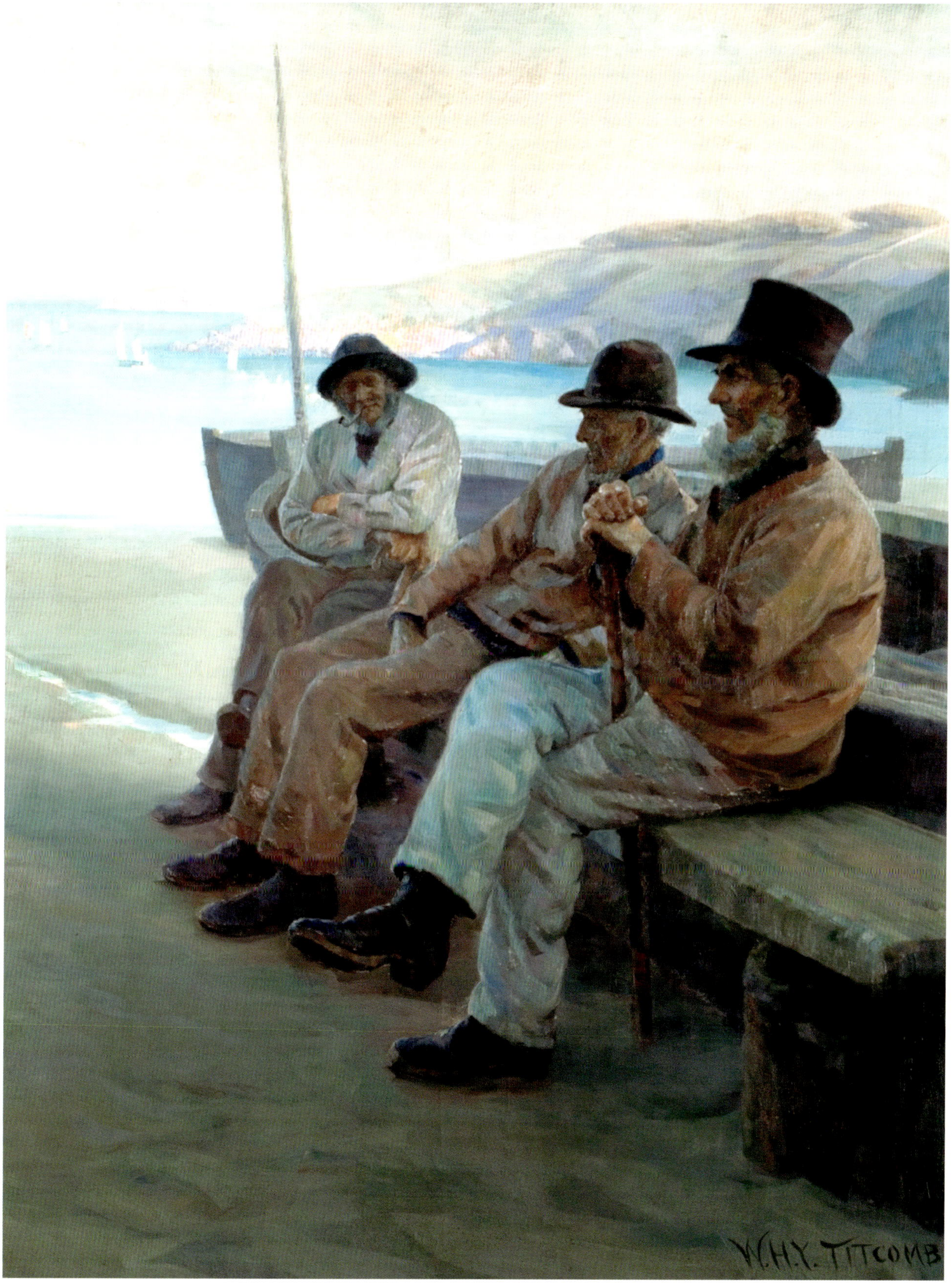

pl. 43 **William Titcomb**
Old Sea Dogs
1891 • oil on canvas • 157.5 x 122 cm
Nottingham City Museums and Galleries

Ephraim Perkin was one of the St Ives artists' most regular models, whilst the real name of 'Prussian Bill', who was also known as 'Old Worm's Fool', was Wilhelm Schmidt. He came to St Ives originally as the cabin boy on a German sailing ship carrying smuggled goods and stayed on in St Ives with one of the local Primitive Methodist families, after Worm, the Captain of the ship, largely due to Prussian Bill's testimony, was acquitted of smuggling.

Titcomb depicts the three old men sitting on a bench on the harbour beach enjoying their memories as the light fades over St Ives Bay. Conversation is limited. In addition to their contrasting poses and bushy beards, Titcomb has highlighted their distinctive headgear. This must be the period – which Stanhope Forbes later recalled with horror – 'when a hideous fashion in hats set in – a hard, black abomination in place of the usual soft sailor-like head gear or quaint old sou'wester'.[39]

The French influence on the artist's technique is clear, particularly in his depiction of the clothing of the right-hand figure, whose trousers are a riot of mauve, green and blue, applied in bold, thick, seemingly random brushstokes. The eye is left to meld the colours together, and to recognise creases and folds. Edges are not defined, and the painting would have been considered by academic painters to be rough and unfinished. The widespread use of mauve to depict the shadows under the bench, inside the boat against which they lean and on the headland in the background also highlights Titcomb's awareness of the French Impressionists and this colour is picked up in the clothing of the fishermen.

Market Day, Etaples aka ***Baby's First Market Day*** (pl. 42, private collection): Etaples, in Normandy, was another popular art colony, and, in 1891, Titcomb visited it, possibly on the recommendations of fellow St Ives artists, Middleton Jameson and Sigisbert Bosch Reitz, who had worked there previously. Whilst studying at the local art school in the town, he met and fell in love with a Scottish artist, Jessie Morison, and the pair became engaged there – the celebrations of their fellow students, which involved banging on tin kettles with their mahl sticks, proving so noisy as to cause the whole group to be summoned before the local magistrates for disorder! Having got married in St Ives in April 1892, they returned to Etaples on their honeymoon, during which William produced this extravagantly impasto-ed, colour-filled painting, in a style that was, for him, unique.

The young baby, the focal point of the work, is dressed in white, in contrast to the immensely colourful clothing of the women, but demands attention due to the heavily paint-laden brushstrokes that have been used. The head-dress and shoulders of the young girl on the right, with the basket on her back, are again depicted in heavy impasto and the foreground is a mass of rough, strong brushstrokes of blue, pink and white. In the tumult of colour, the young girl's white pinafore is streaked with greys, blues and touches of yellow and the old woman's brown dress has purple, orange and blue tinges. Blues and pinks are predominant in the background depictions of the houses in the square and the crowds at the market.

The painting, which was exhibited at the Royal Academy in 1893 under the title, *Baby's First Market Day*, was donated by Titcomb to the Royal West of England Academy on his election as a member but, when needing extensive restoration, was sold back to the artist's family.

TUKE, Henry Scott RA, RBA, RWS, NEAC

YORK 1858–1929 FALMOUTH

Tuke, who had worked previously in Newlyn, was one of two Falmouth-based artists included in the 1894 exhibition. That year, he had surpassed all other Cornish artists in having a second work bought by the Chantrey Trustees, and

39. 'A Newlyn Retrospect', *Cornish Magazine*, vol. 1, 1898, p. 86.

his distinctive paintings of the male nude in bright sunlight were beginning to be widely praised.

Family Quakers, who frequented Falmouth due to ill health during Tuke's childhood. Educated at Quaker School in Weston-super-Mare.
1875–80: Studied at the Slade School under Edmund Poynter and Alphonse Legros, becoming friends with Thomas Cooper Gotch (q.v.).
1880: Worked in Florence.
1881–3: Studied in Paris under J.P. Laurens.
1884–5: Worked in Newlyn in a style similar to his colleagues.
1886: Settled in Falmouth and acquired a brigantine as a studio. Involved in the formation of New English Art Club.
1888: Elected member of RBA.
1889: His Newlyn School influenced painting *All Hands to the Pump* bought by the Chantrey Trustees.
1890: Participated in the Cornish Artists show at Dowdeswells.
1894: *August Blue*, one of his male nude paintings, bought by the Chantrey Trustees. Involved in formation of Falmouth Art Gallery.
1900: Elected ARA (RA 1914).
1904: Elected ARWS (RWS 1911).
1905–29: Remained stalwart of the Falmouth colony.

WALLIS CORRESPONDENCE

In a letter dated 29 May 1894, written from Lyndon Lodge, Hanwell, Tuke commented, 'I think all the pictures you invite are exhibiting at the moment, or out of my control. I will however try to send you something, but cannot promise definitely.' Quite how the final selection was made is unclear, but the works arrived late. In response to a desperate telegram from Wallis, Tuke wrote on 8 September 1894, 'I am so sorry that you have had so much bother about my pictures. It is entirely owing to the stupidity of the agents here.' They had apparently not only been tardy in sending them off but had sent them by goods train. Tuke was resigned to not being represented at all in the show, but Wallis managed to get them hung in time.

1894 EXHIBITS

- ***The Fisherman*** [138]
- ***Making the Stew*** [139]
- ***The Message*** [140]
- ***The Bathers*** (Leeds) [141]

The Fisherman was one of only two works bought from the exhibition by Nottingham Castle for its permanent collection. *The Message* is now owned by Falmouth Art Gallery. *Making the Stew* has not been located.

***Nottingham Evening Post*, 6 October 1894**: 'Falmouth may boast in all sincerity of the possession of such an artist as Mr Henry S Tuke, whose brilliant picture *August Blue* in this year's Academy was bought by the Chantrey Trustees, it being the second work by this painter that they have acquired. At the present day, he stands probably unrivalled in the painting of flesh seen under strong sunlight. He delights in the painting of boys bathing in the sunny harbour of Falmouth. *The Bathers*, a study of three nude boys on a boat, one just about to dive into the sea, is a capital example of his power in this direction. His *Fisherman* is full of fine quality. A red-bearded man, clad in white jersey and blue trousers, is seated in a boat holding a long line. The oars are out, resting upon his knees, he stooping over them. The character in his face is the most powerful feature of the picture, which has for a background the sea, showing green under the white hulls of the vessels in the harbour. Mr Tuke has his studio upon the sea, and the fresh salt air

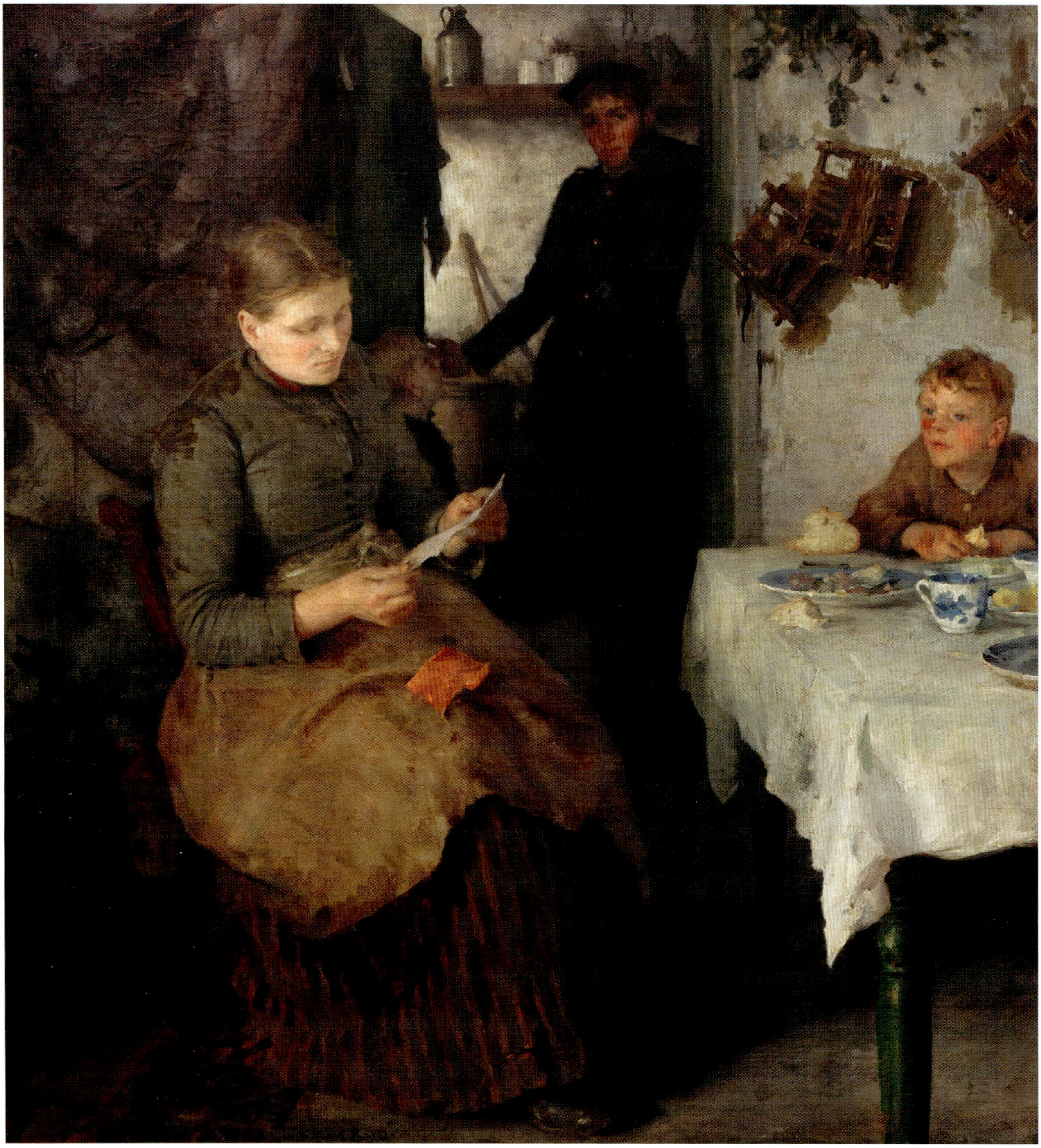

pl. 44 **Henry Scott Tuke**
The Message
1890 • oil on canvas • 100 x 89 cm
Falmouth Art Gallery Collection

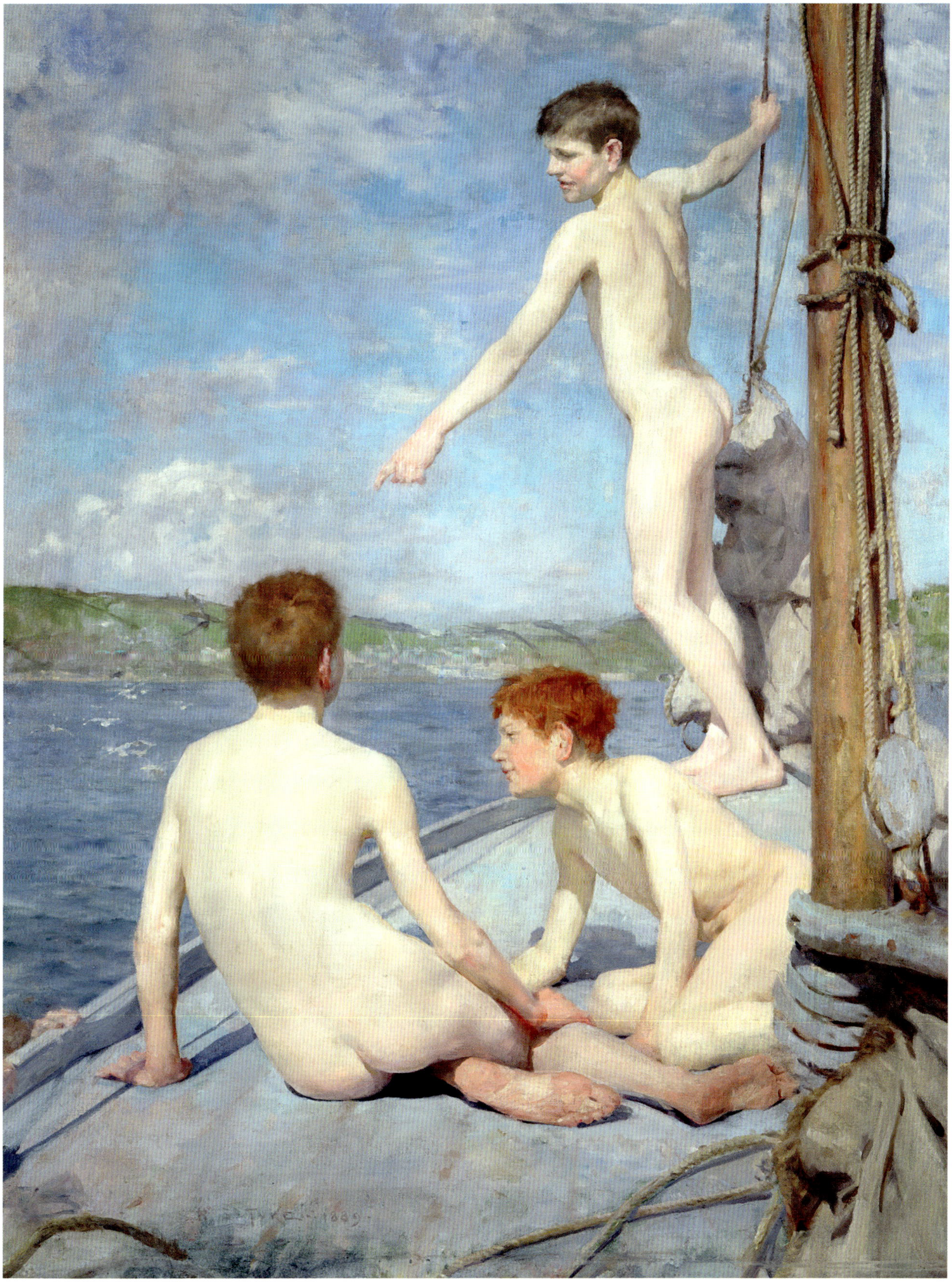

pl. 45 **Henry Scott Tuke**
The Bathers
1889 • oil on canvas • 117 x 86 cm
Leeds Museum and Galleries (Leeds Art Gallery)

pervades his pictures. Another work, *Making Stew*, is a study in browns, of a cook boy taking a lid off a saucepan, with a glimpse of the sea and a big ship showing through the open doorway. He also sends *The Message*, a cottage interior, with a woman reading a letter that a young sailor has just brought her, while a boy sits at a table covered with blue tea-things. Both these pictures have much good quality in them.'

2015 EXHIBITS

The Bathers (pl. 45, Leeds Museum & Galleries – Leeds Art Gallery): This work, dated 1890, is a very early example of his male nudes and was acquired immediately by Leeds Art Gallery. The boys are shown on the deck of *Julie of Nantes*, the French brigantine that Tuke owned from 1886 to 1892 and made his studio.

The Message (pl. 44, Falmouth Art Gallery): This painting, also dated 1890, depicts Mrs Fouracre, Tuke's devoted housekeeper, who served him from 1886 until her death in 1916. His notebook records in relation to this painting, 'Done at Swanpool Nov. 90. Mrs Fouracre sits in front, Geoffrey at the table with Richard behind while Martin leans in the doorway.'[40] The two smaller boys were her sons. The painting was part of a group gifted to Falmouth Art Gallery in 1923 by Alfred Aaron de Pass (1861–1952), a South African businessman and art benefactor, in memory of his sons, Sub-Lieutenant Crispin De Pass, who died in 1918 at Cambrai serving with the tank corps, and John De Pass who was killed in a skiing accident on the Chamossaire mountain, Switzerland, in January 1923. It was also included in the seminal 'Artists of the Newlyn School' exhibition in 1979.

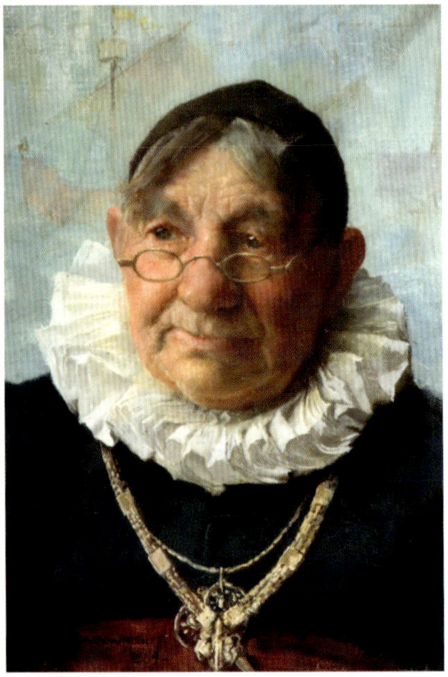

William Wainwright
The Burgomaster
1884 • oil on canvas • 45 x 30 cm

WAINWRIGHT, William John

BIRMINGHAM 1855–1931 BIRMINGHAM

The figure painter, William Wainwright, was one of the 'Birmingham Boys', who were closely involved with the establishment of the Newlyn Art Colony, but, as he had returned to live in Birmingham by 1886, his inclusion in the 1894 exhibition is rather surprising and must be due to the fact that David Hedges, the owner of the work included, was lending other paintings to the show.

Educated at Sedgeley Park College, near Wolverhampton.
1869: Became apprentice at John Hardman & Co, where designed stained glass.
1880: Studied art in Antwerp under Verlat at same time as Frank Bramley and Edwin Harris.
1881–4: Studied in Paris, but visited Newlyn briefly with Walter Langley in 1881.
1884–6: Regular visitor to Newlyn, particularly in 1884.
1886: Returned to live permanently in Birmingham.
1890: Married and had eight children.

1894 EXHIBIT

- ***The Burgomaster*** (David Hedges) [127]

This painting is now owned by Birmingham Art Gallery.

40. Caroline Fox and Francis Greenacre, *Artists of the Newlyn School (1880–1900)*, Newlyn, 1979, p. 140.

Further reading and resources

Books

- Henrietta Boex/Falmouth Art Gallery, *Artists of the First Falmouth Art Gallery*, Falmouth 2014.
- Alfred East, *The Art of Landscape Painting in Oil Colour*, London, 1906.
- Magdalen Evans, *Utmost Fidelity, The Painting Lives of Marianne and Adrian Stokes*, Sansom & Co., Bristol, 2009.
- Caroline Fox and Francis Greenacre, *Painting in Newlyn 1880–1930*, Newlyn, 1985.
- Melissa Hardie (ed.), *Artists in Newlyn and West Cornwall, 1880–1940, Dictionary and Source Book*, Sansom & Co., Bristol, 2009.
- Nina Lübbren, *Rural Artists' Colonies in Europe, 1870–1910*, Manchester 2001.
- Mary O'Neill, *Cornwall's 'Fisherfolk': Art and Artifice*, Sansom & Co., Bristol, 2014.
- Laura Newton (ed.), *Painting at the Edge, British Coastal Art Colonies 1880–1930*, Sansom & Co., Bristol 2005.
- Christiana Payne, *Where the Sea Meets the Land*, Sansom & Co., Bristol, 2007
- Adrian Stokes, *Landscape Painting*, London, 1925.
- David Tovey, *St Ives Art pre-1890: The Dawn of the Colony*, Tewkesbury, 2008
- David Tovey, *Pioneers of St Ives Art at Home and Abroad (1889–1914)*, Tewkesbury, 2008.
- David Tovey, *St Ives (1860–1930): The Artists and the Community – A Social History*, Tewkesbury, 2009.

Websites

- BBC Your Paintings: www.bbc.co.uk/arts/yourpaintings/
- Cornwall Artists Index: www.cornwallartists.org
- Penlee House Gallery & Museum, Penzance: www.penleehouse.org.uk

Index